Deleuze, Cinema and the Thought of the World

Plateaus – New Directions in Deleuze Studies

'It's not a matter of bringing all sorts of things together under a single concept but rather of relating each concept to variables that explain its mutations.'
Gilles Deleuze, *Negotiations*

Series Editors
Ian Buchanan, University of Wollongong
Claire Colebrook, Penn State University

Editorial Advisory Board
Keith Ansell Pearson
Ronald Bogue
Constantin V. Boundas
Rosi Braidotti
Eugene Holland
Gregg Lambert
Dorothea Olkowski
Paul Patton
Daniel Smith
James Williams

Titles Available in the Series
Christian Kerslake, *Immanence and the Vertigo of Philosophy: From Kant to Deleuze*
Jean-Clet Martin, *Variations: The Philosophy of Gilles Deleuze*, translated by Constantin V. Boundas and Susan Dyrkton
Simone Bignall, *Postcolonial Agency: Critique and Constructivism*
Miguel de Beistegui, *Immanence – Deleuze and Philosophy*
Jean-Jacques Lecercle, *Badiou and Deleuze Read Literature*
Ronald Bogue, *Deleuzian Fabulation and the Scars of History*
Sean Bowden, *The Priority of Events: Deleuze's Logic of Sense*
Craig Lundy, *History and Becoming: Deleuze's Philosophy of Creativity*
Aidan Tynan, *Deleuze's Literary Clinic: Criticism and the Politics of Symptoms*
Thomas Nail, *Returning to Revolution: Deleuze, Guattari and Zapatismo*
François Zourabichvili, *Deleuze: A Philosophy of the Event* with *The Vocabulary of Deleuze* edited by Gregg Lambert and Daniel W. Smith, translated by Kieran Aarons
Frida Beckman, *Between Desire and Pleasure: A Deleuzian Theory of Sexuality*
Nadine Boljkovac, *Untimely Affects: Gilles Deleuze and an Ethics of Cinema*
Daniela Voss, *Conditions of Thought: Deleuze and Transcendental Ideas*
Daniel Barber, *Deleuze and the Naming of God: Post-Secularism and the Future of Immanence*
F. LeRon Shults, *Iconoclastic Theology: Gilles Deleuze and the Secretion of Atheism*
Janae Sholtz, *The Invention of a People: Heidegger and Deleuze on Art and the Political*
Marco Altamirano, *Time, Technology and Environment: An Essay on the Philosophy of Nature*
Sean McQueen, *Deleuze and Baudrillard: From Cyberpunk to Biopunk*
Ridvan Askin, *Narrative and Becoming*
Marc Rölli, *Gilles Deleuze's Transcendental Empiricism: From Tradition to Difference* translated by Peter Hertz-Ohmes
Guillaume Collett, *The Psychoanalysis of Sense: Deleuze and the Lacanian School*
Ryan J. Johnson, *The Deleuze-Lucretius Encounter*
Allan James Thomas, *Deleuze, Cinema and the Thought of the World*

Forthcoming volumes
Cheri Carr, *Deleuze's Kantian Ethos: Critique as a Way of Life*
Alex Tissandier, *Affirming Divergence: Deleuze's Reading of Leibniz*

Visit the Plateaus website at edinburghuniversitypress.com/series/plat

DELEUZE, CINEMA AND THE THOUGHT OF THE WORLD

Allan James Thomas

EDINBURGH
University Press

Edinburgh University Press is one of the leading university presses in the UK. We publish academic books and journals in our selected subject areas across the humanities and social sciences, combining cutting-edge scholarship with high editorial and production values to produce academic works of lasting importance. For more information visit our website: edinburghuniversitypress.com

© Allan James Thomas, 2018

Edinburgh University Press Ltd
The Tun – Holyrood Road
12(2f) Jackson's Entry
Edinburgh EH8 8PJ

Typeset in Sabon by
Servis Filmsetting Ltd, Stockport, Cheshire

A CIP record for this book is available from the British Library

ISBN 978 1 4744 3279 5 (hardback)
ISBN 978 1 4744 3281 8 (webready PDF)
ISBN 978 1 4744 3282 5 (epub)

The right of Allan James Thomas to be identified as the author of this work has been asserted in accordance with the Copyright, Designs and Patents Act 1988, and the Copyright and Related Rights Regulations 2003 (SI No. 2498).

Contents

Acknowledgements	vi
1 Introduction: The Problem of Cinema	**1**
Transcendental Empiricism and the '*Cahiers* Axiom'	1
The Monotony of Difference	10
2 The Interval as Disaster	**23**
Terminus, or, Waiting for a Train	23
(Film) History as Montage	33
Cinema as an Anterior History of Violence	43
3 Movement, Duration and Difference	**53**
The Three Theses on Movement	53
The Temporalisation of Difference	61
How to Escape the Dialectic	67
4 What Use is Cinema to Deleuze?	**85**
The Necessary Illusions of Practical Life	85
A Materialist Practice of Metaphysics	91
Transcendental Empiricism as Cinematic Philosophy	104
5 Genesis and Deduction	**119**
Cinematic Being	119
Weak Reasoning, Perversity and Grasping at Threads	132
From 'Primitive' Cinema to Real Movement	141
6 The Thought of the World	**160**
Cinematic Aberration and the 'Great Kantian Reversal'	160
The Classical Cinema as Totalisation	167
Cinema as 'Art of the Masses'	183
7 The Night, the Rain	**201**
Film, Death (the 'Reverse Proof')	201
The Suspension of the World	214
'The Image, the Remains'	224
8 Conclusion: The Crystal-Image of Philosophy	**245**
References	254
Index	263

Acknowledgements

A project such as this incurs many debts, few of which can be properly repaid. Two in particular stand out: William D. Routt, who started me down this path and taught me that thinking begins with not knowing, and Adrian Danks, who as a friend, colleague and mentor has been an unfailing and ever-patient source of wisdom and kindness, both personal and professional. I owe more to him than the conventions and limits of this space allow me to express.

I'd like to thank Daniel W. Smith for his generous feedback on and support for this project. Likewise, to Ian Buchanan, Claire Colebrook, Carol Macdonald and the team at Edinburgh University Press, along with the anonymous readers for this book, my heartfelt gratitude for their guidance. The research leave made available to me by the Research Committee of the School of Media and Communication at RMIT University provided invaluable space for writing and thinking, and the support of my colleagues there was, and continues to be, a great gift. The organisers of the International Deleuze Studies conferences in Cologne, Amsterdam and Istanbul (in 2009, 2010 and 2014 respectively) gave me the chance to present some of the ideas in this book to my peers. Thanks go to Felicity Coleman for always making me feel a part of the community of Deleuze scholars. And needless to say, all error and infelicity herein rests on my head alone.

Finally, to my family and friends, and most of all my wife Bim and daughter Astrid, who have suffered at the hands of my obsessions more than most: thanks are not enough, but I hope that my love may be. This book is dedicated to them, and to the loving memory of my mother, Patricia Margaret Thomas.

1
Introduction: The Problem of Cinema

Transcendental Empiricism and the 'Cahiers Axiom'

Gilles Deleuze's two-volume work on the cinema[1] poses its would-be reader a formidable task. Its proliferation of cinematic references and analyses would stretch the capacities of all but the most dedicated cinephile (of Deleuze's love for cinema there can be no doubt). Furthermore, to engage fully with the historical currents of film theory therein calls for a familiarity with the development of cinema studies as a critical discipline worthy of a dedicated film theorist. Perhaps most challenging of all, it asks that these threads be grasped in relation to Deleuze's own uniquely demanding engagement with the history of philosophy itself, and, more specifically, his own appropriation and transformation of that history and the problems that subtend it as developed across a philosophical career spanning the 1940s to the 1990s.[2] The astonishing scope and ambition of the project are announced in its very title: a work of philosophy (for that is what it surely is) titled simply *Cinema*, as if within its pages Deleuze seeks in some sense to address or draw on the cinema in its entirety and as a whole. The extraordinary nature of this project invites a very simple question: why does Deleuze write about the cinema *as a philosopher*? This is the question the present book seeks to explore.

One path to accounting for this startling fusion might be to locate its origins in Deleuze's own biographical history. His famous antipathy to travel[3] was such that his philosophical career was firmly located within the intellectual and aesthetic life of Paris from the 1950s onwards. By the same token, his cinema-going was embedded in an upswelling of critical, creative and intellectual activity around the cinema that gave rise to one of the great historical and cultural focal points of cinephilia and cinematic exploration, in which the love of cinema took on the form of a critical exploration of the powers of the cinema itself.

As such, one can easily point towards a range of developments located within that specific film culture that had an impact on Deleuze's engagement with and knowledge of film history, theory and criticism, and ultimately on the *Cinema* books themselves. The role of Henri Langlois' *Cinémathèque Française* in the development of Parisian film culture after the war,[4] the critical and pedagogical activities of André Bazin[5] and the foundation and development of the journal *Cahiers du cinéma* under the latter's guidance seem, on the evidence of the *Cinema* books, to have had a particular impact on Deleuze's experience of and interest in the cinema. Certainly it seems plausible to suggest that the *Cinémathèque's* film programmes would have served as one of Deleuze's key (although by no means only) experiences of the cinema and its history from the 1940s onwards, as it did for so many Parisians of the time.[6]

The influence of Bazin's critical and theoretical explorations of the cinema are also clearly evident, not least of all in the *Cinema* books' structuring proposition that post-war Italian neo-realist cinema marks a new and distinct phase in the cinema's history. Although *Cahiers du cinéma* was, and remains, only one of a range of film journals and focal points of film criticism and thinking within Parisian film culture, one can make a strong argument for its particular influence over Deleuze and on the *Cinema* books. Raymond Bellour, for example, notes that Deleuze is 'particularly close' to the authors of the *Cahiers* tradition.[7] Certainly the influence of the critical and creative works of the great Nouvelle Vague critic-filmmakers who were so central to that journal and its impact in the 1950s and beyond is clearly apparent in the cinematic and theoretical reference points of the *Cinema* books, as is the impact of Serge Daney's contribution within *Cahiers du cinéma* and without.[8]

More than this, however, I would locate Deleuze as one of the key inheritors of what Dudley Andrew, following Daney, calls 'the *Cahiers* line' – a conceptual lineage of critical and theoretical thinking in and through which a particular conception of film as a critical activity concerning not just cinema, but the world, takes shape. This lineage is articulated around the backbone of the journal's long history, whose shared proposition Daney presents as follows: 'The *Cahiers* axiom is this: that the cinema has a fundamental rapport with reality and that the real is not what is represented – and that's final.'[9] Just as Bazin serves as the tutelary figure for and progenitor of the *Cahiers* line,[10] his critique of montage in favour of mise en scène and the long take marks a point of origin for this 'axiom': for Bazin, where montage presents us with a ready-made analysis of the world comprehended within its formal patterns, the latter seek merely to expose the world to the eye and to thought as a problem to which they must respond, rather than seek to capture or master.[11] Given the vicissitudes of French political, theoretical and philosophical thought from the 1950s to now, the terms in which the *Cahiers* axiom is dealt with and expressed within that line necessarily vary. However, those treatments all share a concern for the relationship between image and world understood not in terms of representation or reflection, but as a problem offered to the eye and to thought.

If Deleuze's work on cinema can be regarded as a continuation of this 'line',[12] it is not only because of the evident impact of that line on his ideas, but because Daney's axiom also serves as an apt description of the concerns of Deleuzian philosophy as a whole, irrespective of any discussion of the cinema. Indeed, the significance of this axiom may be clearer, at least in an immediate sense, in the context of Deleuze's work than in relation to the theoretical traditions of cinema studies. Deleuze's transcendental empiricism, understood as the attempt to come to grips with the conditions of real, and not merely possible, experience, can be glossed as a concern for the real as that which cannot be adequately grasped or responded to by means of any representation *of* that reality. But it is for precisely this reason that I would argue that the *Cinema* books must be understood not as a response *to* the cinema, or as a product of Deleuze's love *for* the cinema, but as a response to a properly philosophical problem within and for Deleuzian philosophy itself approached by means *of* the cinema: if the *Cahiers* axiom bears on Deleuzian thought, it is as an axiom not of the cinema, but rather of philosophy.

However, although such an answer may tell us why cinema is of relevance to Deleuze's philosophical project, given that difference and a concern for thinking in terms of difference lies at the heart of everything he writes, it does not tell us much about *why* the cinema in particular draws his attention. The clearest indication Deleuze offers comes when he tells us that philosophical problems 'compelled' him to 'look for answers in the cinema'.[13] Unfortunately he does not say what those problems are, or what it is about cinema that enables him to respond to them in a way that philosophy on its own does not.

The constantly growing secondary literature surrounding the *Cinema* books makes it abundantly clear that they are both continuous and deeply intertwined with the philosophical concerns and approaches explored across the entire body of Deleuze's work. David Rodowick, Ronald Bogue and Paola Marrati, for example, have in their different ways done invaluable work unpacking these connections and explicating the layered complexities of cinematic and philosophical refrains Deleuze presents to the reader.[14] In doing so they locate the work of the *Cinema* books both firmly within the broader trajectory of Deleuzian thought and in relation to specific facets and problems explored therein. But for all their success in this task, the question of why Deleuze turns to the cinema for answers to philosophical problems, or what those problems are, remains unanswered.

Thus, for example, David Rodowick identifies the task of his *Gilles Deleuze's Time Machine* (which provides one of the most sustained, substantial and successful examples of such work) as the attempt to 'treat the two [*Cinema*] books as philosophical works and to try to understand them as a logical development through cinema of Deleuze's more general concerns' in so far as the latter's philosophy is 'in the deepest and most complex ways, a philosophy of time'.[15] Rodowick achieves precisely that, and in doing so makes a major contribution to our grasp of the ways in which the *Cinema* books develop these 'concerns'. But given that 'time' understood as Bergsonian duration (as it is in the *Cinema* books) is simply another way of saying 'difference', and that difference underpins all that Deleuze writes, this contribution bears on and informs but does not bring into focus the *specificity* of those books and their problematic within the Deleuzian œuvre. It does not enable us to answer the question 'why cinema?'

Similarly, the substantial body of individual essays that engage with the *Cinema* books in many cases provide valuable insights into particular aspects, problems or issues arising from them in their relation to Deleuzian philosophy (and perhaps to a lesser extent, in their relation to problems within the research tradition of cinema studies).[16] However, their very specificity limits their capacity to respond to the question of the project of those books as a whole.[17] The task of this book is specifically to redress this absence: not only to answer the question 'why does Deleuze write about cinema as a philosopher?', but to do so *in terms of the specific philosophical problems that compel him to do so.*

It seems worth asking why this absence in the critical literature remains, more than twenty-five years after the second volume of the *Cinema* books became available in English.[18] Nearly two decades ago, Rodowick noted that the *Cinema* books were regarded as 'anomalies' by the research communities of both philosophy and

Introduction: The Problem of Cinema

cinema studies,[19] seen by both as 'outside' their legitimate field of interest or perhaps even as an unwarranted expansion of one field into the other (although possibly more so for cinema studies than philosophy). The manner in which Deleuze approaches issues and arguments 'belonging to' or arising out of the cinema studies research tradition as and in terms of philosophical problems, or presents his own philosophical arguments as though they were internal to the cinema, means that readers from both traditions can find themselves alienated from and critical of those arguments, even (or especially) when they appear to concern issues 'proper' to the reader's own field.

'Philosophical' responses to the *Cinema* books have tended to acknowledge in passing, and with a greater or lesser degree of sympathy, the claim Deleuze makes for the philosophical significance of the cinema while still tending to treat the books as one more example among others of his tendency to engage with philosophy through and with a vast diversity of non-philosophical materials drawn from science, mathematics, literature and art. In doing so, the specificity of his engagement with the cinema has tended to be pushed to the background in favour of a focus on the more familiar philosophical concepts, problems and personae that arise therein.

Where the question of Deleuze's contribution to the study of the cinema is concerned, there is a growing body of work from authors with varying degrees of Deleuzian philosophical commitments who have drawn on his work productively to explore aspects of the cinema he touches on in passing, or not at all. Quite reasonably, however, their concerns have tended to be more with what one can do with Deleuze in relation to the cinema than with questioning what the cinema makes possible for Deleuze. The 'non-Deleuzian' cinema studies community has been more directly critical of the lapses, gaps, incongruities or limits they perceive in Deleuze's treatment of 'their' tradition (especially, although not exclusively, in the Anglophone world).[20] Even Rodowick himself, who is clearly deeply engaged with and sympathetic to the philosophical project of the *Cinema* books, argues (with some justice) that Deleuze's 'knowledge of film history departs little from the general histories that have been so profoundly challenged and revised by the new film history of the past fifteen years', and that his attitude towards film authorship 'represents one of the worst aspects of Parisian cinephilisim . . . [while] his analyses are often derivative of other works'.[21]

David Bordwell's argument that Deleuze uncritically repeats the dominant research tradition of cinema studies from the perspective of an arbitrarily imposed theoretical and philosophical framework[22] offers itself as a kind of synecdoche for such criticisms, in so far as behind them all is the question of why the cinema (its histories, theories and the films on which they bear) can or should be approached in terms of philosophy at all.[23] The specific terms of Bordwell's critique foreground the difficulty of responding to the *Cinema* books in terms adequate to the demands of the intellectual and critical traditions of both philosophy and cinema studies. Bordwell characterises the philosophical framework he sees Deleuze as imposing as implicitly Hegelian (by which he largely means 'teleological in orientation'), which will immediately strike anyone familiar with Deleuze's philosophy as somewhat surprising, at least without some very careful and nuanced supporting argument – which Bordwell does not provide. Bordwell is one of the most significant figures in Anglophone cinema studies, and although hostile to what he calls 'grand theory' as a framework for approaching cinema,[24] is a wide-ranging and exacting thinker and writer on the formal, industrial and theoretical dynamics of the cinema and its histories. As such, his failure to support his assertion of Deleuze's Hegelianism in terms that might satisfy (if not necessarily convince) a reader grounded in Deleuzian philosophy seems to me less a reflection of a lack of rigour on his part than it is of the difficulty of dealing with a work (the *Cinema* books) that refuses to distinguish between cinema and philosophy. Any response from a position rooted within only one of those two research traditions runs the risk of missing, misreading or misplacing the goal or the context of the arguments therein, or, more dangerously, the problems those arguments respond to or are grounded in. To read the *Cinema* books as if they were about *either* cinema *or* philosophy is to miss the point entirely.

It seems worth noting that even if Bordwell's use of the adjective 'Hegelian' can be seen as problematic, this does not mean that his overarching criticism – that Deleuze 'imports' a conceptual framework external to the cinema to the analysis of it – can therefore be dismissed out of hand. A more adequate response to Bordwell's critique (and to the wider question of why the cinema can or should be approached in terms of philosophy) and to its philosophical counterpart (why and how the problems of philosophy should be approached by means of the cinema), would be to demonstrate how and why the philosophical problems Deleuze responds to by means of the cinema are internal to the cinema itself. This, of course, goes to the very heart of the problem the *Cinema* books pose to the reader,

Introduction: The Problem of Cinema

regardless of their intellectual and aesthetic commitments. It is not only that the simultaneous depth of cinematic and philosophical erudition that Deleuze demands of the reader has been such that few have been either equipped or willing to engage fully with both aspects, as Rodowick points out.[25] It is also that the *Cinema* books are premised on the principle that the cinema 'thinks' in its own right, and that that thought bears directly on philosophy – and that the basis on which that 'principle' is asserted remains obscure within the books themselves.

The barriers to engagement that Rodowick describes with such clarity have, it must be said, lowered somewhat in recent years, and the reach of the *Cinema* books' impact and influence has in consequence expanded considerably. The continuity and consistency of the *Cinema* books with Deleuze's other work have been skilfully unpacked in the intervening period (not least by Rodowick himself) and, as Robert Sinnerbrink has argued, Deleuze's work on cinema has been a significant contributor to the emergence of 'film-philosophy' as an area of research in the Anglophone world.[26] Within the field of cinema studies more narrowly conceived, the question of how, or indeed why, Deleuze's work could or should be brought to bear on research problems generated from within that field at all has been a more contested issue. Even here, however, we can note that the reconsideration of Bazin's critical fortunes after their nadir in the 1970s and '80s (a reconsideration driven in part by the work of Daney, and reinforced within the Anglophone world by the efforts of Dudley Andrew) has at least to some extent been propelled by Deleuze's treatment of Bazin's work and ideas in the *Cinema* books.[27] Beyond this, the work of authors such as Laura Marks, David Martin-Jones, David Deamer, Elena Del Rio, Nick Davis and Nadine Boljkovac (to name only a few) have in very different ways and contexts shown how Deleuzian concepts can be appropriated to offer productive new ways to approach the cinema.[28] And Patricia Pisters' work on the 'neuro-image' has projected Deleuze's work on the cinema beyond the cinema itself into the realm of the twenty-first century's digital and transmedia reconfigurations of the moving image.[29] Nevertheless, even if the conjunction of cinema and philosophy found in the *Cinema* books appears less anomalous now than it once did, the specific basis on which Deleuze himself constructs this conjunction constitutes no less of a problem now than before.

The difficulty of identifying and specifying this basis is, I think (and perhaps inevitably), rooted in difference itself as the very ground of

7

Deleuzian philosophy, and the corresponding critique of representation and identity that accompanies it. This difficulty manifests itself on multiple levels. To begin with, there is a general methodological problem that faces anyone wishing to write on, or with, Deleuze and Deleuzian concepts. The primacy of difference for Deleuze means that his own philosophical practice cannot simply describe, analyse or discuss difference, since to do so would in various ways be to seek to represent it, to treat it as something identical to itself and so not difference at all. Rather, his philosophical practice must differ from itself if it is to engage with difference *as* difference: it offers, as Bellour says, a 'heterogenesis' whose consistency lies in its difference from *itself*.[30]

In so far as difference grounds all that he writes, Deleuze is the most systematic and consistent of philosophers, but that system is fundamentally disjunctive in so far as each 'moment' or 'event' within it is one of creation, given as the variation of the system itself. In short, as Daniel W. Smith says, 'there is a becoming of concepts not only within Deleuze's corpus, but in each book and in each concept, which is extended to and draws from the history of philosophy, and is repeated in each act of reading'.[31] Attempting to identify or specify what Deleuze is doing at any given point (say, in the *Cinema* books) is thus always problematic, not only because it always slips from our grasp, but also because doing so risks falling into the trap of representation ('Deleuze says ...', 'Deleuze means ...') and so missing the point.

One response to this in the secondary literature has been to claim that one's commentary marks an 'appropriation' of or 'deviation' from Deleuze's work and ideas, rather than a representation or critique of them – to be consistent with Deleuze by differing from him.[32] Deleuze himself encourages us to treat a theory 'exactly like a box of tools',[33] to take what is useful from it in relation to one's own frame of reference and do something with it, rather than seek to fix or pin down what it 'means'. Both of these paths have produced valuable insights into, and uses of, Deleuzian philosophy. However, they are limited in their capacity to investigate and respond to the coherence and consistency of that philosophy.

As Alain Badiou has noted, Deleuze's commitment to difference as the univocity of being is such that it appears throughout his work repeatedly in different guises and via different terminology.[34] Badiou emphasises this repetition as part of his own interpretation of Deleuze as a philosopher of the One, but in doing so Badiou

Introduction: The Problem of Cinema

suppresses difference itself as the single voice in which being speaks, and so distorts the consistency of Deleuzian philosophy (egregiously, to my mind), rather than seeking to understand it in its own terms: the univocity of being is given not as unity, as Badiou would have it, but as multiplicity.[35] What is needed instead is an approach that recognises the repetition Badiou identifies, but this time as an expression *of* difference as the ground of the coherence and consistency of Deleuzian philosophy.

Deleuze offers us a path to fulfilling this demand in so far as he characterises the specificity of any given 'thing' in terms of the difference of the thing itself. The specificity of the colour red, for example, lies not in its difference from green or blue or even of all the 'other' shades of red, but in its participation in the differing from itself of 'pure white light' (which 'contains' all the colours as nuances of that difference).[36] The consistency of Deleuzian philosophy – the repetition of the 'same' concept under different names (movement, duration and difference for example) – is thus given in the specificity of each 'name' as a nuance or differing from itself of that concept, such that they are vitally connected without being interchangeable.

One path to grasping that nuance, that specificity, is to examine the relation between the variations of the concept as it appears throughout the Deleuzian corpus in order to grasp the specificity of the task or problem to which that nuance responds. In more straightforward terms, if you want to work out what Deleuze is doing at any given point, and why, you need to locate the 'moment' you are examining in the context of its difference from related concepts, problems or arguments that appear throughout his work. In relation to the task at hand, this suggests that to identify the problems that drive the argument of the *Cinema* books is to identify the specificity or nuance of difference that they unfold, and to do so in relation to the difference that grounds the consistency of Deleuzian philosophy.

The necessity of such an approach is only amplified if one accepts Michael Hardt's argument that 'often, Deleuze's arguments appear incomplete because he takes for granted and fails to repeat the results of his previous research',[37] thus obscuring the problem or concept each work in turn responds to and differs from. Reading Deleuze in the manner I have outlined requires that we look for our cues and clues in the relationships between texts – what might, in traditional terms, be called a hermeneutic methodology. If such an approach can usefully be brought to bear on Deleuze it is because the repetition of a concept or problem across texts marks the differing of that concept or problem, and in that differing lies the specificity of the instance under examination. Such an approach is not merely a case of attempting to define and restate what Deleuze already says – in this case, the arguments presented in the *Cinema* books. To prefigure arguments made in the body of this book regarding Deleuze's own philosophical practice, this approach can rather be conceived of as kind of montage – a cutting up and reordering of relations between texts in order to enter into the movement of the *Cinema* books by counter-actualising the event of thought actualised within them.

The Monotony of Difference

Given the demands the *Cinema* books place on their reader, I cannot help but be aware of the hubris implicit in the undertaking of this project. Although I love the cinema and know its history moderately well, I do not count myself a true cinephile and most certainly not one on the scale of Deleuze. My academic specialisation is the history of film theory, not philosophy, and in the best light I might be regarded as an informed outsider with regard to the field of Deleuze studies – although perhaps better informed at the end of this project than at its beginning. But there are, I hope, some advantages to such a position, at least in the sense that it allows me to offer a pair of fresh eyes to the question of the relation of the *Cinema* books to Deleuze's philosophical œuvre.

It must be said that there is a great deal that might have been addressed in this book that is not. The usual caveats as to the shortness of time, space and life apply, of course, but it should also be noted that a great deal has already been said about the *Cinema* books. I have tried to avoid repeating analyses already done better elsewhere, except where they might be brought to a new conclusion. For reasons that will become clear over the course of the book, the focus of my argument is on the terms of the break or gap between the two *Cinema* books, and on the relation this break constructs *between* the different images of thought proper to each of them. It is that relation, and not the details of Deleuze's taxonomy of the classical and modern cinemas and their films, that interests me here. As such, the specifics of Deleuze's arguments regarding the classical and modern cinemas individually play little part in my discussion, except where they bear on this break and relation.

Of the great Deleuzian triumvirate of Bergson, Spinoza and Nietzsche – all of whom play a role in the *Cinema* books – I give

Introduction: The Problem of Cinema

sustained attention to Bergson alone. This is not to diminish the importance of the others, but because by my reading it is the 'return to Bergson' presented in the *Cinema* books that points us towards the philosophical problems Deleuze turns to the cinema to resolve. It is this Bergsonian problematic that therefore forms the primary focus of my argument. The Spinozian vector of the *Cinema* books remains largely absent from my treatment because it bears less directly on the philosophical problems that I argue Deleuze turns to the cinema to resolve. If Nietzsche plays a more overt (though still minor) role in my argument, it is because he bears more directly on the question of *how* the cinema allows Deleuze to solve these problems. Thus, for example, although my analysis of the break between the two volumes of the *Cinema* books offers a foundation for understanding the Nietzschean powers of the false Deleuze attributes to the modern cinema, those powers themselves are mentioned largely in passing.

Perhaps most striking of all for a book on a two-volume work titled *Cinema,* the discussion of films and their interpretation plays virtually no part in my analyses. Although my own intellectual background and the origins of my interest in the *Cinema* books are rooted in the traditions of cinema studies rather than philosophy, it is one of the underlying contentions of this book that Deleuze's engagement with and relevance to cinema studies can only be adequately grasped in terms and by means of an understanding of the *philosophical* problems that drive Deleuze to the cinema. That is, although Deleuze himself thinks with and through the cinema and a vast proliferation of examples thereof, I aim to understand the *philosophical* terms on which this cinema-thought takes place and can be understood. It is therefore these problems, and in particular their roots in the very ground of Deleuze's philosophical project, that are the focus of this book. Any exploration of what one might say about specific films on that basis is a task for another time. It is, however, my hope that unpacking these problems may help lay out the terms in which the relation between cinema and philosophy Deleuze constructs might be brought to bear productively on the research problems and traditions of both.

How then can we begin to approach the specificity of the philosophical problems that drive Deleuze to the cinema? Bellour makes the observation that the *Cinema* books stand out as something distinct within the Deleuzian œuvre, singular or perhaps even unique in so far as they concern themselves with a single art form in its entirety – the cinema as such, and as a whole.[38] Where other of

Deleuze's works turn on encounters with specific authors or artists,[39] or entrain congeries of the most diverse artistic and scientific materials as grasped by and for philosophy,[40] the *Cinema* books summon all of a single art form. They do so not in order to produce a philosophy *of* cinema (an idea Deleuze regards as plainly 'stupid'[41]), but to discover what cinema can enable philosophy to think for itself that it otherwise could not. 'I was able to write about cinema', he says, 'not because of some right of consideration, but because philosophical problems compelled me to look for answers in the cinema.'[42]

Now this statement tells us very clearly that if we wish to understand the *Cinema* books and what is at stake in them for Deleuze, we must read them *as* philosophy and specifically in the context of Deleuze's own philosophical history. The necessity of such an approach is implicit in Hardt's observation that each new work by Deleuze tends to assume its predecessors as a given. As such, Deleuze's reasoning at any given moment can remain obscure if the reader is not familiar enough with its antecedents to place both the terms of an argument, and the problems it responds to, in the context of his work as a whole.[43] Immediately, however, we find a curious tension at play: the *Cinema* books, as a 'unique' and 'singular' event within Deleuze's career, are nevertheless inextricably a part of that career, continuous with it and inexplicable outside of it.

The two poles of this tension (the unique and the continuous) might be read as an echo of Badiou's characterisation of Deleuze's career as one devoted to the repetition of the singular, in which Deleuze's account of universal creation as univocal difference gives rise to

> conceptual productions that I would unhesitatingly characterise as monotonous, composing a very particular regime of emphasis or almost infinite repetition of a limited repertoire of concepts, as well as a virtuosic variation of names, under which that which is thought remains essentially identical.[44]

In this vein we could say that Deleuze's thought is devoted to accounting for the unique and the singular, in each and every case, in terms of a single and singular thought: that of being which is everywhere and always given in the same way and in the same sense, as difference that differs from itself. Peter Hallward points us in a similar direction when he notes that 'the real challenge in writing about Deleuze's philosophy lies not in the remarkable diversity of materials that he considers but in the monotony of the underlying logic he invokes

Introduction: The Problem of Cinema

to understand them.'[45] In other words, all of Deleuze's writing, all of its dizzying proliferation of subjects and terminology and topics and fields of inquiry, unfolds from the single assertion that the difference of the unique subsists not in its difference from anything or everything else, but in the difference of being from itself first of all. In this sense, then, the uniqueness of the *Cinema* books does indeed demand to be grasped as a production, or indeed a repetition, of the very same univocal difference that animates all of Deleuze's writing.

The danger of such a formulation, however, is that left undeveloped it remains purely abstract and thus, in a properly Deleuzian sense, incapable of grasping the difference that the *Cinema* books repeat concretely and for itself. In other words, the concept of difference would remain transcendent to the differences collected under its name (i.e., to the cinema) and thought would consist of going 'from the concept to the variety that it subsumes',[46] *recognising* this or that difference as just another case of the concept. This is, of course, a model of thought Deleuze rejects: for him, thought is creation, not recognition.[47] To put it more concretely and pragmatically, to say that the *Cinema* books are just another example of Deleuzian difference doesn't tell us very much about them – it tells us nothing of the 'nuance' Deleuze demands of a thought adequate to the concrete, the 'how, how many, when and where'.[48] The task at hand, then, is to account for the singularity of the *Cinema* books – their difference – in terms of the singular, monotonous thought that animates them: breathes life into them, causes them to move *of their own accord*.

The two poles of this task unfold from a single question: what use is cinema to Deleuze? At one end, this question seeks to account for the singularity Bellour finds in the *Cinema* books (what is it about cinema that makes Deleuze want to write about it, in a way that is different from all his other works?). At the other, it looks towards the monotony of thought Badiou and Hallward find in Deleuze (how do the *Cinema* books fit with, develop, draw on, assume, repeat the thought of his other work?). Asked 'When did you begin to love cinema and when did you begin to consider it a domain worthy of philosophy?', Deleuze responds that he was 'compelled' to look to cinema for answers to philosophical problems.[49] He is interested in cinema because it is able to give philosophy something *strictly philosophical* that philosophy nevertheless lacks. In particular, it is movement that crosses or is given back and forth in the movement between philosophy and cinema, and which draws him to the latter: 'I liked those authors who demanded that we introduce movement to thought, "real" movement (they denounced the Hegelian dialectic as abstract movement). How could I not discover the cinema, which introduces "real" movement into the image?'[50]

In the first sentence of this quote, we find, *ab ovo*, all of Deleuze's philosophy and all that it flees. We will have cause to expand on the themes embedded in it throughout this book, but in their compacted form, they are as follows. On the one hand, there is the positive assertion of the primacy of the being of becoming as the founding principle of Deleuzian philosophy: the difference from itself of being *is* real movement. On the other, there is its critical moment, figured by Hegel as the most extreme version of philosophies of identity and representation – those that begin with being and only then seek to account for its becoming (which gives only an abstract movement). Finally, and most important of all, there is the positing of a thought for which real movement will always be a *demand* and not a right, such that its proper task is always and only to become adequate to such movement, that is to say, to difference *as such* or, as Peter Hallward puts it, to *creation*: 'The main task facing a creature capable of thought is to learn how to think.'[51] To become adequate to movement, then, is to escape the lures of representation and identity, to wrest oneself free of abstraction in the struggle to think movement as differing difference. Hence the dramatic nature of so much of Deleuze's philosophy: in each of its endless proliferation of cases, it is a story of the struggle of thought to think.

Thus, in his second sentence, Deleuze tells us it is cinema's capacity for real movement that draws him to it. It is not, however, that cinema makes thought adequate to such movement in and of itself. He goes on to say that

> something bizarre about the cinema struck me: its unexpected ability to show not only behaviour, but spiritual life as well . . . Cinema not only puts movement in the image, it also puts movement in the mind. Spiritual life is the movement of the mind. One naturally goes from philosophy to cinema, but also from cinema to philosophy.[52]

Immediately, the story is more complex (the plot thickens): to put movement into the image is merely to show behaviour, but cinema also puts movement into the mind, into thought – it *shows* us the movement of the mind or 'spiritual life'. Cinema is not simply thought, but shows us thought thinking, presents it to us directly. This, it seems to me, would be the special virtue of the cinema for Deleuze. Philosophy, surely, can think for itself and may put these

Introduction: The Problem of Cinema

thoughts into words, but it cannot *show* us thought in its struggle to think. Cinema, then, does not merely think, but presents us with the *dramatisation* of thought's struggle to become adequate to becoming, to real movement: the drama of the struggle to construct concepts or ideas adequate to the being of becoming. As Deleuze says elsewhere, it is through 'dramatisation [that] the Idea is incarnated or actualised'.[53] This, then, is the proposition of the *Cinema* books: cinema as the dramatisation of philosophy itself.

Indeed, this is precisely Bellour's answer to the problem posed by the uniqueness of the *Cinema* books: 'why the cinema, why the cinema at that point? Quite simply so that philosophy can thus itself write its novel.'[54] And as he points out,[55] this dramatisation or 'novelisation' of philosophy is prefigured long before the *Cinema* books, in *Difference and Repetition*, where Deleuze argues that

> a book of philosophy should be in part a very particular species of detective novel, in part a kind of science fiction ... The search for new means of philosophical expression was begun by Nietzsche and must be pursued today in relation to the renewal of certain other arts, such as the theatre or the cinema.[56]

What Bellour does not add is that Deleuze then goes on to say: 'It seems to us that the history of philosophy should play a role roughly analogous to that of *collage* in painting.'[57] Christian Kerslake draws our attention to the preface of the English edition of *Cinema 2*, where Deleuze 'claims that cinema is a repetition, in speeded-up form, of an experience that has already occurred in the history of philosophy'.[58] What is 'repeated' here is what Deleuze calls the 'great Kantian reversal' of the subordination of time to movement.[59] This 'reversal', as it appears in and for the cinema, and in the *Cinema* books, does so in terms of the break between the classical and modern cinemas, which is itself repeated in the break or gap – or indeed, the *cut* – between *Cinema 1* and *Cinema 2*. The *Cinema* books, then, offer us a 'cinematic' history of philosophy, not as collage, but as *montage*: the gap or interval between the two volumes, between the classical and the modern cinemas, the pre- and post-war periods, as a cutting together or splicing apart to create the film of the history of philosophy.

But what is this break or 'reversal', this 'experience' that has already occurred in the history of philosophy and is repeated in the history of the cinema? In this reversal, 'time ceases to be the measurement of normal movement ... [and] increasingly appears for itself and creates paradoxical movements. Time is out of joint: Hamlet's words signify that time is no longer subordinated to movement, but rather movement to time.'[60] In the *Cinema* books, this reversal takes place as or in the break between the cinemas of the movement-image and the time-image: in other words in the break or interval between two regimes of montage, the second of which reverses the subordination of time to movement characteristic of the first. But what this reversal reveals is thought's confrontation with the impossibility of thought, of its 'impower', 'this powerlessness at the heart of thought',[61] as Deleuze says. Thus the dramatisation of thought's struggle to become adequate to movement, the dramatisation of the history of philosophy itself, is not one of thought's ascension to power or mastery but of thought's confrontation with its own impossibility.

The pivot of this drama is the demand for the introduction of real movement into thought. Inasmuch as it is a *demand*, and not something thought possesses by right, it is driven by the failure, the inadequacy, of thought itself. Thought that retains a merely abstract conception of movement – thought that subordinates time to movement – is, to invert Hallward's formulation, the thought of a creature that has not yet learnt to think. Yet to accede to this demand, to introduce into thought a movement now subordinated to time – what we see in the time-image of *Cinema 2* – is to cause it to suffer the disordering, destabilising, decentring powers of time 'out of joint'. A thought that truly thinks, it seems, is a thought for which thought is no longer a power that it holds, but powerlessness that it suffers. Thus the appearance of 'the Mummy' in *Cinema 2*, 'this dismantled, paralysed, petrified, frozen instance which testifies to "the impossibility of thinking that is thought"'.[62] Thought, then, either fails to think, or else can think only and always its own failure.

But what is it that thinks, and thus doubly fails to think, in each of these two ways? The human being, whose task it is to 'learn how to think'. And what is it that the human being thus fails to think twice over? Being as such, being as difference that differs from itself. Thought that insists on the subordination of time to movement is a thought tied ultimately to a static conception of being, which moves only on the impulsion of an abstract movement imposed from without (the becoming of being, whose most extreme avatar is Hegel's dialectic). But a thought that introduces real movement, the movement that is the being of becoming, is a thought that suffers its own impossibility. If, as Badiou says, the *Cinema* books sing Deleuze's monotonous refrain of univocal being, it is because they do

Introduction: The Problem of Cinema

indeed return us to his single and singular thought of being as self-differing difference. The singular nature that Bellour finds in them, their nuance and concreteness, lies in their dramatisation not merely of thought, but of thought understood in terms of human being's confrontation with being.

This, in a sense, is the essential theme of all ontological speculation, in so far as ontology is, and can only be, a problem posed to and of being *by* beings, and from within being, by human beings themselves (there is no one else to ask the question and nowhere else to ask it from).[63] In contrast, the specificity of Deleuze's formulation of the ontological question lies in his positing of a being that is univocal, such that beings, and thus human beings, are given in the same terms as being itself and not transcended by it. Transcendence only appears to or in thought to the extent that movement remains abstract and thus separated arbitrarily from being. When real movement is introduced into thought, being appears in and as that movement (that is to say, as real difference): thought becomes adequate to movement at the moment it places itself within that movement, when it thinks *with* or *in* movement rather than *of* it. What the cinema gives us, what it thinks and shows us then, is, as Deleuze says, the 'relationship between man and the world, nature and thought'.[64] This is 'the thought of the world', understood as the problem of thought's thinking *of* being, and its struggle to become adequate *to* being. What I hope to demonstrate is that it is this struggle that lies at the heart of the philosophical problems Deleuze turns to the cinema to solve.

Notes

1. I will refer to these works collectively hereafter as 'the *Cinema* books', and individually as *Cinema 1*; *Cinema 2*.
2. Although the *Cinema* books themselves were published in the 1980s, the problems in question and their treatment in those books nevertheless bear on, inform and can be productively informed by the works that came after them – Deleuze and Guattari's *What is Philosophy?* in particular.
3. See, for example, 'V as in Voyage', *Gilles Deleuze from A to Z*.
4. For an account of the history of Langlois and the *Cinémathèque Française*, see Roud, *A Passion for Films*.
5. Dudley Andrew's 1978 biographical study *André Bazin* remains a key reference point for those wanting to grasp Bazin's impact on and significance for the *Cahiers* tradition and cinema studies more generally,

while the 2011 collection *Opening Bazin* is testament to Bazin's continuing relevance and importance to cinema studies today. Andrew, *André Bazin*; Andrew and Joubert-Laurencin, *Opening Bazin*.
6. Film scholar William D. Routt once proposed to me in conversation that it should in principle be possible to work out which programmes of the *Cinémathèque Française* Deleuze had attended, on the basis of the films referred to in the *Cinema* books.
7. Bellour, 'Thinking, Recounting', 69.
8. Daney was a contributor to *Cahiers du cinéma* from 1964 and its co-editor and editor from 1973 to 1981. He was also instrumental in inviting philosophers such as Michel Foucault, Jacques Rancière and Deleuze himself to contribute to the journal, and so marks an important point of contact between the trajectories of French philosophy and cinema studies. For more on what Garin Dowd describes as the 'traffic of ideas and concepts between Deleuze and Daney', and the specificities of Parisian cinephilism within which this traffic took place, see his 'Pedagogies of the Image Between Daney and Deleuze', 41, and 41–56 more generally.
9. Andrew, *What Cinema Is!*, 4–5; Andrew cites as the original source of this quote Daney, *L'Exercise a Été Profitable, Monsieur*.
10. As Andrew puts it, this 'line' 'is neither perfectly straight, nor is it singular (having many threads), nor is it necessarily tied to this one periodical [*Cahiers du cinéma*]; however it does identify an orientation that owes most to Bazin'. Andrew and Joubert-Laurencin, 'A Binocular Preface', x.
11. Bazin, *What Is Cinema? Volume 1*, 1:23–40.
12. In a quite separate context Thomas Elsaesser and Malte Hagener identify within the traditions of film theory 'a French line of thought linking Jean Epstein, André Bazin and Gilles Deleuze'. Elsaesser and Hagener, *Film Theory*, 2.
13. Deleuze, 'The Brain Is the Screen', 367. Even this hint is offered outside the *Cinema* books, in an interview for *Cahiers du cinéma*. I will be referring throughout this book to the English translation of this interview included in Gregory Flaxman's anthology *The Brain is the Screen*, which borrows its title from that of the interview in question. 'Le Cerveau, C'est L'écran', 24–32; 'The Brain Is the Screen', 365–73.
14. Rodowick, *Gilles Deleuze's Time Machine*; Bogue, *Deleuze on Cinema*; Marrati, *Gilles Deleuze: Cinema and Philosophy*.
15. Rodowick, *Gilles Deleuze's Time Machine*, xiii.
16. Gregory Flaxman's anthology *The Brain is the Screen* is a key source of such material, but numerous significant examples can be found in a diverse range of compilations and journals – many of which are cited throughout this book. From a quite different perspective, the essays collected in Ian Buchanan and Patricia MacCormack's *Deleuze and*

Introduction: The Problem of Cinema

the *Schizoanalysis of Cinema* look to Deleuzian sources beyond the *Cinema* books to think the relation of Deleuzian philosophy to cinema on other terms and in relation to other problems than those Deleuze sets himself in the *Cinema* books.

17. If there is an exception to this rule it is Bellour's remarkable essay 'Thinking, Recounting: the Cinema of Gilles Deleuze'. For my money, this essay is the best short analysis of the *Cinema* books available and perhaps the finest at any scale – the subtlest, the most graceful, the most able to grasp their fusion of cinema and philosophy and respond in kind.
18. Given that I neither speak nor read French, this project has an unavoidable bias to the Anglophone reception and discussion of the *Cinema* books. Although this constitutes a real and present limitation on its scope, the enthusiasm with which French philosophical/cinematic thought and writing have been engaged with in the English-speaking world means that a significant (although necessarily selective) body of relevant French-language material is available in translation.
19. Within the Anglophone world at least, although Tom Conley suggests this confusion was shared to some degree by French readers as well. 'Film Theory "After" Deleuze'.
20. See for example, Luc Moulett's attack on what he describes as Deleuze's 'schoolboy' errors in the latter's treatment of the cinema. Moullet, 'The Green Garbage Bins of Gilles Deleuze'.
21. What Rodowick doesn't acknowledge here is how thorough Deleuze's grasp of this tradition is or, indeed, that most of the 'revision' of this tradition he refers to in this passage took place after the *Cinema* books were written. Rodowick, *Gilles Deleuze's Time Machine*, x and xiii–xvi.
22. Bordwell, *On the History of Film Style*, 116–17.
23. Indeed, a similar criticism can be made in reverse with regard to the relevance of the cinema as a means of exploring philosophical problems. In particular, Deleuze's assertion that the history of the cinema in some sense repeats or recapitulates the history of philosophy risks seeming no less arbitrary an imposition in the absence of an account of how and why this parallel is either justified or required, or indeed what is meant by 'history' in this context – an issue that, as we shall see, has a particular resonance with the project of the *Cinema* books.
24. Bordwell, 'Lowering the Stakes: Prospects for a Historical Poetics of Cinema'.
25. Rodowick, *Gilles Deleuze's Time Machine*, ix–x.
26. Sinnerbrink identifies Deleuze and Stanley Cavell as the 'founding figures' of this area (their very different philosophical contexts notwithstanding.) Along with the work of Sinnerbrink himself, we might point to Daniel Frampton's book *Filmosophy*, Danial Yacavone's *Film Worlds*,

or the journal *Film-Philosophy* (along with its eponymous conference) as some of the markers for this 'emergence' in the English-speaking world. Sinnerbrink, *New Philosophies of Film: Thinking Images*, 4.
27. As evidence for Deleuze's role in this revival we can note, for example, that the index of names in 2011's *Opening Bazin* lists no fewer than eighteen references to Deleuze therein – the second highest, on equal footing with Orson Welles and beaten only by references to Jean Renoir with twenty-five. Moreover, both Welles and Renoir are key cinematic reference points for Bazin's own writing, in a way Deleuze is not and could not be. Such metrics are a blunt tool at best, but they at the very least support Elsaesser's contention that Deleuze's work on cinema warrants the description of him as one of Bazin's key 'successors'. Andrew and Joubert-Laurencin, *Opening Bazin*, 339–44; Elsaesser, 'A Bazinian Half-Century', 5.
28. Marks, *The Skin of the Film*; Martin-Jones, *Deleuze, Cinema and National Identity*; *Deleuze and World Cinemas*; Deamer, *Deleuze, Japanese Cinema and the Atom Bomb*; *Deleuze's Cinema Books*; del Río, *Deleuze and the Cinemas of Performance*; Davis, *The Desiring-Image*; Boljkovac, *Untimely Affects*.
29. Pisters, *The Neuro-Image*. I find Pisters' book to be a particularly productive extension and appropriation of Deleuze's work on cinema. If I don't refer to her work in what follows, it is only because I am concerned here with where the *Cinema* books come from, whereas to my mind Pisters is more concerned to map out where we might take them.
30. Bellour, 'Thinking, Recounting', 70.
31. Smith, *Essays on Deleuze*, 124–5.
32. Brian Massumi is often cited in justifying this kind of approach to the use or interpretation of Deleuze's work. See, for example, his 'Foreword' to *A Thousand Plateaus*, xiv–xv; or his *User's Guide*, 8.
33. Foucault and Deleuze, 'Intellectuals and Power', 208.
34. Badiou, *Deleuze: The Clamour of Being*, 15.
35. As Jon Roffe points out in his book-length critique of Badiou's treatment of Deleuze, 'In Badiou's account of Deleuze's ontology, the word multiplicity only ever appears in places where it is clearly interchangeable with the word multiple . . . which erases, at the level of terminology, a decisive Deleuzean theme.' *Badiou's Deleuze*, 9.
36. Deleuze, 'Bergson's Conception of Difference', 54. He 'repeats' this argument in a different context and in slightly different terms some years later, in *Difference and Repetition*: 'The Idea of colour, for example, is like white light which perplicates in itself the genetic elements and relations of all the colours, but is actualised in the diverse colours with their respective spaces.' Deleuze, *Difference and Repetition*, 206. In both cases, he is drawing on a passage from Bergson's essay 'The Life and Works of Ravaisson', 225–6.

37. Hardt, *An Apprenticeship in Philosophy*, xix.
38. Bellour, 'Thinking, Recounting', 57.
39. Hume, Spinoza, Kafka or Bacon, and so on.
40. *Difference and Repetition*, *The Logic of Sense*, the work with Félix Guattari.
41. Deleuze, 'The Brain Is the Screen', 366.
42. Ibid., 367.
43. Hardt, *An Apprenticeship in Philosophy*, xix. As we have seen, Rodowick points out that this 'obscurity' is perhaps exacerbated in the case of the *Cinema* books – readers drawn to them by an interest in cinema may lack the requisite expertise not only in Deleuze's work, but in philosophy more broadly conceived, while those drawn by Deleuze and an interest in philosophy may find their knowledge of film and film history lacking. Rodowick, *Gilles Deleuze's Time Machine*, x–xi.
44. Badiou, *Deleuze: The Clamour of Being*, 15.
45. Hallward, *Out of This World*, 2.
46. Badiou, *Deleuze: The Clamour of Being*, 14.
47. The genuinely new – creation – is of necessity unrecognisable, since it has no model that could precede it in our understanding. Thus 'things and people are always forced to conceal themselves, have to conceal themselves when they begin. What else could they do? They come into being within a set that no longer includes them.' Deleuze, *Cinema 1*, 2–3.
48. Deleuze, *Bergsonism*, 44–5.
49. Deleuze, 'The Brain Is the Screen', 365–7.
50. Ibid., 366.
51. Hallward, *Out of This World*, 2. It is worth noting that although I agree with many of the premises of Hallward's reading of Deleuze, I do not agree with his conclusion – specifically, I do not agree that Deleuzian philosophy offers nothing to the human or to properly human concerns.
52. Deleuze, 'The Brain Is the Screen', 366.
53. Deleuze, 'The Method of Dramatization', 94.
54. Bellour, 'Thinking, Recounting', 64.
55. Ibid., 72.
56. Deleuze, *Difference and Repetition*, xx–xxi.
57. Ibid., xxi.
58. Kerslake, 'Transcendental Cinema', 7.
59. Deleuze, *Cinema 2*, xi.
60. Ibid.
61. Ibid., 166. Note that the English translators of the *Cinema* books use both 'impower' and 'inpower' to translate the French '*impouvoir*'. Where I make use of quotes including the latter term, I have followed their translation with regard to the relevant passage.

62. Ibid.
63. It is a fairly common convention to capitalise 'Being' when using it in its ontological sense, in contrast to the lower case 'being', used to refer to a particular being or beings. This usage tends to imply a transcendent conception of being, inasmuch as the necessity of distinguishing between the two suggests that 'Being' is of a different order to 'beings'. In keeping with Deleuze's univocal conception of being (in which being and beings are necessarily of the same order), I do not follow this convention here, relying rather on context to provide the reader with the relevant sense in which the term is being used.
64. Deleuze, *Cinema 2*, 163.

2

The Interval as Disaster

Terminus, or, Waiting for a Train

> ... *my waiting, whatever it be, expresses duration as mental, spiritual reality.*[1]

If the path to unfolding the problem that drives this book lies in the examination of the relation between texts, then the proposition of this chapter is that the starting point for this hermeneutic investigation lies in the relation between the two volumes of the *Cinema* books themselves. In particular, it lies in the relation between the movement- and time-images that dominate the first and second volume respectively. This relation is far murkier than it might at first seem, and constitutes in itself a significant interpretative problem for the reader. It is this interpretative problem and the terms in which it is to be resolved that marks the path I will follow in order to show how, and why, the cinema offers Deleuze the means to resolve a strictly philosophical problem.

We can start this investigation with a fable of origin: that of the cinema itself. Here, then, at the beginning, we are waiting. We stand patiently on the railway platform at Ciotat, at the railway terminus, waiting for the train to arrive. We sit patiently in the audience at the Grand Café in Paris, 1895, waiting for the cinema to arrive, tired, bored, restless, fidgeting, waiting for *something* to happen.[2] Now, a waiting whose object can be determined and met, that is, a waiting for something that will arrive (a train, perhaps), is no more than a pause or delay in a system of action and reaction. To this extent, this waiting might be understood in terms of the sensory-motor schemata that Deleuze describes as characteristic of the movement-image. Its figure would be that of a railway timetable, measuring only the time it takes until the next train will arrive, constituting or reconstituting time and this time of waiting simply as a function of movement (the regular and regulated movement of trains between stations).[3] Inherent in this waiting, however, is the possibility that its object can always not arrive – not only that the train may not arrive on time, but that it will *never* make it to the station. Thus waiting as pause or delay finds itself inhabited, haunted by another potentially unlimited or interminable waiting which has lost its object, which corresponds to no timetable and whose only figure would be that of time itself. Here, in this interminable waiting we find ourselves closer to something like the time-image Deleuze describes in *Cinema 2*. Implicit in such a formulation (of a sensory-motor waiting inhabited by the possibility of an interminable or unlimited waiting) is the conclusion that, despite Deleuze's presentation of a movement-image which is succeeded more or less historically by the time-image after the Second World War, this time-image is present in some sense at the very earliest point of the cinema, waiting there at the very beginning, inhabiting the movement-image, tracing within it the echo of what Deleuze describes as 'that Proustian dimension where people and things occupy a place in time which is incommensurable with the one they have in space'.[4]

It seems useful, then, to take this moment of arrival (of a train at Ciotat station, of the film of this arrival, of the arrival of the cinema itself) and the mythology of origin that surrounds it as a place from which to begin to explore the ambiguous and ambivalent relations between the movement- and time-images that Deleuze uses to divide the cinema into a 'classic' pre-war and a 'modern' post-war phase. To the extent that Deleuze uses this historical periodisation to mark the path of a development of the cinema (from the movement-image to the time-image) one might comfortably expect to assume that the early Lumière films, *L'Arrivée d'un Train à la Ciotat* (1895)[5] among them, would present the characteristics Deleuze attributes to the cinema of the movement-image. This would seem at least to a certain extent to be true, both in terms of the internal relations of the elements of the image, and in terms of the relations of those images to the audience. The hustle and bustle of the train arriving, passengers getting on and off and milling around on the platform, would seem to meet the minimal criteria for a movement-image, inasmuch as it at least points towards a setting or situation which could form an element in a schema of action and reaction.

Moreover, the film is clearly capable of engaging its audience in a sensory-motor situation. As Dai Vaughan recounts, in a 'story so frequently repeated as to have assumed the status of folklore ... members of the first audiences [of this film] dodged aside as [the] train steamed towards them into [the] station'.[6] This response has little to do with any excess of naïveté or credulity on the part of this first audience. As Vaughan notes,

> we cannot seriously imagine that these educated people ... expected the train to emerge from the screen and run them down ... What this legend means is that the particular combination of visual signals present in that film had had no previous existence *other* than as signifying a real train pulling into a station.[7]

In terms of Deleuze's model, in the absence of any other context through which they might filter and suppress it, the habitual sensory-motor engagement that this image articulated for its first audiences outweighed any intellectual recognition that this was only an *image* of movement before them, and not the real movement of an actual train. And lest we fall into the temptation to separate the sophisticated viewing responses of contemporary audiences from the primitive responses of those first spectators, it's worth noting that despite the knowledge that it is 'only a movie', the movement-images that, as Deleuze points out, make up the bulk of contemporary cinema[8] are nonetheless still entirely capable of inducing today's audiences to jump in their seats, shriek in horror or weep with sadness. To this extent at least, *Arrival of a Train* offers itself to be seen as a figure, even if a mythical one, for the origins of a cinema of sensory-motor engagement that is active even now.

Nonetheless, despite these potential reasons for assimilating this and perhaps the other early Lumière films to a cinema of the movement-image, there are certain issues which problematise the possibility of such an assimilation. Not the least of these is that Deleuze quite specifically rules out the early cinema from the constitution of a movement-image, thereby excluding it from his theorisation of the cinema and effectively relegating it to the status of cinematic 'pre-history'. Tom Gunning has pointed out that 'The history of early cinema, like the history of cinema generally, has been written and theorised under the hegemony of narrative films',[9] to the extent that one of the major questions asked of these films is whether and to what extent they might be considered to constitute a minimal or originary form of cinematic narrative. Despite clearly discounting Christian Metz's linguistically based account of cinematic narrative, Deleuze holds enough common ground with Metz to be able to follow him in noting that 'The historical fact is that cinema was constituted as such by becoming narrative, by presenting a story, and by rejecting its other possible directions.'[10] The cinema is constituted *as* cinema in becoming narrative; if films like *Arrival of a Train* belong to the pre-history of the cinema for Deleuze, this exclusion is tied to their inability to constitute a cinematic narrative. In order to grasp the significance of this for the position of the early or primitive cinema within Deleuze's schema, however, we must first examine what narrative itself constitutes for Deleuze.

One of the noteworthy features of Deleuze's history of the cinema (to the extent that it is such) is that it begins well after the 'beginning', with a discussion of the films of D. W. Griffith, circa 1915, and progresses, in *Cinema 1* at least, in a roughly chronological fashion from there, thereby largely eliding the early or primitive cinema. This is less a gap or omission than it is a logical consequence of the importance of montage and the use of the mobile camera in Deleuze's theory of the movement-image, and of Griffith's role in articulating these elements into a coherent model of cinematic narration. Deleuze quite specifically excludes the early cinema from the constitution of the movement-image, defining what he calls the 'primitive state of the cinema' as one 'where the image is in movement rather than being movement-image', suggesting that the static unedited shot (like those of the Lumière films presented at the Grand Café) can at best contain the tendency or potential for 'the mobilisation of the camera in space, or ... montage in time' that the movement-image requires.[11] It thus can never articulate a movement-image as such.

Now, although both montage and the mobile camera make their appearance some time after the Lumière films, their appearance in the cinema substantially pre-dates their use by Griffith, as do more or less fragmentary attempts to use these techniques within the context of a filmic narration (Edwin S. Porter is the director most likely to spring to mind in this context). Nonetheless, Griffith is generally credited with their integration into a systematic and unified mode of specifically cinematic narration, the so-called 'classic narrative' form. Moreover, this form is, according to Deleuze, derived directly from the organic composition of the different kinds of movement-image through montage and 'according to the laws of a sensory-motor schema', a system of possible responses to perception which maintains a correspondence between the action received and the reaction generated in response to it.[12]

If the French, German and particularly Soviet counterparts of Griffith that Deleuze discusses produce narrative forms that differ in various ways from the model that Griffith sets up, this is a consequence of the differing conceptions of the composition of movement-images articulated in their various models of montage.[13] These offer us varying degrees of difference in styles of narrative while still remaining narrative as such. For example, Deleuze suggests that parallel alternating montage in Griffith articulates a set of differentiated parts unified only by their common membership of the same organic whole: 'men and women, rich and poor, town and country, North and South, interiors and exteriors etc.'[14] Eisenstein on the other hand offers a 'montage of opposition', through which rich and poor, for example, cannot be paralleled simply as separate elements of the same whole, but which are, rather, opposed to each other dialectically to produce a unity at a higher level of explanation, in a third shot. This higher level of explanation is, as Deleuze points out, that of social exploitation.[15]

The differing conceptions and uses of montage that Griffith and Eisenstein present us with each produce a whole determined by a different sensory-motor schema, a different system of action and reaction, and hence a different model of narration. Thus Deleuze is able to note that, if Eisenstein condemns Griffith's conception of the whole as 'bourgeois', this is not merely on the basis of Griffith's 'way of telling a story or of understanding History',[16] but relates directly to Eisenstein's own conception of montage (and note the implications of this statement: by the concept of montage Deleuze presents us with, it is not only story but also *history* that is secondary to montage, a product of it and not a given).

For Deleuze, narrative thus 'results from the sensory-motor schema, and not the other way round',[17] as the organisation of movement-images according to a sensory-motor schema (articulated in montage) which itself constitutes a whole that changes. This whole 'isn't any set of things but the ceaseless passage from one set to another, the transformation of one set of things into another',[18] as for example in the changing set of relations between objects in a single mobile shot, and more generally in the transformation in relations articulated between two fixed or mobile shots. To this extent the whole is not closed, but open, as the never-completed transition from one set to the next (and the next and the next. . .). With each movement the whole changes qualitatively, and what this change expresses is time as duration. As such, Deleuze suggests that 'it is montage itself which constitutes the whole, and thus gives us the image *of* time [and] is therefore the principal act of cinema'.[19]

We are now in a position to perhaps understand Deleuze's comment that the cinema as such, the cinema *as* cinema, is constituted in becoming narrative. Narrative, understood as the organisation of movement-images (which are themselves formed at the level of the shot) according to a sensory-motor schema articulated at the level of montage, is thus constitutive of the changing whole that gives us the indirect image of time and which, as Deleuze says, is the 'principal act of cinema'. The question is now, where does this leave the Lumières? Given that *Arrival of a Train* is made up of a single fixed shot, there is little possibility of it presenting a narrative in Deleuze's sense, that is, as a sensory-motor schema articulated at the level of montage. Furthermore, for Deleuze, it cannot articulate a whole which changes, since in a single fixed shot, 'the whole is identical to the set in depth',[20] with the consequence that there can be no transformation in relations between the elements of the set or shot, so that the set remains closed and immutable. There can thus be movement within the image, but not a movement-image as such.

On these grounds, one might reasonably follow Deleuze in taking the position that *Arrival of a Train* belongs more to the pre-history of the cinema than its history proper, a mere step in the development of the techniques which would allow it to display its true character in the presentation of a movement-image. There remains, however, the problem of that first audience, the one so engaged by the sensory-motor scheme presented in the image that its members jumped out of the way as the image of the train pulled into the image of the station. For a cinema of the movement-image, the sensory-motor schema is articulated at the level of montage, as the coordination of perception and action across the different sets or shots which ensures their coherence and rationality, and thereby maintains a unity across the totality of the transformations of the open whole. In the absence of montage, however, it becomes difficult to speak of a *system* of action and reaction, or a sensory-motor *scheme* as such, since there is no whole to coordinate, no multiplicity of shots to articulate into a coherent totality.

Thus in the case of *Arrival of a Train*, we might say that, rather than a *system* of action and reaction, we are offered an *incident*. The audience leaping out of the way of the moving image of the train clearly indicates a sensory-motor engagement, but it seems closer to the isolated movement of a reflex response than a participation in a coherent world presented in the relations between images, inasmuch as it does not extend itself beyond that initial shock. Equally, the represented action of the arrival of the train, passengers getting on and off, etc., could certainly present itself as an *element* within a sensory-motor schema (one determined by a railway timetable, for instance). However, for this potential or tendency to become manifest in even a minimal sense requires either a second shot – of the train leaving the station for instance, thereby creating a montage of arrival and departure – or else the use of a mobile camera effecting a montage *within* the single shot by a continuous framing and reframing of the train as the camera follows it leaving the station.

Of course, this means that the single fixed shots of the Lumière films always contain the potential for the production of a movement-image. All that is required to draw this potential out is the montage produced in the addition of this second shot. As such, Deleuze argues that the movement-image was always present, even in the primitive cinema, as a potential as yet unable to express itself, a tendency or demand waiting to be filled. Thus he notes that

> this movement [expressed by the mobile camera and/or montage] was already characteristic of the cinema, and demanded a kind of emancipation, incapable of being satisfied within the limits set by the primitive conditions – so that the so called primitive image, the image in movement, was defined less by its state than by its tendency.[21]

Despite this tendency, however, it would seem overly hasty to then simply assimilate the early cinema to that of the movement-image that follows it. The tendency *towards* montage and the mobile camera nonetheless does not yet actually constitute either of them as such. As it stands, what we are offered in a film like *Arrival of a Train* would seem to present at best a *fragment* of a sensory-motor schema articulated in montage.

Here some interesting possibilities begin to present themselves. Deleuze's account of the transition from the cinema of the movement-image to that of the time-image begins precisely with the fragmentation and collapse of the unity of action and reaction presented in the sensory-motor schema. In this fragmentation, 'perceptions and actions cease to be linked together, and spaces are now neither coordinated nor filled'.[22] Montage no longer produces a continuity of world across and between shots, but produces aberrant movements articulating non-localisable relations, such that perceptions can no longer be extended into action. There is no longer a world to which characters can respond, but only 'pure optical and sound situations' to which there can be no response or reaction. As Deleuze says, 'These [characters become] pure seers ... given over to something intolerable which is simply their everydayness itself.'[23]

If *Arrival of a Train*, as a single static shot, does not yet present us with a movement-image, does it, as a *fragment* of a sensory-motor schema, move towards the presentation of a time-image? It must be said straight off that a 'fragment' as such probably cannot be taken as being of the same order as a 'fragmentation'. Fragmentation still presumes a system, albeit one whose connections are weakening or have fallen apart altogether. Even in a situation of total fragmentation, that fragmentation only has a sense to the extent that there are gaps between a number of fragments which are not crossed; that is to say, fragmentation presumes or is predicated on the interstices between fragments. Where the sensory-motor links presented in a film are weak or non-existent, and thus in the absence of a unifying system, the fragment each shot presents becomes incommensurable with the next, and montage, rather than offering the open totality of the whole, produces the false continuities and aberrant movements which give rise to the time-image. It is in this sense that Deleuze notes that the time-image presupposes montage just as much as the movement-image.[24]

It follows from this that an isolated fragment, a single-shot film like *Arrival of a Train*, cannot produce aberrant movement or false continuities as such. Nonetheless, the fragment of a sensory-motor schema that it presents is equally incapable of extending itself into the open totality of a whole. It cannot yet extend itself into action, leaving it apparently in the realm of neither the time nor the movement-image. It is interesting to note in this context the responses of some of the early audiences to these films. Vaughan refers to Georges Sadoul's *Histoire Générale du Cinéma* for the observation that

> what most impressed the early audiences was what would now be considered the incidentals of scenes: smoke from a forge, steam from a locomotive, brick-dust from a demolished wall. Georges Méliès, a guest at the first Paris performance . . . made particular mention of the rustling of leaves in the background [of a shot of the infant Lucie Lumière being fed her breakfast].[25]

Siegfried Kracauer also makes a point of the enthusiasm with which 'the ripple of leaves stirred by the wind' were received in discussion of the Lumières' work.[26] It seems to me that what is being identified in these instances are the elements of the image beginning to exist for themselves, rather than in relation to their place in a world of action and reaction: the steam from the train rather than the transport of passengers from one stop to the next, the brick dust from a fallen wall rather than the labour of the workers responsible for its demolition, the rustling of the leaves rather than the necessities of parenthood. Isolated from either a unified whole or a fragmented system articulated in montage, the partial elements of action within the single shot film begin to float aimlessly, are emptied out of purpose or function and tend towards an existence for themselves outside of any system, irrespective of their tendency or potential to move towards such a system, fragmented or otherwise.

It seems to me that in this situation we are presented with the limit case of what Deleuze refers to as a 'pure optical situation', an opsign, in which

> the viewer's problem becomes 'What is there to see in the image?' (and not now 'What are we going to see in the next image?'). The situation no longer extends into action through the intermediary of affections. It is cut off from all its extensions, it is now important only for itself, having absorbed all its affective intensities, all its active extensions.[27]

The opsign (and its aural correlate, the sonsign) are the genetic elements of the time-image; it is with their appearance in the films of the post-war period, particularly in Italian neo-realism, that Deleuze marks the beginning of the modern cinema and the appearance of the time-image. They mark the dispersion of the movement-image, the weakening of the links of action and reaction such that 'objects and settings take on an autonomous, material reality which gives them an importance in themselves ... [so that] the action floats in the situation, rather than bringing it to a conclusion or strengthening it'.[28] As already noted, however, this weakening of links, and even their complete collapse, is nonetheless articulated in and through montage. It is through the false continuities and aberrant movements generated *between* opsigns and sonsigns that the cinema gives rise to the different varieties of time-image. How then are we to understand the isolated opsign, the singular fragment that a film like *Arrival of a Train* seems to present us with?

In his discussion of the appearance of the time-image in the cinema of the post-war period, Deleuze notes briefly and with little discussion that the time-image has *always* inhabited the cinema as a possibility or implicit presence, saying that

> it took the modern cinema to re-read the whole of cinema as already made up of aberrant movements and false continuity shots. The direct time-image is the phantom which has always haunted the cinema, but it took modern cinema to give a body to this phantom.[29]

If then, as we have noted, the fixed-single-shot films of which *Arrival of a Train* is representative contain at best the tendency or potential for the presentation of a *movement*-image, we must also say that, to the extent that they represent an isolated opsign, a fragment without a system to fragment, they also offer themselves as the genetic element of a direct *time*-image which was implicit in the cinema from and at the very beginning.[30]

As a first approximation, then, we might say that the classic cinema, that of the movement-image, suppresses this implicit tendency by subsuming it to a system of action and reaction, a sensory-motor schema, without fundamentally altering this potential. When this system comes into question, when it begins to lose its capacity to maintain coherent relations between images, to produce an organic unity, the time-image as fundamental *possibility* of the cinema begins to rise up from beneath the movement-images under which it has been buried and suppressed. This is the sense in which the time-image haunts the cinema like a phantom, as Deleuze says, in that it always remains implicit in any world or whole unified by a system of action and reaction, waiting to assert itself when that system begins to fragment. Thus the time-image is not opposed to the movement-image, but rather inhabits it, subsists within it.

The multiplicity of waiting I described at the beginning of this section thus offers itself as a kind of model for the cinema itself. As we find ourselves back at the railway platform, still waiting for the *Arrival of a Train*, still waiting for the arrival of the cinema, we wait in a fashion that is of necessity indeterminate. Waiting for a train which will arrive, scheduled and coordinated to the system determined by its timetable, we engage in a sensory-motor waiting which participates in the schema of action and reaction aligned with the movement-image. We wait until our train arrives, on time or not, get on and travel to our destination, arriving either on schedule or at a time which is late or early only relative to that schedule.

But as we wait and still the train does not appear, we begin to wonder, 'when *will* the train arrive?' and sensory-motor connections begin to slacken and unravel, until finally we realise that our waiting will never be met by the arrival of any train, and that our waiting has become interminable. Thus the interminable, the non-figurative figure of the time-image, inhabits the limited and delimited waiting of the movement-image, subsists within it. Indeed, there is no way of knowing, no way of telling where one ends and the other begins, since, just as the interminable has no end, no termination, no terminus which can be reached, it also has no point of departure.

Even though the distinction between a train that will arrive and one that will not can be articulated as a binary opposition, the waiting proper to each forms part of a continuum which allows of analogue *difference*, but not digital *distinction*; there is no point at which one ends and the other begins. By the time one realises that one's train is not simply late but is never going to arrive at all, one is already in the middle of the interminable waiting which is the virtual counterpart of the actual waiting measured on a railway timetable, without that waiting ever having begun.

(Film) History as Montage

Such an understanding certainly offers us a model for the mutual imbrication of the movement- and time-images apparent in the conditions of the early or primitive cinema that Deleuze largely excludes from his analysis. The danger with this approach, however, is that we may once again lose the specificity of each image; if we cannot mark the movement-image and the time-image as distinct from each other, how can we account for the distinctly different characteristics Deleuze attributes to each of them? Indeed, what is missing here is precisely the gap itself. Baldly put, the differences between the cinemas of the movement- and time-image turn to a large degree on the role of montage in each or, more precisely, on the interval or gap which montage inserts between images as one which is either crossed (movement-image) or not (time-image), rational or irrational, coherent or dispersive.

Indeed, the movement that Deleuze posits from movement-image to time-image is itself a form of montage; there is a cut, gap or interval between these two images conceptually, between the classical and modern cinemas historically, and between the two books physically and materially (in the separate volumes devoted to the movement-image and time-image respectively.) Thus Angelo Restivo points out that

> Gilles Deleuze's work on the cinema is marked by a grand caesura, not only conceptually (movement-image giving way to time-image) and 'historiographically' (World War II as the name for the historical moment of this giving way), but also, even, *materially*.[31]

This homology suggests that an adequate account of the relationship between the movement- and the time-image requires a theory of the interval or gap not only as it applies to cinematic montage proper, but also in relation to the conceptual, historical and material 'montage' that the *Cinema* books themselves put into play (and 'material' must be understood with absolute literality as their physical separation into two volumes, *Cinemas 1* and *2*). The terms in which Deleuze accounts for the transition from movement to time-image in the cinema make it clear that the theory (or theories) of cinematic montage he presents are fundamentally intertwined with concrete material and historical formations, and cannot be understood in isolation from them. The cinema of the movement-image, for example, is characterised by a montage organised according to a sensory-motor schema, which ensures that relations between perception, action and reaction remain coherent; it posits a world that we know how to respond to, in which we know true from false, and in which time moves in one direction only.

It is in the collapse of this sensory-motor schema that the time-image begins to appear, following the Second World War. As Deleuze makes clear, however, this transition is not merely a matter of a change in the way films are edited before and after the war. Rather, the collapse of the sensory-motor schema as it expresses itself in cinematic montage is an expression of a world historical (as opposed to merely film historical) change in our relation to the material conditions of our existence. Thus:

> the post-war period has greatly increased the situations which we no longer know how to react to, in spaces we no longer know how to describe ... what tends to collapse, or at least to lose its position, is the sensory-motor schema which constituted the action-image of the old cinema.[32]

Clearly the sensory-motor schema Deleuze refers to here is not simply a system for organising relations between the shots in a film: it describes a way of relating to and understanding the world we live in, one which begins to break down after the war and which finds one of its expressions in the cinema. More precisely, what is at stake in this transition from the pre to the post-war era is the status of the relations between the elements of the whole, and of the consequent nature of that whole itself. When Deleuze tells us that the cinema of the movement-image expresses 'the sensory-motor relationship between world and man, nature and thought',[33] he describes a world in which we know how to act, a world to which it is possible to respond, which we may grasp in thought and master in action – 'a sensory-motor unity of nature and man'.³⁴ In the post-war cinema, however, we find no such unity; we are confronted precisely with a world, a whole, to which we do not and cannot know how to respond, which thought is powerless to master, and which reveals only the powerlessness of thought to think either itself *or* the whole: the whole as the outside.³⁵

My point here is not the fairly self-evident one that the *Cinema* books aren't just about the cinema. It is rather that the theories of montage, of the interval or gap, that Deleuze presents in relation to the cinema must themselves be understood and accounted for not only in terms of the cinema, but also in terms of the 'relation between man and the world, nature and thought' or, more precisely, in terms of the transformation of the whole and of this relation with the whole expressed within the conceptual, historical and material 'montage' that the *Cinema* books put into play. Furthermore, our account must be capable of sustaining both the specificity of the movement- and time-images (and therefore of the gap between them) *and* the necessity of their mutual imbrication, the spectral relationship in which the time-image haunts the movement-image 'like a phantom'.

Any analysis of the 'historical' face of the *Cinema* books, however, hits its first snag the moment it begins: the very first thing Deleuze tells us when we begin to read his two volumes on the cinema, in the preface to the French edition, is that 'This study is not a history of the cinema.'³⁶ The force of the statement is clear: the stakes of this argument are not historical or at least not 'film-historical'. To attempt to read into the *Cinema* books any form of historical thesis is, it seems, to wilfully ignore the express intentions of their author. Despite this injunction, however, for many readers the temptation to understand the two books in precisely this manner, as a history, has been difficult to resist (at least partly for the very good reason that they look and read very much like a history). For example, András Bálint Kovács has argued that 'owing to his theoretical starting point, as well as his analytic methods, Deleuze inevitably discusses his subject matter in historical, as well as taxonomic terms',³⁷ while for Jon Beasley-Murray, the *Cinema* books outline 'a formal history of tendencies inherent in the very idea of cinema . . . a history of the cinematic image along the lines of a conception of "total cinema" as overdetermining myth'.³⁸ At the very least, it seems reasonable to argue that Deleuze's 'discussion' is historical in the sense that it posits a progression from a 'classical' period distinguished by the movement-images which characterise its films, to a 'modern' period in which a new kind of image presents itself (the time-image), and identifies the break between them with a precise historical moment (the Second World War).

Certainly this progress gives. *Cinema 1* its structure. Deleuze begins with a presentation of the philosophical ground of the movement-image as a concept that is in a fundamental sense cinematic, and then proceeds to articulate a taxonomy of images and signs produced by the cinema in a gradual ramification of the possibilities implicit within its fundamental character as movement-image.[39] His exposition of this process begins more or less with Griffith in 1915, opening with a definition of montage as the composition of movement-images into an indirect image of time. Since, in Deleuze's schema, different modes of composition form different kinds of indirect images, Deleuze contrasts Griffith's use of montage (which Deleuze calls 'organic') with differing styles or practices of montage represented in various historically and geographically distinct 'schools' of montage: the Soviet school (dialectical composition); the pre-war French school (quantitative composition); and the German Expressionist school (intensive composition).[40] Deleuze then begins the process of differentiating the movement-image into three component images: the perception-image, the affection-image and the action-image. He then divides these three images further according to a taxonomy derived from Charles Sanders Pierce's model of semiotics. Here again, his exposition takes the form of an examination of specific 'schools', genres and filmmakers. As he progresses through his discussion of each image and its varieties in turn, he also progresses through the history of the cinema (albeit with a variety of loops and circles backwards), towards the final chapter in which the 'classical' period of film reaches its culmination and completion in the work of Alfred Hitchcock, who 'accomplishes and brings to completion the whole of the cinema by pushing the movement-image to its limit'.[41]

However, this 'completion' is also a precursor of the crisis that marks the classical cinema's break or transition to the modern period. Deleuze specifies the crisis or break in which these new images begin to arise not only historically, but also geographically: 'The timing is something like: around 1948, Italy; about 1958 France; about 1968, Germany.'[42] In this sense, Deleuze's typology of images in *Cinema 1* presents itself indirectly as a kind of historical progression from 1915 to 1968, as if the history of the cinema were one of a progressive discovery or uncovering of the implicit capacities held in reserve by each

36

variety of the movement-image, leading finally to the appearance or discovery of the time-image.

This sense of historical progression in the books is so marked that Jaimey Fisher feels justified in describing it as 'a teleological march through cinema',[43] a process of progressive mastery akin to those histories of science which present it as a timeline marked off at the appropriate points by the cumulative mastery of the laws of nature in an inevitable historical movement towards final and complete knowledge or, to put it in more Hegelian terms, 'absolute knowledge'. All this is simply to say that, implicit in the composition of *Cinema 1* itself, in its 'montage' of chapters and sections, there is an indirect image of time, of time as subordinate to movement, time as progress, time as action.

This, of course, is a central or defining characteristic of the movement-image itself, as it is discussed in the second chapter of *Cinema 2*, on the condition that the movement in question is 'normal':

> What we mean by normality is the existence of centres: centres of the revolution of movement itself, of equilibrium of forces, of gravity of moving bodies, and of observation for a viewer able to recognize or perceive the moving body, and to assign movement.[44]

Time is thereby subordinated to movement to the extent that that movement is assigned to a centre, a scheme, a system which organises it and keeps each movement 'in proportion' with the others; thus the system of movements corresponds to an organisational principle which determines the relation of one movement to another and makes them coherent.

The system of movements deployed in *Cinema 1* appears simply to be that of 'progress', the inevitable mastery of the inherent possibilities of the cinema *as* movement-image, from a 'primitive state' to the 'discovery' of montage, the mobile shot and then the varieties of the movement-image and their various combinations, up to its most complex form in a cinema of 'mental images' (represented by the work of Hitchcock). The evaluation of one form of cinema as 'primitive' and another as 'complex', and of the relationship between them as one of a progressive development from the former to the latter, implies a goal-oriented development, a *telos* which serves as the principle or scheme of organisation which thereby produces the 'movements' described in *Cinema 1* as 'normal'.

Indeed, Fisher is not alone in reading the *Cinema* books in this fashion – not merely as a history,[45] but specifically a teleological history, whose end or goal is the time-image as the 'essence' of the cinema, that which orients and guides its development towards its final uncovering or revelation. Thus Greg Lambert refers to 'Deleuze's teleology of modern cinema',[46] while Kovács argues that not only is Deleuze's model of film history linear, but that 'the incarnation of the time-image . . . is also the incarnation of a goal (*telos*) in the broad cinematographic evolution'.[47] Indeed he goes even further, quoting with approval Alain Ménil's comment that 'Deleuze considers the time-image "the object of a singular conquest, the point at which the cinema would come into possession of its essence"',[48] and later asserting that 'Whether we like it or not, Deleuze's model [of cinema, and cinema history] is linear.'[49] If we say then that time is subordinated to movement here, it is in the sense that, from the perspective of this goal or end, film-historical time is articulated *as* chronological progression towards this goal, as a movement along a line travelling from past to present, from primitive to complex, and is thus given as no more than a measure of this movement, this progress.

However, if we attempt to follow this film-historical timeline from the period covered in *Cinema 1* into *Cinema 2*, the situation becomes rather more complex. To the extent that *Cinema 1* and *Cinema 2* function *together* as a whole, a single work which presents a theory of the cinema or a set of philosophical concepts which are in some sense 'cinematic', and to the extent that the groundwork laid out in the first volume provides the basis for ideas developed in the second, one might reasonably expect that there would be a coherence or continuity across or between them. This coherence would derive from a shared centre or system of organisation that would determine *Cinema 2* as a continuation and expansion of the concepts laid out in *Cinema 1*. The shift from the 'organic' regime of the movement-image described in the first volume (where the constituent images form a whole or totality according to principles of differentiation and integration) to the 'crystalline' regime laid out in the second (where integration and differentiation are replaced by serialisation and relinking on irrational divisions) would then simply represent a continuation of the 'teleological march' Fisher describes. In this sense, then, the time-image would simply be the newer, more advanced, more perfect expression of the possibilities inherent in the cinema, a continuation of the development mapped out in *Cinema 1*. Indeed, Bordwell makes precisely this argument, claiming that 'Deleuze's . . . belief that a cinematic essence unfolds across history' constitutes not merely a teleological but an explicitly Hegelian conception of film history.[50]

For all that the books seem to allow and even welcome such a reading, however, the teleological and Hegelian approach that it identifies would be strikingly at odds with the anti-Hegelian[51] and anti-teleological tenor of Deleuze's philosophy in general. Rodowick emphasises this point when he argues that 'For Deleuze, the history of cinema is in no way a progression toward an ever more perfect representation of time',[52] while Gregory Flaxman notes that

> Deleuze condemns history as an enterprise that stakes out origins and anticipates conclusions, the result of which is a chronological series. This model organizes history as an *organic* process – history as story (*histoire*) – whose naturalization rings with a note of Hegelian inevitability: in other words, history reveals the prototypical movement of Spirit (*Geist*).[53]

Flaxman thus implies that any reading of the *Cinema* books as a model of film-historical *progress* towards some end or essence illegitimately conceives of them, to a greater or lesser extent, as Hegelian and teleological in orientation and fails to adequately acknowledge the anti-Hegelian tendencies of Deleuzian thought.

However, I would argue that the 'historical' reading of the *Cinema* books that Fisher et al. present is not simply wrong, or at least is not wrong in a way that is itself simple. Where *Cinema 1* does indeed appear to offer itself to be read as a chronological history of the cinema as the development of the possibilities latent within the movement-image, *Cinema 2* not only fails to continue that history post-1968 (or '58, or '48), but describes a regime of the image which is neither opposed to the movement-image nor subsumable to it as a simple continuation of its development. Moreover, this 'crystalline' regime of the time-image not only fails to provide a centre which normalises movement, but rather is essentially *de*centring; not only does it not continue the chronology of *Cinema 1*, but it revisits or displaces that history, fragments it, de-chronologises it such that movement that was 'normal' now becomes 'aberrant'. Thus the 'new' image which arises in the crisis or break announced at the end of the first volume in precise geographical and historical terms then appears in more or less dispersed and fragmentary forms throughout the *whole* of cinematic history in the second volume. Elements accounted for in terms of the taxonomy of the movement-image are then understood or worked through as somehow characteristic of the time-image. Thus Marie-Claire Ropars-Wuilleumier notes that

> the very foundations of the first volume tumble down in the second: The first volume proceeds by means of categories leading to traditional

divisions in the history of cinema, while the second proceeds by operations that void the traditionally established typologies . . . [for example] Eisenstein's conflictual hypotheses are treated in terms of organic synthesis in volume one, and are necessarily re-examined in volume two . . . [in terms of] a problematic of discontinuity and disconnection.[54]

However, for all that the historicist tendencies of the first volume find themselves fundamentally disrupted in the transition to the second, we are nevertheless left with the very specific historical timing Deleuze gives for the break between the regime of the movement-image and that of the time-image. This begs the question: why then? What is it in the war or its aftermath that prompts the time-image to separate itself out from the movement-image? Deleuze poses this question for himself in the preface to the English edition of *Cinema 2*:

> why is the Second World War taken as a break? The fact is that in Europe, the post-war period has greatly increased the situations which we no longer know how to react to, in spaces we no longer know how to describe . . . what tends to collapse, or at least to lose its position, is the sensory-motor schema which constituted the action-image of the old cinema.[55]

As we can see, there is something of a slippage between the question Deleuze asks and the answer that he actually gives. What his answer describes are the conditions out of which the time-image arises *after* the war. What his question seems to be asking, however, is 'why is the war itself the break? What happens *in* the war to create this break, to set up these new conditions?' He gives us an effect ('situations we no longer know how to react to . . . spaces we no longer know how to describe'), but not a cause. We are left to infer the fact of the break from its symptoms, while the break itself slides out of view.

It's possible to read this slippage as a necessary manifestation of the ambivalence of the relation between the pre- and the post-war cinema, between the movement- and the time-image. On the one hand, if the break is posited as a historical event that takes place, thereby producing the conditions under which the time-image begins to appear, then a causal chain is mapped out linking the movement-image to the time-image (a 'rational cut', to use terminology Deleuze adopts and adapts from mathematician Richard Dedekind[56]). However, relations of cause and effect, of action and reaction, belong properly to the movement-image, to the pre-war cinema. Were it possible to posit a chain of cause and effect across the break between pre- and post-war cinema (*this* event takes place during the

The Interval as Disaster

war, leading to *these* changes) the time-image in effect would once again be reduced to a simple continuation of the movement-image. As such, there would be no new image at all: just an extension of the old sensory-motor schema of the movement-image.

On the other hand, if the time-image is indeed anterior to the movement-image, always already subsisting within it, this causal chain is unavoidably disrupted. At a specific level, relations of cause and effect are themselves disturbed if the effect (time-image) is posited as anterior to its causal predecessor (movement-image). That is to say, if the appearance of the time-image is a function of the disruption of the sensory-motor schema of the movement-image, then for the time-image to precede the movement-image would be to disrupt causality itself.

More generally, if the time-image is anterior to the movement-image, then one must assume that the decentring, disordering power of the time-image would disrupt any sensory-motor schema before it ever formed and so the movement-image itself would never appear. This would resolve the problem of a causal chain linking the appearance of movement- and time-images (by disordering all causal chains), but at the price of effacing the movement-image altogether and positing the entire cinema, both pre- and post-war, as one of the time-image. Depending on how one looks at the problem, then, either the time-image is subsumed by the movement-image as a causal extension of it, or else the movement-image has always in fact been a time-image. Clearly neither option is satisfactory.

For all that these complexities seem to suggest that, at some level, the relationship between the time- and movement-image is non-totalisable, unamenable to being fully determined or delimited as such, the problematic that this relationship arises out of can at least be stated with some precision. The difference (that is to say, the *gap*) between the movement- and the time-image (whether conceptual, historical or material) is nothing other than their differing accounts *of* the gap, of the interval, of montage. On the one side of this gap we find 'rational' cuts, ordering coherent relations between images in terms of sensory-motor schemata; on the other, 'irrational' cuts give rise to a disordering, decentring montage in which relations between action and reaction collapse.

The impossibility of determining the relationship between movement- and time-image is precisely that if we attempt to grasp the difference between them in the terms of the account given in *either Cinema 1* or *Cinema 2*, we necessarily efface, and thereby lose, the other. As I've argued, if the gap between movement- and time-image, the transition from one to the other, is rational and coherent, then the irrationality of the time-image is constrained to and by the order of the movement-image and is thus reduced to a simple continuation of it. If, however, the gap between them is irrational, then the movement-image itself is disordered and disrupted to the extent that there is and only ever has been a time-image.

As such, to attempt to reconcile this conflict, or alternatively to attempt to show that it truly is irreconcilable and that Deleuze's conceptual framework is therefore incoherent, would be to neglect both the content and the form of the work itself, inasmuch as this tension between coherence and incoherence runs to the heart of the definitions of and relations between the movement- and the time-image themselves. In short, we can read the *Cinema* books as a whole neither coherently nor *in*coherently, since to do either is to collapse the theoretical framework of one of the two volumes into that of the other. They are, in a strict sense, *impossible* to read.

Deleuze indirectly suggests a way of approaching this problem in his comment that 'It took the modern cinema to re-read the whole of cinema as already made up of aberrant movements and false continuity shots.'[57] If the whole of cinema is re-read as a cinema of the time-image ('already made up of aberrant movements and false continuity shots'), then the movement-image is indeed effaced, inasmuch as in that act of re-reading it is produced as a time-image. From this perspective, the time-image is indeed anterior to the movement-image, in that it effaces it altogether, so that the time-image was always already there from the very beginning.

However, it is only so *retrospectively*. It is a process of *re*-reading which reinscribes the movement-image as a time-image only *after* the break in which the time-image begins to appear. To get to the time-image you must pass through the break between movement- and time-image; once you fall under the regime of the time-image, however, the movement-image is effaced and there can no longer be any break. The break between pre- and post-war cinema must therefore take place as an event that does not take place, can only 'take place' in the interminable event of its own absence. Interminable waiting: nothing happens and does not stop happening. In *The Writing of the Disaster* Maurice Blanchot gives us a name for just such a non-eventual eventuality: the disaster, 'advent of what does not happen, of what would come without arriving',[58] or again, 'that which does not come, that which has put a stop to every arrival'.[59] The break, the interval, the cut (and thus montage), the disaster.

Cinema as an Anterior History of Violence

'The interval as disaster': what does this phrase tell us about the cinema, or indeed about the *Cinema* books? Under what circumstances can it be considered legitimate? Gerald L. Bruns points out that *The Writing of the Disaster* is 'usually perceived as a book about the Holocaust'[60] in the sense that the Holocaust and the death camps in some sense lie at its centre. It is not that the Holocaust functions as a paradigmatic or exemplary instance of the disaster: 'the Holocaust is *not a species* of the disaster'.[61] Rather, the impossibility of thinking or doing anything which could respond to, account for, or even grasp such an event in a way which could ever be adequate to it exposes us to the disastrousness of thought when thought itself is lost. The disaster is so disastrous it destroys all possibility of response or comprehension, evades any thematisation, and in doing so destroys even itself, erases any possibility of taking it as an object of or for thought.

> The holocaust, the absolute event of history – which is a date in history – the utter-burn where all history took fire, where the movement of Meaning was swallowed up ... How can it be preserved, even by thought? How can thought be made keeper of the holocaust where all was lost, including guardian thought?[62]

Such a disordering of thought and action has clear correspondences with the decentring power Deleuze attributes to the time-image, and he does note briefly that 'the great post-war philosophers and writers demonstrated that thought has something to do with Auschwitz, with Hiroshima, but this was also demonstrated by the great cinema authors from Welles to Resnais – this time in the most serious way'.[63]

Deleuze does not expand on this idea in the *Cinema* books. However, as Flaxman argues, it is implicit that the collapse of the sensory-motor schema in which the time-image is 'released' is, in some sense, a function of the discovery of the Nazi death camps and the images of them that filtered out of Europe after the war:

> especially in the aftermath of the Holocaust, which effectively obliterated any attempt to 'make sense', the old-style narrative seems impossible. The system of Truth or sensory-motor schema, which was entrusted with intelligibility even at the cost of illusion, is no longer up to the task: no explanation, no statement, can adequately respond to these images.[64]

The closest Deleuze comes to saying this, and even then indirectly, is in his 'Letter to Serge Daney', where he attributes the idea to Daney himself: 'You've pointed out that this form of cinema didn't die a natural death but was killed in the war ... in circumstances where horror penetrated everything, where 'behind' the image there was nothing to be seen but concentration camps.'[65]

To say 'the interval as disaster', then, would be to attribute the break between the classical and modern cinemas to the loss of faith in the capacity of action or thought to respond or correspond adequately to the world as a result of such an event within this very same world. However, for all that such an attribution may perhaps be justifiable on many levels, and potentially capable of accommodating the conceptual, historiographical and material caesuras in the *Cinema* books that Restivo points us towards, it remains inadequate or incomplete. It accounts for only one aspect of 'the interval' as such, and moreover does so on the basis of an event which is, strictly speaking, external to the cinema itself.

What is lacking here is a means to understand the sense in which the interval internal to the cinema – that is to say, montage – may also be said to be 'disastrous'. If, as I've argued, the transition from the classical to the modern cinema is not merely a matter of a change in the ways films are edited before and after the war, neither can that change be explained without reference to Deleuze's conception of what cinema, and in particular montage, itself is. Deleuze's treatment of the cinema turns on quite precise technical or empirical determinations, or rather, takes elements traditionally given in such a fashion – specifically, framing, shot, montage – and grasps them in terms of a specifically Bergsonian treatment of the relationship between movement and time. That is to say, framing, shot and montage are taken by Deleuze as the material elements of a metaphysical problematic: the cinema as a question of, and *to*, ontology.

Moreover, the break between the classical and the modern cinemas (whether we grasp it conceptually, historiographically or even materially) is itself intimately tied to the transformation in the operation of such elements. To say 'the interval as disaster', then, is not merely to be confronted with a disaster external to the cinema (the Holocaust) that finds its reflection or representation in a disaster internal to the cinema (given in terms of framing, shot and montage). Rather, it is to posit a disaster that must be found, in some sense, in the cinema itself, as if the Holocaust and the death camps could be deduced on the basis of cinema alone: the death camps as the realisation of 'cinema's dream, in circumstances where horror penetrated everything, where "behind" the image there was nothing to be seen but concentration camps'.[66]

Such a claim seems at best problematic, and at worst a grotesque overvaluation of the importance of 'the movies', unless one recognises in the cinema what Nicole Brenez (paraphrasing Vachel Lindsay) describes as 'not . . . a simple reflection, the redoubling of something that already existed, but . . . *the emergence of a visionary critical activity*'.[67] This is the cinema as an anterior history of violence, in so far as, according to Goddard, it 'does not show, it previsions'.[68] If this conception of the cinema as 'visionary critical activity' appeals to Deleuze in relation to his two volumes – which are philosophical in the same terms and at the same time that they are cinematic – it is because he has already found in philosophy just such a 'critical and anticipatory power',[69] a 'science fiction' of philosophy in which it is 'neither a philosophy of history, nor a philosophy of the eternal, but untimely, always and only untimely'.[70]

The elaboration of Deleuze's treatment of the cinema as just such a 'visionary critical activity', one possessed of a properly 'critical and anticipatory power' (which is the project of this book), begins necessarily with and from Bergson, inasmuch as it is the latter's treatment of movement and time that for Deleuze 'prefigure[s] the future or essence of the cinema'.[71] Indeed, one of the most paradoxical features of the theoretical framework Deleuze constructs across the *Cinema* books revolves around the very centrality of the position Bergson occupies throughout both volumes. The difficulty lies in the transformation in the nature of the whole that occurs in the transition from the classical to the modern cinema. Bergson's treatment of the relationship between movement and time turns ultimately on his definition of the whole within which movement occurs, not as a closed set, but as an *open whole*. Where a set contains a number of fixed and determined elements that are static and unchanging, and thus can be given in advance, an open whole neither contains determined elements, nor has any consistency other than its continuous and continual difference from itself. The open whole is that which constantly transforms, and this transformation is duration itself, is time:

> Bergson's always saying that Time is the Open, is what changes – is constantly changing in nature – each moment. It's the whole, which isn't any set of things, but the ceaseless passage from one set to another, the transformation of one set of things into another.[72]

If the classical cinema is defined by its relation to the open whole, it is because the movement-image is given in relation to its openness to that whole, such that movement is nothing more than an expression of duration, or change in the whole itself. Now Deleuze presents these ideas in the very first chapter of *Cinema 1*, which offers a commentary on Bergson's theses on movement, and at the end of that chapter he makes it clear that the time-image, no less than the movement-image, is ultimately derived from these very same theses:

> Now we are equipped to understand the profound first thesis of *Matter and Memory*: (1) there are not only instantaneous images, that is, immobile sections of movement; (2) there are movement-images which are mobile sections of duration; (3) there are, finally, time-images, that is, duration-images, change-images, relation-images, volume-images which are beyond movement itself.[73]

This seems hardly surprising, given that Bergson's work provides the foundation for the ideas presented in *Cinema 2* no less than in *Cinema 1* – except, however, in one respect. Halfway through *Cinema 2*, in his chapter on 'Thought and Cinema', Deleuze makes the point that, in the shift from the classical to the modern cinema, the status of the whole changes; where, for the movement-image, the whole was the open, for the time-image *the whole is the outside*.[74]

The open whole is defined in the third and final of Bergson's theses on movement presented at the start of *Cinema 1* and is in many senses the foundation on which all the others rest, the foundation of Deleuze's conception of the cinema. Moreover, as we have just seen, both the movement- and the time-image are derived on the basis of those theses. And yet for the modern cinema, for the time-image, *the whole is no longer open*. Inasmuch as the classical cinema works explicitly to articulate the 'relation between man and the world, nature and thought' – the relation of man and the whole, thought and the whole – this transformation in the nature of the whole itself reflects a fundamental shift in these relations. How then are we to understand the Bergsonism of the time-image, of *Cinema 2*, when Deleuze removes its Bergsonian foundation?

'The outside' is of course not a Bergsonian concept. Deleuze adopts it, rather, from the work of Blanchot:

> The whole thus merges with that Blanchot calls the force of 'dispersal of the Outside', or 'the vertigo of spacing': that void which is no longer a motor-part of the image, and which the image would cross in order to continue, but is the radical calling into question of the image.[75]

Blanchot, in his turn, also tells us that 'the outside' and' the disaster' are in some sense terms for the same 'thing' (were it not for the fact that what both name is simply the differing of difference from itself): 'These names, areas of dislocation, the four winds of spirit's absence, breath from nowhere – the names of thought, when it lets itself come undone and, by writing, fragment. Outside. Neutral. Disaster. Return.'[76] One might wish to differentiate them, hastily perhaps, by saying that in relation to the *Cinema* books at least, 'the outside' is concerned with the nature of the whole ('the whole as the outside'), whereas 'the disaster' concerns the interval, the gap ('the interval as disaster').

Yet it is clear that, to the extent that the whole is the outside, it is precisely the interstice, the gap that is not crossed, that itself comes to constitute the whole. To the extent that it 'is' anything, the disaster is, precisely, the interval *as* the whole or, more properly, the *absence* of any whole that thought could think, to the point to which 'The modern fact is that we no longer believe in this world . . . The link between man and the world is broken.'[77] The interval as disaster; the whole as the outside; 'The names of thought when it lets itself come undone'; interminable waiting for waiting to begin.

All of this happens 'against' Bergson, inasmuch as his notion of the open whole provides the theoretical foundation of the *Cinema* books and it is this whole which is suspended, fissured, cracked in the shift from the open to the outside. And yet Bergson remains untouched by all of this, inasmuch as the time-image no less than the movement-image belongs to, is articulated by Deleuze in terms of, a specifically and overtly Bergsonian thought of cinema.

In some sense, then, *Cinema 2* asks us to think 'against' or indeed outside Bergson *on the basis of Bergson*, as if Bergson's thought were somehow subject to the aporetic logic of the disaster, of the outside, of Blanchot, 'from within' as it were, in a way that leaves it nonetheless untouched.[78] Indeed, if the relation between the two volumes of the *Cinema* books is, as I've argued, 'disastrous', then to the extent that the disaster happens (in the non-event of its own happening), it happens as a *result* of the first volume, happens 'after' having read it, as if it somehow led us or drew us towards the disaster in its 'teleological march through cinema' and having happened, has not happened, has never happened, has never stopped (not) happening. It is in this sense that, for all that it is the outside and the disaster that Blanchot poses 'together', in order to read the *Cinema* books (impossible task) we must 'find' the disaster on the basis, not of Blanchot and the outside, but of Bergson and the open whole itself.

In fact this task can (must) be formulated more precisely, as that of 'finding' the disaster on the basis of Deleuze's own Bergsonism. It is something of a commonplace to note that the roots of Deleuzian philosophy are to be found in his engagement with Bergson,[79] most particularly in relation to the founding principles of his philosophical approach: the primacy of difference over identity and the corresponding ontological principle of being as that which differs with itself first of all. This gives our task a quite specific frame: the problems posed by the *Cinema* books are not 'merely' problems concerning their entanglement of cinema, thought and history, but are posed in the context of a return by Deleuze, *via cinema*, to problems that constitute his own origins or foundations. As such, these foundations and their transliteration into cinematic terms are the subject of the next chapter.

Notes

1. Deleuze, *Cinema 1*, 9.
2. The reference here is of course the first public appearance of Auguste and Louis Lumière's cinematograph, and the audience reaction to the films screened at that event – in particular, the film known as *Arrival of a Train (L'Arrivée d'un Train à la Ciotat)*. The stories passed down about this event deserve to be called 'fables' partly because stories of origin are always an oversimplification. In this case, not only are there a range of proto-cinematic technologies that pre-date and map a path towards the Lumière brothers' 'invention', but as John L. Fell points out, there are a range of competing claims for different kinds of 'firstness' with regard to motion picture technology from Germany, England, the United States and within France itself. But this 'scene of origin' is also a fable because the events recounted with respect to it have less to do with actual historical detail than they do with the mythologies accreted around them. For example, as Martin Loiperdinger has demonstrated, although a film of a train arriving at a station may have been part of the evening's programme, there is good reason to doubt that *L'Arrivée d'un Train à la Ciotat* was actually part of the Grand Café screening at all. Indeed, it seems likely that that film most probably had its first screening some time in 1896. Successive retellings of this myth of origin seem to have collapsed a range of early experiences of the cinema into one conveniently packaged story. This does not, however, detract from its utility for my purposes. Fell, *Film Before Griffith*, 9; Loiperdinger, 'Lumière's Arrival of the Train', 103.
3. This correlation of time given as a function of movement and the operational organisation of a railway timetable should be taken

concretely and literally. As Stephen Kern points out, the adoption of World Standard Time towards the end of the nineteenth century has as its direct antecedent the imposition of a uniform time by railroad companies in the United States and elsewhere seeking to rationalise and simplify their operations. The train, and its regular and regulated movement between stations, thus serve as a figure for technological modernity's subordination of time to movement. Kern, *The Culture of Time and Space: 1880–1918*, 11–12.
4. Deleuze, *Cinema 2*, 39.
5. Lumière and Lumière, *L'Arrivée d'un Train à La Ciotat*. Although 1895 is the year usually given for the production of this film, as noted above (n.2), there is good reason to believe that the actual production date is more likely 1896.
6. Vaughan, 'Let There Be Lumière', 63.
7. Ibid.
8. Deleuze, *Cinema 2*, 168.
9. Gunning, 'The Cinema of Attractions', 56.
10. Deleuze, *Cinema 2*, 25.
11. Deleuze, *Cinema 1*, 24–5.
12. Deleuze, *Cinema 2*, 26.
13. Deleuze, *Cinema 1*, 55.
14. Ibid., 30.
15. Ibid., 32–3.
16. Ibid., 32.
17. Deleuze, *Cinema 2*, 272.
18. Deleuze, *Negotiations*, 55.
19. Deleuze, *Cinema 2*, 34.
20. Deleuze, *Cinema 1*, 24.
21. Ibid., 25.
22. Deleuze, *Cinema 2*, 40–1.
23. Ibid., 41.
24. Ibid.
25. Vaughan, 'Let There Be Lumière', 64–5.
26. Kracauer, *Nature of Film: The Redemption of Physical Reality*, 31. These leaves have entered the 'folklore' of cinema's origins no less than the arriving train and its putative shock effect. In Robert Stam's gloss of early silent film theory, the two come together as a kind of generalised synecdoche for early responses to the event of the cinema: 'We find in some journalistic critics, for example, a discourse of wonderment, a kind of religious awe at the sheer magic of mimesis, at seeing a convincing simulacral representation of an arriving train or of the "wind blowing through the leaves."' Stam, *Film Theory: An Introduction*, 23.
27. Deleuze, *Cinema 2*, 272.
28. Ibid., 4.

29. Ibid., 41.
30. Indeed, Rodowick does observe in a brief endnote that the 'primitive cinema' displays elements associated with the time-image. He does not give the reasoning behind this claim, nor explain what these elements are, beyond directing the reader to the work of Noel Burch, Tom Gunning and the essays collected in Thomas Elsaesser's *Early Cinema*. Rodowick, *Gilles Deleuze's Time Machine*, 214 n.6.
31. Restivo, 'Into the Breach', 171.
32. Deleuze, *Cinema 2*, xi.
33. Ibid., 163.
34. Ibid., 162.
35. The theoretical framework Deleuze sets up here seems to parallel many accounts of the transition from modernity to postmodernity. For example, the collapse of sensory-motor schemata that precipitates the arrival of the time-image in Deleuze's schema seems substantially akin to the loss of faith in master narratives by which Jean-François Lyotard characterises the postmodern era in *The Postmodern Condition* – especially when one keeps in mind the role of such sensory-motor schemata in the constitution of (cinematic) narrative. Against this similarity, however, one must place the profoundly modernist tendencies of the cinematic examples by and through which Deleuze characterises the time-image and indeed the total absence of 'postmodernity' as a concept or theme in Deleuze's work.
36. Deleuze, *Cinema 1*, xvi.
37. Kovács, 'The Film History of Thought', 153.
38. Beasley-Murray, 'Whatever Happened to Neo-Realism? – Bazin, Deleuze, and Tarkovsky's Long Take', 38.
39. Deleuze, *Cinema 1*, xiv.
40. Ibid., 29–55.
41. Ibid., 204.
42. Ibid., 211.
43. Fisher, 'Deleuze in a Ruinous Context', 62.
44. Deleuze, *Cinema 2*, 36.
45. Indeed, several authors have pointed out that Deleuze's approach to the cinema in many respects reproduces an extremely conventional view of film and film history. See, for example, Rodowick, *Gilles Deleuze's Time Machine*, xi–xii; Bordwell, *On the History of Film Style*, 116–17.
46. Lambert, 'Cinema and the Outside', 267.
47. Kovács, 'The Film History of Thought', 156–8.
48. Ménil, 'Deleuze et Le Bergsonisme Du Cinéma', 29; Quoted in Kovács, 'The Film History of Thought', 156.
49. Kovács, 'The Film History of Thought', 158.
50. Bordwell, *On the History of Film Style*, 117.
51. Deleuze's oft-cited comment that 'What I detested most was Hegelianism

The Interval as Disaster

and dialectics' seems to sum up his attitude towards Hegel succinctly. *Negotiations*, 6.
52. Rodowick, *Gilles Deleuze's Time Machine*, 13.
53. Flaxman, 'Introduction', 24.
54. Ropars-Wuilleumier, 'The Cinema, Reader of Gilles Deleuze', 257–8.
55. Deleuze, *Cinema 2*, xi.
56. Deleuze adopts the distinction between 'rational' cuts' (associated with the movement-image) and 'irrational cuts' (associated with the time-image) from mathematician Richard Dedekind's work on irrational numbers and the continuity of the real number line. Ibid., 181. For an account of rational and irrational cuts in mathematical terms, see Boyer, *A History of Mathematics*, 607–8. Given the importance of Dedekind's innovations in this area for the development of set theory, Deleuze's characterisation of the shot as set, and the role Russell's paradox of the set of all sets plays in Deleuze's notion of the whole, an examination of the role of set theory in the *Cinema* books would be of interest – but it will need to take place somewhere other than this book.
57. Deleuze, *Cinema 2*, 41.
58. Blanchot, *The Writing of the Disaster*, 1.
59. Ibid., 5.
60. Bruns, *Maurice Blanchot: The Refusal of Philosophy*, 212.
61. Ibid., 213.
62. Blanchot, *The Writing of the Disaster*, 47. Italics and use of lower-case 'h' for 'holocaust' in original.
63. Deleuze, *Cinema 2*, 209.
64. Flaxman, 'Introduction', 41.
65. Deleuze, *Negotiations*, 69. At the end of the same paragraph, Deleuze also makes note of Daney's comparison of Alain Resnais' work to that of Blanchot in *The Writing of the Disaster*.
66. Ibid.
67. Brenez, 'The Ulitmate Journey'. Emphasis added.
68. Quoted in ibid.
69. Rodowick, *Gilles Deleuze's Time Machine*, xvii.
70. Deleuze, *Difference and Repetition*, xxi.
71. Deleuze, *Cinema 1*, 3.
72. Deleuze, *Negotiations*, 55.
73. Deleuze, *Cinema 1*, 11.
74. Deleuze, *Cinema 2*, 179.
75. Ibid., 180.
76. Blanchot, *The Writing of the Disaster*, 57–8.
77. Deleuze, *Cinema 2*, 171–2.
78. And doesn't Blanchot tell us that 'The disaster ruins everything, all the while leaving everything intact' – in this context, ruins Bergson, ruins

the open whole and nevertheless leaves them intact? Blanchot, *The Writing of the Disaster*, 1.
79. See for example Hardt, *An Apprenticeship in Philosophy*, xvi; Boundas, 'Deleuze-Bergson: An Ontology of the Virtual', 81; Alliez, 'On Deleuze's Bergsonism', 228.

3
Movement, Duration and Difference

The Three Theses on Movement

The drama of thought presented in the *Cinema* books begins in a fashion Horace would surely approve of: as Flaxman points out, 'to read the cinema books is to lapse, almost in media res, into Deleuze's assurance that "Bergson does not just put forward one thesis on movement, but three."'[1] This is, as Flaxman says, a somewhat disorienting beginning: immediately we 'begin to lose our bearings, thrown from one strange milieu – what was billed as a philosophy of the cinema – into another: the theses of Henri Bergson.'[2] The disorientation, of course, comes from the fact that we don't know how we got there: looking for an answer to the question 'why Deleuze and cinema?' we are thrown instantly instead into the question 'why Bergson and cinema?'

The importance of Bergson's work to Deleuzian philosophy is well attested, but equally so is Bergson's critique of cinematographic movement as an illusion constructed out of abstractions.[3] An apparent act of perversity by Deleuze then, or perhaps even a paradox: two volumes on cinema built on the theses of a philosopher who rejects it. Deleuze fully accepts both this critique of abstraction and the terms in which it is offered. However, he suggests that, although thought and philosophy do indeed suffer this illusion, Bergson's choice of the cinematograph as a metaphor for it is misguided. In fact, Deleuze argues, the movement we see on screen at the cinema is real, not abstract: in some sense, the cinema serves to 'correct' the cinematographic illusion.

Although the secondary literature is sometimes critical of the arguments Deleuze offers to justify this claim,[4] such commentaries by and large content themselves with noting the paradoxical or problematic nature of the conjunction of Bergson and cinema that Deleuze presents, and then move on to issues that seem more pressing. The effect of this is that the cinematographic illusion is often treated in practice as peripheral to the primary concerns of the

Cinema books. By my reading, such an approach is almost entirely wrong. In fact, the cinematographic illusion and its relation to both thought and cinema are central to the project of the *Cinema* books and to the philosophical problems they respond to, in ways that I will discuss in detail further on in this book. Moreover, as this chapter will demonstrate, the *Cinema* books mark a return not just to Deleuze's early interest in Bergson, but more precisely to the cinematographic illusion itself and the role it plays in establishing the foundations of Deleuzian philosophy. The three theses on movement that serve as the opening salvo of those books provide us with the key to demonstrating this link.

Bergson's first thesis can be summarised as follows: actual movement cannot be determined spatially, that is, as a passage over or across a given territory;[5] rather, it must be determined temporally as a passage of time, and as such is the expression of a concrete duration. If we attempt to determine movement in terms of space covered, we lose the actual movement itself, a conclusion implicit in Zeno of Elea's 'Arrow' paradox and in Bergson's resolution of it. If you define movement in terms of space covered, no matter what units you use to measure that space – no matter how finely you divide it up – there is no point at which an object supposedly in motion (such as an arrow in flight) actually moves, since at any given instant, or point, that object can only occupy the same space as itself.[6] If we spatialise movement we fall into what Bergson refers to as 'the absurd proposition, that movement is made of immobilities'.[7] Deleuze puts it like this: 'you can bring two instants or two positions together to infinity [that is to say, subdivide space more and more finely, even to infinity]; but movement will always occur in the interval between the two, in other words behind your back'.[8] Indeed, Zeno's aim with this paradox is to prove that movement is logically impossible, and that its appearance is therefore an illusion.

Bergson was clearly aware that the tools to resolve Zeno's paradoxes mathematically had been developed throughout the nineteenth century.[9] However, while such approaches can offer mathematically consistent resolutions of Zeno's paradoxes, they do not of themselves show that such mathematical abstractions are in fact an adequate description of concrete physical reality.[10] The key issue here is the way that mathematics defines motion in its resolution of the paradoxes. In his discussion of this question, Wesley C. Salmon tells us that 'Motion may be described in mathematical terms as a functional relation between space and time.'[11] This is the basis of the 'at-at' theory of motion: at any given time t, the object in motion will be at a position x, so that Zeno's 'arrow moves when for every time – that is, every value of t – x(t) has a value such that there are no "jumps" in x as t varies. At every t, the arrow is at some x.'[12] Thus, from a mathematical perspective, movement is indeed composed of an appropriately ordered series of immobilities or instantaneous states – the value of x for every possible t, which form an infinitely divisible, but nonetheless continuous and finite series. However, from a Bergsonian perspective, the mathematical resolution of Zeno's paradoxes simply reproduces the same flawed conception of motion as the paradoxes themselves – taking actual movement to be the same thing as space covered. Although one may say that a 'moving body occupies, one after the other, points on a line, motion itself has nothing to do with a line'.[13]

Bergson's resolution of this problem is to argue that although it is possible to *represent* a movement from point A to point B abstractly via a line drawn from one to the other, the movement itself is qualitatively different to that representation:

> The truth is that mathematics ... deals and can deal only with lengths. It has therefore had to seek devices, first, to transfer to the movement, which is not a length, the divisibility of the line passed over, and then to reconcile with experience the idea ... of a movement that is a length, that is, of a movement placed upon its trajectory and arbitrarily decomposable like it.[14]

We can see, then, that both Zeno's paradoxes and the modern mathematical resolutions of them share the same error, that of thinking of movement *abstractly*, conceiving of movement in terms of the line drawn by movement, rather than thinking the movement itself. However, the means of abstraction is not the same in each case. Bergson's second thesis on movement is in fact an account of the different ways that ancient and modern thought produced this same error. The ancient version, which he identifies with Platonism and with finalism more generally, consists of defining movement in terms of the transition from one ideal form to another, as a series of privileged instants or poses whose transformations are ultimately summed up in or as the movement *towards* a pre-given transcendent ideal, and whose essential moment is thus this 'final term or culminating point (*telos, acme*)'.[15] Thus the ancient conception of movement has both its physics, which tells us how movement works (the transition from one privileged moment to the next), and its metaphysics, which tells us why it works that way (it derives from the transcendent eternal forms which these moments instantiate). The movement itself is designated as of little interest to ancient science, since it thinks that *'it knows its object sufficiently when it has noted of it some privileged moments'*.[16] What counts for this model are the poses themselves (and not the transitions between them) and the end or goal towards which movement is oriented: it is a teleological, or finalist, conception.

The modern version of this error relates movement not to significant or privileged instants, but to what Deleuze, following Bergson, calls 'any-instants-whatever'. This is the approach of 'modern science', derived in large part from precisely the kind of mathematical techniques referred to above, in which time is treated as simply another dimension equivalent to the three properly spatial ones and thus as analysable in the same terms. Modern science presents its spatialisation of time in formulae that explicitly correlate time with the movement of an object in space – whether it be the formula for the orbit of a planet around the sun, the rate of fall of an object or the trajectory of a cannon ball.

Such formulae give a precise position relative to any-instant-whatever, such that time is reduced to 'a sequence of instantaneous states linked by a deterministic law'.[17] As opposed to the finalism of the ancient conception, the modern presents us with a deterministic model of mechanical causality. Despite their differences, however, both the ancient and the modern approach rely on the 'absurd' assumption that movement can be reconstituted from immobilities, whether they be privileged points or any-instant-whatevers. What is significant about this for us here is that the finalism and mechanism Bergson critiques in the ancient and the modern conceptions of movement respectively are both constituted in relation to a whole which is in some sense given in advance as a *totality*. Thus 'in both cases, one misses the movement because one constructs a Whole, one assumes that all is "given", whilst [real] movement only occurs if the whole is neither given nor giveable'.[18]

Finalism determines movement in relation to its *telos*, the *'formal transcendental elements'*[19] or poses which its privileged moments instantiate, such that each moment in that movement is determined in relation to that ideal form or goal, and thus given by it in advance. In contrast, from the modern perspective (that of mechanism), the whole is given in terms of the formulae that determine the movements of its elements. This kind of mechanistic determinism makes the 'future and past calculable functions of the present, and thus claims that *all is given*'.[20] Inasmuch as the whole is given, there can be no change, no production of the new or unforeseeable, since every moment is in some sense 'given in advance'. To take the whole as given is, in effect, to spatialise time, to treat it as if it *has no duration*. Bergson says of the mechanistic formulae of modern science that 'nothing would have to be changed in our scientific ideas of things if the totality of the real was deployed all at once and instantaneously ... [Thus] positive science essentially consists in the elimination of duration.'[21] That this is equally so for finalism is even more explicit, since for it the 'totality of the real' *is* deployed all at once and instantaneously in its transcendental and ideal form. Movement understood as the transition between poses instantiating ideal forms is thus given in advance and for all time in the eternal, transcendent realm where those ideal forms dwell. In these terms, the unforseen, the production of the new, is impossible.

Thus, as Deleuze puts it in *Bergsonism*:

> the confusion of space and time, the assimilation of time into space, make us think that the whole is given, even if only in principle, even if only in the eyes of God. And this is the mistake that is common to mechanism [the modern conception of movement] and to finalism [the classical conception]. The former assumes that everything is calculable in terms of a state; the latter, that everything is determinable in terms of a program: In any event, time is only there now as a screen that hides the eternal from us, or shows us successively what a God or superhuman intelligence would see in a single glance ... this illusion is inevitable as soon as we spatialize time.[22]

As he put it in *Cinema 1*, 'as soon as a whole is given to one ... there is no longer room for real movement'.[23]

These first two theses together define the terms of the cinematographic illusion. In terms of this metaphor, the individual frames of the film strip abstract the real movement of the objects that pass before the motion picture camera to a series of still images, just as finalism and mechanism reduce movement to a series of static points (first thesis). The movement we see when that film is projected on screen is not the movement of the things themselves, but is something added to the still frames of the film strip by a strictly external motor – that of the projector (second thesis). Finalism's external motor is the ideal form or goal that constitutes the quintessence or synthesis of the static poses in which it culminates. For modern science, the motor is causality: an object only moves because something else – something external to it – causes it to do so.[24]

There is an important difference, however, between the ancient and the modern conceptions of movement. The former gives movement as the transition between instantiations of pre-given, eternal and unchanging ideal forms; these forms are the whole, the transcendent ideal form of reality. There is by definition no space for the creation of the new in this model, since everything is given once and for all time, and movement is only the movement towards these final and perfect idealities. The modern conception, on the other hand, although its whole is equally given in advance, does not do so in terms of pre-given forms towards which movement tends, but rather in the mechanical working through of causality, which does not move towards a pre-given *telos*, but is, rather, determined by its past, which leads *necessarily* to its future. The importance of this difference for Bergson is that, if one can show that the arbitrarily closed frames of reference of modern science in fact subsist within the framework of a necessarily *open* system, then the genuinely unforeseen becomes possible, since movement is thereby determined neither by the finalism of ideal forms nor by the determinism of mechanical necessity. The creation of the new becomes possible, at any-instant-whatever.

This demonstration is precisely what we find in the third thesis on movement, which seeks to show that the whole is not a totality given in advance, but is instead an unceasing variation or differing from itself that can neither be closed off nor totalised. This is what Bergson calls the 'open whole'. In fact, this final thesis is largely implicit in the first theses' definition of movement as the expression of a concrete duration. If movement expresses a passage *of* time rather than a passage *through* space, then that movement cannot be divided without changing qualitatively, since every movement expresses a concrete duration in which change takes place. The important factor here is that this change is not related to the spatial translation of elements, but rather concerns the transformation of the *relations* between objects or elements.

If I move from Melbourne to Paris, this does not happen 'abstractly' but concretely, for a purpose – perhaps there is a job in Paris and none in Melbourne. This movement cannot be captured in a spatial translation, a line on a map, since what defines that movement is not the distance covered, but the transformation that movement expresses: I change from unemployed to employed, the job from available to taken, I change from a local to a foreigner, my family misses me rather than being sick of the sight of me and so on. Moreover, it is not 'me' that changes in this movement, nor my employers, nor any of the other 'elements' involved. Rather, it is the *relations* between these elements that are transformed. As Deleuze points out, 'Relation is not a property of objects, it is always external to its terms'[25] and exists *between* elements, not as a part of them. I am only employed in relation to my new employer; I am only missed in relation to my family; I am only a foreigner in relation to the locals. The movement that has taken place here is not that of a change in relative position of a set of elements in space so much as it is a transformation of the relations between them. Movement as an expression of duration is nothing other than the expression of this change in relations. Thus, 'We can say of duration itself or of time, that it is the whole of relations.'[26]

Now implicit in this definition is that any given movement expresses itself in the change of relations between a given set of elements, which is in itself finite. Of course, that set may be expanded, new elements added, new relations entered into, but just as movement cannot be divided without changing in kind, so too it cannot be 'added to' without changing in quality. Consider Bergson's example of the glass of sugared water: if we look at the set of elements which includes only the glass, the water and the sugar, then the movement (that is to say, the duration) which pertains to it expresses nothing more than the relation of 'solubility' between the sugar and the water, and the relation of 'container' to 'contained' between the glass and them both. If, however, I expand that set to include myself, I find that, having put the sugar in the water, 'I must, willy-nilly, wait until the sugar melts.'[27] The relations expressed in this expanded set are something other than merely solubility or containment. They express the relation of my own temporality to that of the sugar, the water, 'my impatience . . . a certain portion of my own duration';[28] in other words, my *waiting*: 'My waiting, whatever it be, expresses duration as mental, spiritual reality.'[29]

If at any point the set of elements could be closed, this kind of qualitative change would itself be foreclosed, inasmuch as the whole (of the set) would indeed be given. In such an instance there would be no real movement, only translation without transformation (the difference here is, as Bergson puts it, 'between an evolution and an unfurling, between the radically new [temporal transformation] and a rearrangement of the pre-existing [spatial translation]'[30]). The problem here, of course, is that sets as such are necessarily closed, since the rules of membership that define a given set determine the elements of that set completely.[31] The third thesis on movement presents Bergson's solution to this problem: movement is a mobile section of duration (and as a 'section' is necessarily limited), which expresses a qualitative change in the whole (a change in relations), but that whole in itself is neither given nor giveable, 'because it is the Open, and because its nature is to change constantly, or to give rise to something new, in short, to endure'.[32]

What then is this whole, and what is it that constitutes its 'openness'? Deleuze has already given us at least a partial answer: 'If one had to define the whole, it would be defined by relation.'[33] Although any given set of elements is necessarily closed by virtue of its rules of membership, relations are external to their terms and thus not a property of sets or their elements. They belong to the whole, which has no parts and is itself not a set.[34] Where sets are constituted of discrete and separate elements extended spatially, relations, and therefore the whole, are continuous and temporal. Every change in relations – every expression of real duration – is continuous with the whole as such, and propagates no less to the most distant and the nearest aspect of the whole. As Bergson puts it:

> our sun radiates heat and light beyond the farthest planet. And, on the other hand, it moves in a certain fixed direction, drawing with it the planets and their satellites. The thread attaching it to the rest of the universe is doubtless very tenuous. Nevertheless it is along this thread that is transmitted down to the smallest particle of the world in which we live the duration immanent to the whole of the universe.[35]

As the transformation of relations between elements of a set which is itself closed, movement is an expression of duration and thus of the whole, which 'changes and does not stop changing'. It thereby links or opens that set to the openness of the Whole, and so prevents the set from closing in on itself. We may grasp the flight of an arrow abstractly as a simple translation from here to there, but this passage and the transformation of relations it expresses concretely are nothing other than a 'mobile section' or 'partial view' of the whole with which it is continuous. As Bergson puts it, 'The systems we cut out within ... [the whole] would, properly speaking, not then be *parts* at all; they would be *partial views* of the whole.'[36] This is the basis of the 'metaphysics' Bergson seeks to add to the account of modern science, the 'correction' which enables it to account for genuine creation, the production of the new:

the whole is not a closed set, but on the contrary that by virtue of which the set is never absolutely closed, never completely sheltered, that which keeps it open somewhere as if by the finest thread, which attaches it to the rest of the universe.[37]

The openness of the whole is simply time as the endurance or duration of matter that plunges it into memory, into time, into the past as that which differs from itself first of all. To put it in Deleuzian terms, it is the being of difference itself.

The Temporalisation of Difference

One of the aspects that make these theses such a startling and potentially disorienting opening to the *Cinema* books is that their significance is not immediately apparent. The arguments that follow are derived from them clearly enough, but the problem that they themselves respond to is not: the stakes of the game are hidden. Apropos of Hardt, if we wish to find them we must look elsewhere, in the previous arguments Deleuze 'assumes' in this opening volley. In particular, we must look to arguments presented some thirty or so years earlier in his essay 'Bergson's Conception of Difference'.[38] The link between this essay and the three theses is the cinematographic illusion itself. The cinematographic illusion is never mentioned by name in 'Bergson's Conception of Difference', or indeed anywhere in Deleuze's work prior to the *Cinema* books. However, as we shall see, Bergson's critique of that illusion underpins the entire argument of this early work. To the best of my knowledge this link has not been noted in the secondary literature, and this is, I think, an important oversight.

Giovanna Borradori has argued that 'Bergson's Conception of Difference' has been unjustly neglected as 'one of Deleuze's least known essays',[39] with Hardt one of the few authors to draw attention to it. More recently, however, Hallward has noted that 'From start to finish, Deleuze's philosophy is everywhere consistent with the point of departure he adapts from Bergson in opposition to Hegel.'[40] 'Bergson's Conception of Difference' is that point of departure and in it are outlined the foundations on which Deleuze's philosophical project rests: the critique of philosophies of identity and representation, and thus of negation; his own purely positive alternative, given in terms of the being of difference; and finally the demonstration that his critique of the errors of negation and the negative is given in terms that allow Deleuze to derive or deduce those errors on the basis of real difference – which, as we shall see, is essential if Deleuze's own philosophy is to retain its purely positive character.

Let us start, then, from this positivity. Deleuze's philosophy is, as Hallward suggests, a *philosophy of creation*,[41] such that the Deleuzian question *par excellence* is 'how is something new possible?'[42] The task he essays in 'Bergson's Conception of Difference' is to provide a firm foundation for such a philosophy by demonstrating the *necessity* of a purely positive conception of being, one in which negation and the negative have no place.[43] ('Necessity' is used here in a properly philosophical sense, as opposed to the accidental or the contingent.) More precisely, Deleuze seeks to demonstrate that a purely positive conception of ontology is the only one capable of retaining the necessity of being itself.

As the title of Deleuze's essay suggests, the key term here is difference, in so far as any philosophy that seeks to grasp being must account in some way for difference. This is, in an everyday sense, self-evident, in that one need only open one's eyes to see a world that changes, that differs: things move and are thus other than they were. Immediately there is an intimate relationship between movement and difference: that which moves, differs, and that which differs, moves. The question, then, is how to account for that movement: how is it that being moves, how is it that it differs? Thus, for Deleuze, it is the reality of movement, of difference *as that which is*, that is at stake in ontological speculation.

The argument presented in 'Bergson's Conception of Difference' is dense, and contains the seeds of many of the themes that Deleuze returns to throughout his career in order to unpack and develop them. Hardt's commentary on that essay provides an excellent entry point and my reading of it is indebted to his analysis (although my presentation of it below places an emphasis on the identity of movement and difference that owes more to Borradori than it does to Hardt).[44] Hardt notes that Deleuze's argument begins by drawing on Bergson to construct a critique of mechanism and Platonism (or finalism). These targets are criticised for accounting for difference (change, that is to say, movement) in terms of something strictly external to the thing that moves. In the case of mechanism, this 'something' is causality: it posits a world of things that move (which differ) only under the impetus of other things.

Where mechanism accounts for movement in terms of a material cause (this billiard ball hits that one), Platonism, on the other hand, accounts for it in terms of a movement towards a *telos*, a finality, an end or goal: 'the difference of the thing comes from its use, its end, its destination, The Good'.[45] As such, the differences between things are given only in relation to their end: 'only the Good accounts for the difference of the thing and lets us understand it in itself'.[46]

In either case, difference is reduced to a determination imposed from without: things change, move, being *becomes* only by means of something outside of them. Difference remains *external* to being, a 'motor' that is added to it 'after the fact'. And since being is all there is, an external conception of difference also implies both that difference *has* no being and that being has no *difference*. Being is thereby reduced to a static, sterile immobility: all that there is is the One, a closed totality with neither change nor movement. External conceptions of differences such as those offered in Platonism and mechanism are thus incapable of accounting for the being of difference, and thus the reality of movement and of change.

The discussion in 'Bergson's Conception of Difference', then, turns primarily on the contrast of internal and external difference. The term 'movement' is clearly identified in the text with duration and real difference, but in general remains something of a background figure in the argument. Deleuze does, however, make the observation that

> movement is qualitative change and qualitative change is movement. In short, duration is what differs and what differs is no longer what differs from something else, but what differs from itself ... movement is no longer the character of something, but has itself taken on a substantial character, it presupposes nothing else, no moving object.[47]

Thus duration is that which differs from itself, and is given in and as qualitative change, as movement. This is what Borradori calls Deleuze's 'temporalisation of difference'. The importance of this for Deleuzian philosophy cannot be overstated: for Deleuze, the being of difference is simply time itself as the form of change.[48] Thus both movement and duration must be understood here as substantives, as something in and of themselves, and not in relation to any other thing: movement is real only in so far as it *is* something for itself, rather than being the movement *of* some other thing. Remember that it is the internal character of difference, of movement, that allows it to retain its necessity: the reality of movement *is* its necessity. Real movement – movement as qualitative change, as duration – *is* internal difference.

If these arguments seem familiar, it is for good cause. The 'three theses on movement' from the first pages of *Cinema 1* are in fact a transliteration of the arguments of 'Bergson's Conception of Difference', in which the terminology of difference has been replaced by that of movement,[49] and unless we recognise this, we risk missing the ontological force of their arguments. Specifically, we find 'internal difference' posited in the first thesis in terms of movement as the expression of duration and contrasted with 'external difference' given as movement understood as a series of static points, points *abstracted* from real movement. The demonstration in the second thesis that both the classical/finalist and modern/mechanist conceptions of movement lead only to a static and unchanging model of the universe – a closed whole, given in advance – is equally a demonstration that such conceptions of movement are incoherent: they conceive of movement as something static. Real movement is neither movement imparted *by* something else (mechanism), nor movement *towards* something else (finalism). For movement to be movement, it must be *necessary* that it move in and of itself, rather than being the movement of some thing. This leads us directly to the conclusion offered in the third thesis: being must be open, must *be* movement, duration, difference that differs from itself first of all.

We can see then that the 'return to Bergson' we find in the *Cinema* books is more precisely a return to the founding premises of Deleuzian philosophy itself, and to the role of the cinematographic illusion in establishing these premises. However, recognising this does not, as yet, allow us to understand the *reason* for this return; we do not yet know the stakes of the game. These stakes, it seems to me, belong to a more subterranean link between the three theses and the concerns of 'Bergson's Conception of Difference'. The aspect of the latter that the three theses *don't* seem to invoke is, for Hardt, the very core of that essay: the ontological critique of Hegel and the dialectic that Deleuze constructs out of the arguments Bergson turns against mechanism and Platonism. It seems to me that this critique points us towards the stakes of the game that are left unspoken in the opening chapter of *Cinema 1*. However it is not so much the critique of Hegel itself that lurks behind this opening, as it is the dangers inherent in such a critique and, more specifically, the manner in which Deleuze escapes those dangers.

Before we can get to this point, however, we need to understand the critique itself and the specific challenges it poses to Deleuze in posing his own alternative. Hardt locates the latter's critique of

Hegel within the context of the 'generalized anti-Hegelianism' that Deleuze describes as dominating continental philosophy from the 1940s through to the '60s,[50] and which Vincent Descombes traces in large part to the influence of Alexandre Kojève's work on Hegel throughout the 1930s and '40s.[51] Hardt thus points out that

> for the generation of Continental thinkers that came to maturity in the 1960s, Hegel was the figure of order and authority that served as the focus of antagonism. Deleuze speaks for his entire cohort: 'What I detested above all was Hegelianism and the dialectic.'[52]

Such a rejection is, however, perilous. As Hardt takes care to make clear, to oppose Hegel (that is, to stand in a relation of negation to him) is to risk being subsumed by him once more in the totalising synthesis of the dialectic.[53] He directs us to Judith Butler's analysis of the relations between Hegel and contemporary French philosophy, in which she points out that 'References to a break with Hegel are almost always impossible, if only because Hegel has made the very notion of "breaking with" into a central tenet of his dialectic.'[54] The rejection of Hegel that Deleuze speaks of on behalf of his 'cohort' can thus only ever be a fraught one, since 'the act of repudiation more often than not requires the continued life of that which is repudiated, thus paradoxically sustaining the "rejected Hegel"'.[55] As Blanchot puts it, 'One cannot "read" Hegel, except by not reading him. To read, not to read him – to understand, to misunderstand him, to reject him – all this falls under the authority of Hegel or doesn't take place at all.'[56] As such the question of difference, and how to articulate a difference *from* Hegel which nevertheless does not constitute a negation *of* him, takes on a signal importance for Deleuze.

Deleuze begins to essay this task in 'Bergson's Conception of Difference', despite Bergson having little or nothing to say about Hegel himself. Indeed, Hardt presents this apparently curious choice as part of a tactical distancing of Deleuze and his arguments from Hegel and the territory of the dialectic, the better to avoid opposing Hegel directly.[57] Rather than attack Hegel head on, he adopts what Hardt calls a 'method of triangulation'.

> [Deleuze] does not attack the dialectic directly, but rather he introduces a third philosophical position that he locates between Bergson and the dialectic. Deleuze then engages this proximate enemy on the specific fault that marks its insufficiency, and then he proceeds to show that Hegel, the fundamental enemy, carries this fault to its extreme.[58]

In 'Bergson's Conception of Difference', the 'proximate enemies' that Deleuze critiques via Bergson are those of mechanism and finalism (in the form of Plato). It is the Hegelian dialectic, however, that is the fundamental target of these critiques, and that according to Deleuze takes these flaws to their extreme.[59] The essence of the dialectic 'is constituted by a dynamic in which the cause is absolutely external to its effect',[60] since the negation of one term by another requires that they be absolutely external to each other. As a result, 'The process of the mediation in the opposite necessarily depends upon an external causality.'[61]

Indeed, the defining characteristic of the dialectic is to take external difference, difference *between* things, to its most extreme point. As Hardt puts it, 'according to Hegel, the thing differs from itself because it differs in the first place from all that it is not, such that difference goes to the point of contradiction',[62] that is to say, *all the way to negation*. Thus 'in effect, if we ignore questions of historiography, Hegel appears to gather the faults of Mechanism and Platonism and repeat them in their pure form by taking external difference to its extreme'.[63] As we should now recognise, this also positions the Hegelian dialectic as the most extreme form of the cinematographic illusion Bergson critiques within philosophy.

Hegel's negative ontological determination is thus identified merely as the most extreme end of a spectrum of philosophies in which difference is merely difference in degree, spatialised difference. Deleuze for his part replaces the negative ontological determination of Hegel with a conception of duration as positive ontological *differentiation*: being which differs first of all and immediately with itself, such that difference is thereby both internal and necessary to being. The necessity of being itself is thus conserved by posing its essence as its very inessentiality, by replacing the determination of being offered by the targets of his critique with being as indetermination itself. 'Bergson always insists on the unpredictable character of living forms: "indeterminate, *i.e.* unforeseeable". And with Bergson, the unpredictable and the indeterminate is not accidental, but on the contrary the essential.'[64] The word 'unforeseeable' here bears a significant load, in so far as the creation of the genuinely new is only possible to the extent that its creation is unforeseeable, that is, to the extent that being is open (to the future). More important in this context, however, is that Bergson's conception of being as that which differs from itself offers Deleuze 'a conception of difference without negation, which does not contain the negative – such is Bergson's greatest effort'.[65]

How to Escape the Dialectic

Deleuze's argument contains a further step, which allows him to develop his critique of Hegel towards a fully positive alternative. The importance of this step for his philosophical framework is flagged by the fact that he returns to it several times in his career, although in new terms and in relation to different problems (for example, in *Bergsonism* and in *Difference and Repetition*, whose resources I will draw on where they add to or clarify what is at stake in this issue). The initial 'critical' phase of this manoeuvre draws on the critique of external difference already mapped out in order to define the characteristics of a thought that is adequate to the concrete and to the real.[66] Both Bergson and Deleuze posit such a thought as essential to any philosophy that seeks to account for or think the real as such, rather than mere abstraction.

Platonism and mechanism, despite their inability to grasp internal difference, are at least capable of distinguishing differences of degree; their concept of difference allows for *contrast* between different things without implying a relation of opposition between them. Hegel's dialectic, however, pushes this contrast to its extreme, all the way to *negation*. As Hardt says, 'From the very first moments of *Science of Logic* – from pure being to nothingness to determinate being – the dialectic is constituted by a dynamic in which the cause is absolutely external to its effect: This is the essence of a dialectic of contradiction.'[67] Thus Deleuze points out that

> If the objection that Bergson made against Platonism was that it stopped at a *still external conception of difference*, the objection that he makes to a dialectic of contradiction is that it remains with a *merely abstract conception of difference*. 'This combination [of two contradictory concepts] can present neither a diversity of degrees nor a variety of forms: it is, or it is not.' What comprises neither degrees nor nuances is an abstraction.[68]

Indeed Deleuze points out that, for Bergson, 'the one' and 'the many' are abstract concepts that are simply too general to ever lead us to an understanding of the concrete: 'in this type of *dialectical* method, one begins with concepts that, like baggy clothes, are much too big. The One in general, the multiple in general, non-being in general ... In such cases the real is recomposed with abstracts.'[69] Such generalities lack precision, and so can only account for reality in general terms, while letting the concrete, the singular, the particular 'slip through their net'. Deleuze returns to this theme in *Difference and Repetition* when he argues that

> the one and the many are concepts of the understanding which make up the overly loose mesh of a distorted dialectic which proceeds by opposition. The biggest fish pass through. Can we believe that the concrete is attained when the inadequacy of an abstraction is compensated for by the inadequacy of its opposite?[70]

Even if we think of difference purely in terms of the difference between determined beings,[71] we can see the 'generalising' tendency of the Hegelian dialectic in the way it takes the difference between beings to the most extreme point, 'all the way to negation'. It thereby loses any possible conception even of differences of degree between things (there are no 'degrees' of negation). Such generalising tendencies lose any possible grasp of the concrete quality of reality and thus tell us little, if anything, about it. As Bergson puts it, pure opposition, '*yes* and *no* are sterile in philosophy. What is interesting ... is *in what measure?*'[72] The fish that slip through the dialectical net are thus precisely specificity, detail, 'nuance', as Bergson says. Thus the combination of the one and the many in general misses the essential: '*how, how many, when and where*. "What" unity of the multiple and "what" multiple of the one?'[73]

Deleuze distinguishes Hegel's purely abstract notion of being that becomes via pure negation (dialectical movement as that which first posits being, and only then seeks to account for its movement) from Bergson's conception of being as that which differs with itself first of all (movement as an expression of duration). In contrast to Hegel, Bergsonian ontology seeks to think the real in its concreteness and specificity. This is the very goal of Bergson's philosophy: to escape the illusions of abstraction and to constitute a philosophy, a thought, adequate to the real. The manner in which it is able to do so is implicit in his references to 'nuance' as that which the ready-made generality of the dialectic necessarily misses. Consider the qualities evoked by 'nuance' and its cognates – shade, tone, timbre, grain; they all describe aspects that are difficult to pin down exactly, to assign a precise identity or location to. To put it another way, they allude to something that is 'precisely' indeterminate, which cannot be determined, given a precise content or identity without betraying it, but is nonetheless unquestionably real in some sense.

Imagine a whitewashed wall, illuminated by the sun. Although we might simply call it 'white', that nomination is an abstraction that compresses a variation of shade and tonality that cannot be contained by or reduced to that label.[74] Moreover, as the light of the sun passes overhead, that wall perforce presents a constant variation of shades of 'whiteness' to the eye at different times. Not only does the light change in angle and intensity throughout the day, it bounces off and reflects or absorbs the colours of the plants and flowers nearby, such that the whiteness of the wall presents a subtle and continuous spectrum of difference. Nevertheless, it is impossible to distinguish 'one' shade from the 'next', even if different times of day reveal tones that would be 'clearly' different from each other if placed side by side. Because the angle and intensity of the light on the wall changes in an unbroken and continuous transition, there is no point at which the wall becomes a distinctly 'different' shade: there is only an unbroken and continuous variation throughout the day.

Indeed, to speak of the wall's 'whiteness' is in itself a false determination. To the extent that the wall presents a continuous variation, there is no pure white here at all. There are, rather, various tendencies towards colour and colours, in the sense that cinematographers refer to the 'colour' of a light source: the warm yellow white of the tungsten lamp, the cold blue white of the Sun, the green white of fluorescent light, and so on. Whiteness, in this sense, is like the concept of colour itself, so that the different shades or colours are simply 'the nuances or degrees of the concept itself [of whiteness], degrees of difference itself and not differences of degree'.[75] There is in such variation a differentiation of whiteness, a continuity of nuances of difference without any determination of distinct shades or colours of white.

In the 'indetermination' or continuous variation I've described, 'white' cannot be understood as a singular, abstract idea that is represented in different degrees in its various shades, since these shades cannot be determined as different from each other. If one were to take a series of photographs of the wall at different times of day, each photograph would show a specific and determined shade of white. But as we have seen with Zeno's paradoxes, to attempt to reconstruct a continuous movement of change through the addition of static points is to lose the essential quality of that change, which is change itself. No matter how many photographs you took (even up to and beyond the twenty-four-'photogrammes'-a-second of the film strip), you would only ever have a series of static determinations of the wall's whiteness, without ever capturing the essential difference of that colour from itself – that is to say, its duration. Inasmuch as such a series of photographs does give us a sense of the movement, or change over time, it is because we add to them an abstract concept of movement in general, a concept whose 'bagginess' ensures that the essential aspect of the real movements, its 'nuance', is lost.[76] This abstraction, and the bagginess of the general concepts it gives rise to, are precisely the philosophical illusions Bergson calls cinematographic.

Deleuze characterises this difference between Bergson's difference and that of mechanism and finalism (and, at its most extreme point, Hegelianism) as one between differences in kind and differences in degree. It is important to recognise that what is at stake here is the difference between internal and external difference, and thus between movement understood as an expression of duration or as a mere translation in space. But which type of difference is the difference between these two differences? Is it one of kind or one of degree?[77] A difference of degree – a quantitative or external difference – will never change in kind, no matter how large or small it becomes, and thus will always remain a difference of degree, can never extend to a difference in kind, and thus cannot account for the difference between difference in kind and in degree. Difference in kind, on the other hand – qualitative, or internal difference – differs with itself first of all. That is, it differs even from its own difference to the point that it contains all the degrees of difference between quality and quantity, all the way up to and including differences of degree. Deleuze presents this argument over several pages in 'Bergson's Conception of Difference'[78] but gives it more concisely in the later *Bergsonism*:

> between the two there are all the *degrees of difference* or, in other words, the whole *nature of difference* ... Differences in degree are the lowest degree of Difference; differences in kind (*nature*) are the highest nature of Difference. There is no longer any dualism between nature and degrees. All the degrees coexist in a single Nature that is expressed, on the one hand, in differences in kind, and on the other, in differences in degree.[79]

Put simply, degrees of difference (internal difference) are capable of accounting for or 'containing' differences in degree (external difference). The latter are merely the static points 'extracted' from the continuous variation of the former. And this treatment of difference and thus movement reflects in direct terms the critique presented in Bergson's first thesis on movement.

Both internal and external difference are thus given univocally, in one and the same 'voice', in so far as the genesis of the latter is deduced on the basis of the differing from itself of internal difference: difference in degree is merely the furthest degree of difference. Duration, movement, and thus being, can only be grasped in its reality if it is understood in terms of qualitative difference: real movement is introduced into thought in these terms, and these terms only. To think in terms of quantitative difference or differences of degree, on the other hand, is to lose the reality of the real, to think a merely abstract, static and 'sterile' thought: such is a thought that 'fails to think'.

Here we are close to the secret and the power of Deleuzian philosophy, understood in terms of a precise characterisation of its 'purely positive' nature. Hegel is often described as Deleuze's great 'enemy', on the basis of several highly critical references by the latter to the former, such as that in the 'Letter to a Harsh Critic', where Deleuze makes the comment that 'What I most detested was Hegelianism and dialectics.'[80] The violence of such language certainly suggests the relationship of antagonism often posited between the two. However, to take one's lead from such comments risks missing the subtlety, and indeed delicacy, with which Deleuze's actual arguments respond to the challenge posed by Hegel and the dialectic. As I noted earlier, Hegel poses a specific challenge to those who wish to attack or refute him. To oppose Hegel is to stand in a relation of negation to him, and thus to risk being subsumed by him or, rather, *synthesised* by him via the dialectical movement of negation, to let negation in 'by the back door' as it were. To put it bluntly, to be Hegel's enemy is to be his friend. Hence the vital importance Deleuze places on being able to constitute a purely positive basis for philosophy: a philosophy that seeks to elude Hegel can have neither part nor parcel of the negative or negation.

As Hardt argues, the 'tactical' distance Deleuze places between himself and Hegel in 'Bergson's Conception of Difference' (by critiquing Hegelianism as the most extreme instance of flaws already manifest in mechanism and Platonism) should be understood as a response to this problem. It is, however, a merely *tactical* distance, an argumentative methodology that holds Hegel at arm's length, while still keeping him in reach. The distance it imposes is susceptible of being collapsed if one breaks the argument down and reduces it to its essence – which is exactly what Hardt's reading of 'Bergson's Conception of Difference' does. To truly escape from the dialectical trap that Hegel sets, Deleuze needs something more: he requires a means to *account* for Hegel without *opposing* him. The treatment of difference in terms of degrees of difference that differ all the way to differences of degree provides him with the tools to do just that.

We can see this more clearly in later, more developed formulations of this idea. To do this, however, we require a slight change in terminology. The heterogenesis of Deleuzian philosophy is such that with each new book he seems to invent a whole new range of terms and concepts,[81] without ever entirely leaving the terminology of earlier works behind. More confusingly, the concepts these terms describe often seem to overlap with or repeat those of other works. For example: being, difference, duration, real movement, the pure past, the virtual. All these terms refer more or less directly to Deleuze's founding ontological conception of the internal difference of being. At the same time, they each draw out a nuance or tendency within that model that finds its expression in relation to the specific territory a given argument is exploring.[82]

If we move from 'Bergson's Conception of Difference' to the fifth chapter of *Bergsonism*,[83] we find a shift in emphasis marked by the introduction of three terms (virtual, actualisation, actual) to account for the differences in difference that are dealt with in the earlier work via two ('degrees of difference' and 'difference of degree'). This shift is at least in part a response to the need to give this difference in terms of process, of movement: the two-part model is too conceptually static for the action it describes. The three-part model offers the same argument, but places it more clearly in the movement it describes, and in doing so emphasises the creative character of this movement. This movement is needed here in so far as Deleuze is responding directly to Bergson's notion of *élan vital* as a force of differentiation or evolution: the argument seeks to place its concepts in the same movement it finds within Bergson's creative evolution.[84]

What then does the use of three, rather than two, terms add to our grasp of the notion of difference they all correspond to? It brings out more clearly the status of the actual (as the differences of degree 'contained' within the degrees of difference) and the traps this sets for thought. In this tripartite distinction, the virtual (which is difference that differs from itself) actualises itself according to divergent lines, which become actual only in so far as they 'appear' as a specific degree of difference:

> When the virtuality is actualised, is differentiated, is 'developed', when it actualises and develops its parts, it does so according to lines that are

divergent, but each of which corresponds to a particular degree in the virtual totality. There is here no longer any coexisting whole; there are merely lines of actualisation ... Nevertheless, each of these lines corresponds to one of these degrees that all coexist in the virtual; it actualises its level, while separating it from the others; it embodies its prominent points, while being unaware of everything that happens on other levels.[85]

There are two points to clarify here. First of all, that which is actualised of the virtual is life as it presents itself in and as matter. Actualisation is the mode of being's *creation* of beings such that 'Evolution takes place from the virtual to actuals. Evolution is actualisation, actualisation is creation.'[86] The second point concerns actualisation or, more precisely, the significance of its 'addition' as a third term to the pair of degrees of difference and differences of degree. Deleuze emphasises the fact that the actual does not resemble the virtuality that it embodies. To use Ronald Bogue's analogy, 'Just as the structure of genes bears no resemblance to the structure of an actual animal, so the structure of a virtual idea bears no resemblance to the structure of its actual embodiment.'[87] Thus 'it is difference that is primary in the process of actualisation – the difference between the virtual from which we begin and the actuals at which we arrive, and also the difference between the complementary lines according to which actualisation takes place.'[88]

The difference that is enacted at each stage of this process (the difference that differs from itself first of all, into different 'lines' of actualisation, which manifest themselves in actual beings or creations that bear no resemblance to the action or process in which they are actualised) is essential to Deleuze's requirement that being *be* creative, *be* creation. He emphasises this through a comparison of the 'virtual and the actual' with the 'possible and the real'.[89] One cannot map these pairs onto each other: whereas the possible has no reality at all, both the virtual and the actual are equally real – hence Proust's formula for the virtual: 'real without being actual, ideal without being abstract'.[90] As we have seen, actualisation is a movement of creation, such that the virtual that is actualised in no sense resembles that which is actualised of it, since 'It is difference that is primary in the process of actualisation.'[91]

The realisation of the possible, on the other hand, is governed by the principles of resemblance and limitation; 'resemblance' since 'the real is supposed to be in the image of the possible that it realises. (It simply has existence or reality added to it ... from the point of view of the concept, there is no difference between the possible and the real.)'[92] 'Limitation' since not everything that is possible comes to be realised, so that the real is simply a subset of the possible and pre-exists itself ready-made, so that 'Everything is already completely given.'[93] (Note the echo of the second thesis on movement, where mechanism and finalism are critiqued for conceiving of the whole as 'given in advance'.)

However, as Deleuze points out, this conception of the real as a limited representation of the possible is a fiction, a 'sleight of hand': it is not the real that resembles the possible, but rather the possible that resembles the real. The possible is no more than a fictitious image we produce *on the basis of* the real – that is, on the basis of real actuals divorced from the virtual they are the actualisation of. We then project this image backwards in order to account for the real itself, to be able 'to claim that it was possible at any time, before it happened'.[94] We postulate the possible *on the basis of* the real, 'after' the real and in order to explain the real, and then pretend that the real derives from the possible and not the other way around. The fallacy of the possible and the real is thus the model for any thought that begins from the actual divorced from its movement of actualisation and then attempts to account for it on the basis of what is thus given actually. Such a thought 'projects backwards' the characteristics of the actual and thus 'extracts' the possible from the real 'like a sterile double',[95] and then claims that this explains or accounts for the qualities of the actuals themselves.

Thus we can see that, firstly, the actual does not resemble the virtual that it actualises because actualisation is an act of creation in and of itself. Secondly (and this is the key point), although there is no negation or negativity in this movement of actualisation and creation, if one abstracts the products of actualisation from that movement (that is, if one considers only the actuals themselves and not the virtual that they are the actualisation of), the difference of those isolated actuals from each other *can* be articulated in purely external terms, as a difference *between* two actual and determined elements, which are thus susceptible of appearing in a relation of negation with each other. Thus

> forms of the negative do indeed appear in actual terms and real relations, but only in so far as these are cut off from the virtuality which they actualise, and from the movement of their actualisation. Then, and only then, do the finite affirmations appear limited in themselves, opposed to one another, and suffering from lack or privation.[96]

Movement, Duration and Difference

The actual, inasmuch as it is 'cut off' from the virtual it is the actualisation of – if it is taken independently of the movement of becoming it is the expression of – can be taken to constitute a self-identical element. However, it is an identity whose condition is difference. Rather than deriving difference from identity (as the difference between self-identical elements), difference is given here as the basis *of* identity itself. As a consequence, however, if thought begins from actuals taken on their own, in isolation from the movement of creation and invention in which they are actualised – if thought takes the actualised elements as static points, as self-identical elements – it is able to arrive, however falsely, at a negative conception of being, despite being's purely positive foundation as and in difference. Thus, 'In short, the negative is always derived and represented, never original or present: the process of difference and differenciation is primary in relation to that of the negative and opposition.'[97]

The error of Hegel's dialectical movement of negation and synthesis is that it is premised on the apparent qualities of actual things divorced from the virtual of which they are the actualisation. Thus isolated, these 'finite affirmations appear limited in themselves, opposed to one another, and suffering from lack or privation'.[98] Hegel derives the principle of negation from this apparent opposition and projects it backwards, and then claims that this accounts for the actual world he sees before him. But the world so constructed is merely a cinematographic illusion that loses the reality of both movement and of difference itself.

These are the terms of Deleuze's escape from the 'dialectical trap' of negation: one accounts for the position of one's 'enemy' not in terms of contestation or negation, but rather subsumes them as a limited, abstract and arbitrary[99] construction that can be deduced from one's own strictly positive position, while the failings of one's foe are those of negation and the negative, and the models of identity and representation these give rise to. As he puts in *Difference and Repetition*, it is a case of accounting for 'the *genesis* of the appearance of negation' on the basis of a purely positive genesis of affirmation.[100] Thus Deleuze is able to critique Hegel and demonstrate the insufficiency of the dialectic as a means of responding to the specificity of real being, all the while retaining the virtues of a purely positive movement of affirmation and creation for himself. In doing so, he is able to demonstrate that Hegelian philosophy (and indeed, any mechanist or finalist model at all) may be deduced in principle from his own philosophy of difference, and should be understood as something constructed within an arbitrarily limited or closed set of actual elements 'cut out' or abstracted from the open whole of being. As we shall see, this genetic method, whereby Deleuze deduces and accounts for the target of his 'critique' on the basis of his own philosophical principles, plays an important part in the logic and argument of the *Cinema* books.

For the moment, however, this perspective suggests that the characterisation of Hegel as Deleuze's great 'enemy' both mistakes the nature of their relationship and overlooks the elegance of the means with which Deleuze negotiates it. An enemy is something one seeks to destroy, one whose aims and goals are not only different from yours, or at odds with them, but which go so far as to put yours in danger. One must destroy, kill, negate one's enemy before they negate you (the showdown at the dialectical corral). This is more or less how Hardt characterises the relationship between Deleuze and Hegel. Hardt deals with the danger of dialectical synthesis with and by the enemy by proposing a strictly non-dialectical concept of negation, a *pars destruens* or moment of absolute destruction that 'clears the terrain for creation; it is a bipartite sequence that precludes any third, synthetic moment'.[101]

I find this proposal unconvincing for two reasons. Firstly, as I understand him, Deleuze seeks to account not only for being in strictly positive and creative terms, but also for thought and the powers of thought as creative creations of being in themselves. The introduction of negation, even an absolute or pure negation without hope of synthesis, thus seems to me to rely on an element that is strictly external to Deleuze's own thought (in the sense that it is not derived or derivable from the ontological difference that founds it) in order to explain or account for that thought. By accounting for the thought of his 'enemy' as immanent to his own, he is able to demonstrate the genesis of their thought on the basis of a purely positive ontological conception.

Secondly, to think of the relationship between Deleuze and Hegel in terms of pure enmity is to miss the commonality that they share, a commonality that turns precisely on the issue Deleuze emphasises in his account of what drew him to the cinema: the introduction of movement to thought. As Flaxman points out, 'In modern philosophy, the question of putting movement into thought was effectively broached by Hegel, as Deleuze admits.'[102] This is why the nature of the movement one wishes to introduce into thought, the means by which one understands and conceives of that movement, are so vital for Deleuze: far from being Hegel's enemy, he is, as Hallward says, his *rival*.[103]

Both seek the same goal of putting movement into thought, so that the stakes of their rivalry are given in the competition between their respective conceptions of movement: is the movement of being dialectical or differential? By demonstrating the incoherence and inadequacy of dialectical movement at an ontological level, while simultaneously showing how the dialectical movement can be derived from his own differential conception of movement as a kind of 'epistemological illusion',[104] Deleuze in effect contains or subsumes his rival without destroying or negating him as an enemy. In short, he accounts for an apparent dualism (Deleuze vs Hegel) as a strict monism (the dialectic determined and accounted for in and by Deleuze). Like the winner of a footrace, who in a sense 'contains' all the races run by his rivals within his own, Deleuze thus both 'contains' and dismisses Hegel, without destroying or negating him and thus tripping on the dialectical traps set by the latter. Moreover, the terms in which he does so allow him to account for any philosophy in which negation or the negative play a part – any philosophy premised on notions of identity and representation, any philosophy that falls under the sway of the cinematographic illusion – in precisely the same fashion.

According to Hallward, this mode of engagement is, in fact, 'one of the most characteristic features of Deleuze's work' throughout his career:

> his tendency to present what initially appears as a binary relation [in my example, the relation of 'enmity' between Deleuze and Hegel] in such a way as to show that this relation is in fact determined by only one if its two 'terms'. The difference between active and reactive force, for instance, turns out to be internal to the self-differentiation of active force, which alone *is* . . . In this and every comparable case, 'dualism is therefore only a moment, which must lead to the re-formation of a monism'.[105]

Although Hallward does not identify it as such, what he describes here is the application of a method of genetic deduction that ultimately finds its roots or its ur-form in Deleuze's treatment of the relation of internal and external difference. Deleuze's 'monism' is simply the demonstration of the univocity of being as difference, in so far as the genesis of the 'second' term of a given binary is ultimately deduced in terms of the first. As we shall see by the end of this book, this 'genetic' method bears directly on Deleuze's treatment of the cinema and on its relation to his treatment of Kant.

By repurposing Bergson's critique of cinematographic conceptions of movement into a critique of external conceptions of difference, Deleuze is able to establish the necessity of a strictly internal conception of difference, one that underpins his entire philosophical project. Moreover, although negation and the negative play no role in that project or its foundations, on the basis of that concept of difference he is able to account for his philosophical rivals in purely positive terms, without falling into the illusions and errors that negation and the negative draw those rivals into.

The cinematographic illusion is, then, central to both the positive and the critical dimensions of Deleuzian philosophy. By invoking not just that illusion, but its foundational role for Deleuze's work, the 'three theses' at the very least indicate that the project of the *Cinema* books bears in some sense on problems derived *from* those foundations, and from the place of the cinematographic illusion in them. The task of the next chapter is to identify the key problems that derive from that foundation, how Deleuze responds to them in his work at large, and only then to specify what role the cinema is to play in relation to them.

Notes

1. Flaxman, 'Cinema Year Zero', 87; quoting Deleuze, *Cinema 1*, 1.
2. Flaxman, 'Cinema Year Zero', 87.
3. Indeed, debates over the sympathy or otherwise between Bergsonism and the cinema can be found in French writing on cinema little more than a decade after *Creative Evolution* was published. See, for example L'Herbier, 'Hermes and Silence', 148–9.
4. See, for example, the criticisms Rodowick and Douglass offer respectively on this point, criticisms that I discuss in more detail in Chapter 5. Rodowick, *Gilles Deleuze's Time Machine*, 22 and more extensively 216 n.2; Douglass, 'Bergson and Cinema: Friends or Foes?', 220.
5. It would be more accurate, but awkward, to say in each case of this discussion 'Deleuze's presentation of Bergson's theses'. I will content myself with asking the reader to keep in mind the obvious: it is *Deleuze's* Bergsonism that is at stake here, no matter how many of Bergson's own words are summoned up to explicate it.
6. Salmon, 'Introduction', 10–11.
7. Bergson, *Creative Evolution*, 308.
8. Deleuze, *Cinema 1*, 1.
9. As a student, Bergson excelled at mathematics as well as philosophy.

He was apparently expected to enter the *Ecole Normale* to study mathematics, but chose to focus on philosophy instead. It is unsurprising, then, that Bergson makes explicit reference to at least one of these solutions in his treatment of those paradoxes. Ansell-Pearson and Mullarkey, 'Chronology', vii; Bergson, *Creative Evolution*, 311 n.1.
10. Thus Salmon notes that 'William James, Alfred North Whitehead, and Henri Bergson . . . have held that Zeno's paradoxes, while not proving the impossibility of motion, do validly show that the mathematical account of continuity is inadequate for the description of temporal processes.' 'Introduction', 17.
11. Ibid., 15. Emphasis added.
12. Huggett, 'Zeno: Commentary', 50.
13. Bergson, *Time and Free Will*, 120.
14. Bergson, *Creative Evolution*, 311 n.1.
15. Ibid. The contents of the parenthesis (*telos, acme*) are in ancient Greek in Bergson's original text, but are offered in translation where Deleuze quotes them in the English-language version of the *Cinema* books. Deleuze, *Cinema 1*, 4.
16. Bergson, *Creative Evolution*, 330. Emphasis in original.
17. Rodowick, *Gilles Deleuze's Time Machine*, 19.
18. Deleuze, *Cinema 1*, 7.
19. Ibid., 4. Emphasis in original.
20. Bergson, *Creative Evolution*, 37.
21. Bergson, 'Bergson–James Correspondence', 362.
22. Deleuze, *Bergsonism*, 104.
23. Deleuze, *Cinema 1*, 7.
24. Which is, roughly speaking, Newton's first law of motion.
25. Deleuze, *Cinema 1*, 10.
26. Ibid.
27. Bergson, *Creative Evolution*, 9.
28. Ibid., 10.
29. Deleuze, *Cinema 1*, 9.
30. Bergson, *The Creative Mind*, 21.
31. Of course, it is always possible define a rule of membership that constitutes a constantly expanding and potentially infinite set – the 'set of all people living and dead', for example. Furthermore, the axioms of set theory allow us to add sets to each as much as we like, again to infinity. However, in either instance this infinity is given or giveable in advance in the rules of membership for the set or in the combination of rules when sets are added together.
32. Deleuze, *Cinema 1*, 9.
33. Ibid., 10.
34. To treat the whole as a set is to fall into Bertrand Russell's paradox of the set of all sets. Such a set must either be a member of itself or not:

if it is not a member of itself it is not the set of all sets (since it doesn't include the set that it is in itself); if it *is* a member of itself, it is also not the set of all sets (since the addition of itself to the set creates another, larger set, which must then also be added to the set and so on into infinity).
35. Bergson, *Creative Evolution*, 10–11.
36. Ibid., 31.
37. Deleuze, *Cinema 1*, 10.
38. Deleuze, 'Bergson's Conception of Difference'; according to Hardt, this essay was originally published in *Les études bergsoniennes* in 1956, but was written and presented to the *Association des Amies de Bergson* in 1954. Hardt, *An Apprenticeship in Philosophy*, 2.
39. Borradori, 'The Temporalization of Difference', 1. The English translation of 'Bergson's Conception of Difference' was only published in 1999.
40. Hallward, *Out of This World*, 14–15.
41. Ibid., 15.
42. This is yet another sign, if we needed it, of the deep and abiding Bergsonism of Deleuze's philosophy: as Ronald Bogue points out, 'One of Bergson's central questions is, "How is something new possible?"' The next clause in Bogue's sentence signals something of the origins of the *Cinema* books: 'and the cinema points toward an answer'. Bogue, *Deleuze on Cinema*, 23.
43. In fact, as we shall see, it is more precise to say that it is a conception of being in which negation and the negative are to be found only on the basis of their abstraction by beings from the real difference of being.
44. Hardt, *An Apprenticeship in Philosophy*, 1–10.
45. Deleuze, 'Bergson's Conception of Difference', 52.
46. Ibid.
47. Ibid., 48.
48. Borradori argues that the primary significance of 'Bergson's Conception of Difference' for the trajectory of Deleuzian philosophy lies precisely in this 'temporalization of difference', especially with regard to his subsequent reading of Nietzsche. As we will see in final few chapters of this book, the Bergsonian–Nietzschean axis this constructs also plays an important role in Deleuze's response to Kant, played out in the cinema books in relation to the 'great Kantian reversal' of the relation of movement and time that divides the classical from the modern cinema. Borradori, 'The Temporalization of Difference', 10–15.
49. To be precise, it is the other way around: 'movement' is the original terminology of the Bergsonian sources that Deleuze draws on in these arguments, and which he transliterates into the terminology of 'difference' in 'Bergson's Conception of Difference'.

50. Hardt, *An Apprenticeship in Philosophy*, x; Deleuze, *Difference and Repetition*, xix.
51. Descombes, *Modern French Philosophy*, 10.
52. Hardt, *An Apprenticeship in Philosophy*, x; quoting Deleuze, *Difference and Repetition*, xix.
53. Hardt, *An Apprenticeship in Philosophy*, xi.
54. Butler, *Subjects of Desire*, 183–4.
55. Ibid., 175–6. In his examination of the critique of the dialectic presented in *Difference and Repetition*, Lutz Ellrich uses a similar logic against Deleuze specifically. Ellrich argues that the terms of Deleuze's rejection of Hegel ultimately rest on and require a strictly Hegelian notion of mediation; whether one accepts Ellrich's arguments or not, they both emphasise the difficulties facing Deleuze in his attempt to constitute a mode of thought outside of Hegel and the dialectic, and offer a concrete example of the risks Butler refers to. Ellrich, 'Negativity and Difference: On Gilles Deleuze's Criticism of Dialectics', 486–7.
56. Blanchot, *The Writing of the Disaster*, 46.
57. Hardt argues that this 'distancing' becomes more extreme as Deleuze's career goes on, to the point that 'as Deleuze's thought evolves we will see that he has continually greater difficulty in finding common terrain for addressing the Hegelian position'. Hegel is certainly not an immediate presence in *Cinema 1*'s account of Bergson's three theses on movement. However, as I will argue, Deleuze's relationship to Hegel and the dialectic nevertheless bears on the role Bergson's three theses on movement play in the *Cinema* books. Hardt, *An Apprenticeship in Philosophy*, 4.
58. Ibid.
59. Both Plato and Hegel offer teleological conceptions of the movement of being and are in this sense both forms of finalism. It is the 'extremity' to which Hegel takes his model – all the way to negation – that differentiates his finalism from Plato's.
60. Hardt, *An Apprenticeship in Philosophy*, 7.
61. Ibid.
62. Deleuze, 'Bergson's Conception of Difference', 53.
63. Hardt, *An Apprenticeship in Philosophy*, 7.
64. Deleuze, 'Bergson's Conception of Difference', 50.
65. Ibid., 53.
66. Deleuze returns to this question of 'concreteness' a number of times throughout his career, often in very similar terms to the ones deployed in 'Bergson's Conception of Difference' (another example of his 'monotony') and always with reference to Bergson. I therefore don't hesitate to cite these as well as the article at hand where the former offer a clearer formulation of a given problem or argument.

67. Hardt, *An Apprenticeship in Philosophy*, 7.
68. Deleuze, 'Bergson's Conception of Difference', 53. Emphasis in original; citing Bergson, *The Creative Mind*, 184. Intriguingly, Karl Marx's essay 'On Hegel's Concrete Universal' presents a critique of Hegelian idealism posed in strikingly similar terms. Marx, 'On Hegel's "Concrete Universal"', 314.
69. Deleuze, *Bergsonism*, 44.
70. Deleuze, *Difference and Repetition*, 182.
71. That is, in terms offered by mechanism and Platonism.
72. Quoted in Mullarkey, *Bergson and Philosophy*, 130; the original source is Bergson, *Mélanges*, 477.
73. Deleuze, *Bergsonism*, 44–5.
74. If you're not convinced that 'white' has shades or colours, I direct you to the paint samples section of your local hardware store.
75. What I have presented here is a variation or adaptation (intended to bring out the temporal character of Bergsonian difference more directly) of an argument Deleuze presents in 'Bergson's Conception of Difference' and again in *Difference and Repetition* in slightly different terms ten years later. In both cases, he is drawing on a passage from Bergson's essay 'The Life and Works of Ravaisson'. Deleuze, 'Bergson's Conception of Difference', 54, *Difference and Repetition*, 206; Bergson, 'The Life and Works of Ravaisson', 225–6.
76. It's worth emphasising that Bergson's treatment of 'colour' would not deny that what is captured in the 'snapshot' of passing reality is in some sense part of that reality. The distinct and determined shades captured in the photographs really are there 'in' the continuous multiplicity of the whiteness of the wall. However, they are only 'there' virtually, and to find them there *actually* requires that they be artificially 'cut' out of the continuity they are contained within – as if in a 'snapshot' of them.
77. There's an obvious similarity in the logic of this argument to the terms in which I have posed the problem of the relation between the two volumes of the *Cinema* books. Deleuze's analysis of the relation between differences in kind and in degree will indeed bear directly on my own characterisation of the break that lies between *Cinema 1* and *2*, once the tools needed to do so have been prepared in the chapters to come.
78. Deleuze, 'Bergson's Conception of Difference', 47–54.
79. Deleuze, *Bergsonism*, 93. It should be emphasised that the phrases 'degrees of difference' and 'differences of degree' are not transitive, are not simple inversions of each other, and have radically different senses. 'Degrees of difference' refers to qualitative difference, difference in kind or internal difference, which is the continuous variation of difference differing from itself. The 'degrees' of difference here are

not self-identical extensive units that differ from each other, but rather intensive differences in the self-differing *of* difference. However, in this self-differing difference we find all the differences in the differing of difference, up to and including a different mode *of* difference. This different mode of difference in difference is that of 'differences of degree', which are quantitative and external and can only ever repeat their own self-identical form of difference between 'things'. It is in this sense that the 'degrees in difference' constitute the 'whole' or the 'highest' nature of difference, including 'differences of degree', while the latter remains the 'lowest degree' of difference.

80. Deleuze, *Negotiations*, 6.
81. Bellour notes that Deleuze seems to invent a conceptual language for each new book – which is perhaps an aspect of the 'heterogenesis' or 'becoming of concepts' both Bellour and Smith see as underlying Deleuze's philosophical practice. Bellour, 'Thinking, Recounting', 70; Smith, *Essays on Deleuze*, 124–5.
82. For example, as we have already seen, the argument given in 'Bergson's Conception of Difference' reappears in the opening chapter of *Cinema 1*. In the latter, the terminology of difference and determination of the former is replaced by that of real and abstract, or spatialised movement, so as better to draw out the special character of cinematic movement Deleuze seeks to explore. We can see here the play of monotony and specificity referred to in my opening chapter.
83. Deleuze, *Bergsonism*, 91–113.
84. Thus we find the critique of external difference and abstraction repeated once again, but given this time in terms of the movement of evolution. Evolutionary models that conceive of 'the action of the environment and the influence of external conditions' are only capable of giving us an abstract understanding of the elements that evolve, understood only in terms of 'relations of association and addition'. Evolution understood as a vital differentiation (Bergson's 'creative evolution'), on the other hand, accounts for the diversity of the products of evolution in terms of a vital internal differentiation, so that the evolved creature is not acted on by a purely external environment, but 'co-evolves' with it as part of a constant variation or differentiation. Translated into the terminology of *Cinema 1*, 'the environment' corresponds to 'the open whole'. Ibid., 99.
85. Ibid., 100–1.
86. Ibid., 98.
87. Bogue, *Deleuze and Guattari*, 59–60.
88. Deleuze, *Bergsonism*, 97.
89. Deleuze draws this comparison more or less directly from Bergson's essay 'The Possible and the Real' in *The Creative Mind*, 99–102.
90. Quoted in Deleuze, *Bergsonism*, 96.

91. Ibid., 97.
92. Ibid.
93. Ibid., 98.
94. Ibid.
95. Ibid.
96. Deleuze, *Difference and Repetition*, 207. In this book we find yet another 'return' to the argument laid out in 'Bergson's Conception of Difference' (and again in Bergsonism) via a new terminology (that of different/ciation) and in relation to a new focus: the differential relation between problems and solutions. Thus 'differen*t*iation' deals with the structures difference composes as it differs from itself (virtual problems or ideas), and 'differen*c*iation' with the multiplicity of possible solutions to such problems/ideas in so far as they are actually instantiated in the world (unlike questions and answers, solutions never 'exhaust' the problem they respond to). Like the actual and actualisation, such differen*c*iated solutions bear no resemblance to the problems composed in difference's differen*t*iation.
97. Ibid.
98. Ibid.
99. 'Limited', in the sense that it deals only with actual being, and loses the virtual being of which the actual is actualised; 'abstract' because it reduces the becoming of being to static elements 'torn' from it; and 'arbitrary' because those static elements are extracted from being according to the needs of the thought that seeks to 'capture' or account for being, and not on the basis of being itself.
100. Deleuze, *Difference and Repetition*, 206. Emphasis added.
101. Hardt, *An Apprenticeship in Philosophy*, xiii.
102. Flaxman, 'Introduction', 17.
103. Hallward, *Out of This World*, 6.
104. It is illusory in the sense that it only 'appears' to thought if one divorces the actual from the virtual that it is an actualisation of, and then mistakes the difference between the actual things thus abstracted for a fundamental difference.
105. Hallward, *Out of This World*, 156–7, citing Deleuze, *Bergsonism*, 29. Hallward goes on to offer as further examples of the same dynamic the relation Deleuze proposes between schizophrenic immanence and paranoid transcendence, and the molar and the molecular.

4

What Use is Cinema to Deleuze?

The Necessary Illusions of Practical Life

We can start this chapter with a preliminary problem. As should be clear by now, Bergson's primary concern in positing his cinematographic metaphor has little to do with criticising the cinema. Indeed, he has very little interest in the cinema as cinema and is certainly not in any sense presenting a theory *of* the cinema.[1] Bergson's critique of the cinematographic illusion is aimed at a far larger target than the cinema: it critiques mechanistic science, Platonism and indeed the Western metaphysical tradition itself. Far from being derived from or targeted at the cinema, the cinematographic illusion is, as Ménil puts it, 'in fact so ancient that it is co-extensive with the entire history of Western thought'.[2] Deleuze adopts this evaluation wholeheartedly and articulates it in his own terms in his critique of external conceptions of difference within philosophy. However, even if we accept these arguments, the question remains: *why* does philosophy suffer this illusion so pervasively?

In *Creative Evolution* Bergson tells us that thought, perception and language are all cinematographic in their orientation: 'Whether we would think becoming, or express it, or even perceive it, we hardly do anything else than set going a kind of cinematograph inside us . . . the mechanism of our ordinary knowledge is of a cinematographical kind.'[3] On this basis it would certainly follow that philosophical thought, too, suffers this illusion. However, this simply kicks the can down the road. What is it that necessitates that thought, language and perception are cinematographic in nature? Bergson hints at an answer when he notes in passing the fundamentally practical character of this orientation.[4] But to find a full account of what this means, we have to look not in *Creative Evolution*, but in *Matter and Memory*.

The role of *Matter and Memory* in the *Cinema* books is a complex one. The resources Deleuze draws on to propose his Bergsonian characterisation of the cinema come primarily from that work, rather than *Creative Evolution*. He argues that the movement we are given by cinema presents us with mobile sections of duration, or *movement-images*, 'the discovery of which was the extraordinary invention of the first chapter of *Matter and Memory*'.[5] It is on the basis of this 'discovery' that Deleuze derives the taxonomy of cinematic signs he then unfolds. This, on the surface of it, appears to be the basis on which he argues that the cinema is itself free of the cinematographic illusion, to the point that he appears to berate Bergson for having 'forgotten' the findings of *Matter and Memory* when he comes to discuss the cinematographic illusion in *Creative Evolution* some ten years later.[6] Certainly this is how the secondary literature tends to interpret this passage in Deleuze's discussion of the first of Bergson's three theses on movement. I think this interpretation is flawed, for reasons I explore in detail in the next chapter. For now, however, it suffices to note that the arguments that culminate in Bergson's cinematographic metaphor and his attribution of its role in shaping thought, perception and language to its practical utility find their roots not in *Creative Evolution*, but in *Matter and Memory* itself.

In the latter work the issue arises as follows: having developed his argument for a conception of the world as a 'mobile continuity' on the basis of his critique of realism and idealism, Bergson must nevertheless account for the fact that this is not what our everyday perception of the world presents to us. When we open our eyes, what we see it a world consisting of distinct things, objects and beings, located distinctly in space, and not an unbroken continuity of becoming. He accounts for this apparent discrepancy in the most pragmatic of fashions. Being may be an unbroken becoming, but living beings need to eat, and in order to do so they must first distinguish themselves from this becoming as a thing (constitute themselves as a centre of action) and then find something else to nourish themselves on: perceive it, act on it (hunt it down) and eat it.[7] The necessities of life thus require us to constitute a world of determined bodies, discrete beings or actual elements constituted relative to the demands of action. The pragmatism of this 'cutting up' of the continuity of reality is no more complex than an organism's will to survive; at its most basic level it is the determination of some other body as food, in order to consume it. As Bergson puts it,

> whatever the nature of matter, it may be said that life will at once establish in it a primary discontinuity, expressing the duality of the need and

of that which must serve to satisfy it ... Our needs are, then, so many searchlights which, directed upon the continuity of sensible qualities, single out in it distinct bodies. They cannot satisfy themselves except upon the condition that they carve out, within this continuity, a body which is to be their own and then delimit other bodies with which the first can enter into relation, as if with persons. To establish these special relations among portions thus carved out from sensible reality is just what we call *living*.[8]

What *Matter and Memory* tells us, then, is that in order to live, the living must abstract the unbroken continuity of being into distinct objects cut out artificially according to its practical needs. And inasmuch as social life is also practical life, the world of human actions and interactions and constructions are products of this same illusion. Thus Bergson can say: 'That which is commonly called a *fact* is not reality ... but an adaptation of the real to the interests of practice and to the exigencies of social life.'[9] In order to live we must eat; in order to eat we must act; in order to act we must cut out distinct elements from the continuity of being to act on. In other words, life is *obliged* to grasp the world cinematographically in order to live (even if this term will not be used to describe this phenomenon until much later, in *Creative Evolution*). Now it should be said immediately that this element of Bergson's argument is a secondary theme in *Matter and Memory*. The emphasis is, rather, on establishing the illusory and artificial nature of this 'cutting out' in relation to the unbroken world of images, whose establishment is his major concern. But despite Deleuze's apparent suggestion that the cinematographic illusion articulated in *Creative Evolution* is a 'step backwards' from the 'cinematic' ontology of images presented in *Matter and Memory*, the logic that will lead Bergson to the formulation of that illusion in the former is already clearly present in the latter.

Bergson does, however, develop this logic much further in *Creative Evolution*. In *Matter and Memory*, the argument that will be developed later into the critique of the cinematographic illusion turns on the necessity for perception to abstract static moments from the undivided becoming of being, in order to be able to act. In *Creative Evolution*, this perceptual abstraction is developed as the model for the operations of thought and language. This is what Bergson indicates when he refers to two theoretical illusions, rather than one, in his introduction to the chapter in which he develops the idea of the cinematographic illusion.[10]

The first illusion is the perceptual abstraction to which life is subject as a function of the needs of action, which is already present in the arguments of *Matter and Memory*. The second is the development of language and thought on the basis of the first. Thus this second illusion 'is near akin to the first. It has the same origin, being also due to the fact that we import into speculation a procedure made for practice.'[11] That is, thought develops in relation to life's needs as an extension of life's power over the world, and action in turn is guided by that thought, since 'The function of the intellect is to preside over actions.'[12] Thought perforce starts from a static and abstract grasp on being, derived from the needs of action, and thus builds itself on a cinematographic base. Thus

> the cinematographical method is therefore the only practical method [of thought – but note the emphasis on *practical*], since it consists in making the general character of knowledge form itself on that of action, while expecting that the detail of each act should depend in its turn on that of knowledge.[13]

This cinematographic tendency in thought manifests itself in its focus on capturing the state of things, rather than their change, so that 'the mind derives ... three kinds of representations: (1) qualities, (2) forms of essences, (3) acts'.[14] And to the extent that language is a tool for thought, and for communicating thought, it too takes on a cinematographic form, such that the 'three ways of seeing correspond to three categories of words: *adjectives*, *substantives*, and *verbs*, which are the primordial elements of language'.[15]

If we now have the outline of a plausible account of why and how the cinematographic illusion shapes perception, thought and language, and thus philosophy, this in turn poses another problem, which bears on Deleuze no less than Bergson. The problem is simple: if perception, thought and language are all cinematographic in character, what possible tools are left to us to think or see or speak otherwise? How can we come to grips with being, with becoming or duration, if we are condemned to the cinematographic illusion merely by virtue of being alive, being life, and thus forced to *act*? For thought to think real being, real movement, it seems, the living being must overcome the natural tendencies that constitute both it and its relationship to the world, must overcome itself, since, as Deleuze puts it, 'The illusion ... does not result only from our nature, but from the world in which we live, from the side of being that manifests itself to us in the first place.'[16] For human being to truly think, it seems, it must overcome the human condition.[17]

John Mullarkey poses the quandary concisely:

> the problem is this: according to everything Bergson seems to write about language, thought, and philosophy itself, it is far from evident how he, or anyone for that matter, could ever have been able to write genuinely about time at all . . . An immediate grasp of the temporal which is inexpressible would hardly seem to be a good place to begin one's philosophy.[18]

The moment we attempt to think or talk about real being, about duration, we perforce fall under the sway of the cinematographic illusion, and thus lose the being we seek to speak or think of. And yet in so far as beings, and thus human beings, are part of being they participate in the real movement and duration of that being. This at least seems to allow for the possibility of the intuition by which Bergson seeks to grasp the real, since we are an aspect or expression of that which we seek to intuit and never in reality isolated or separated from it. Even if we allow this possibility, it does not, however, resolve the problem of how we are to communicate such an intuition, or indeed even think of or with it, without reducing it once more to an abstract and static representation that loses its essential quality – its duration.

The solution Bergson offers, at least as far as language goes, is that we must force it 'beyond' itself through a creative use of language and especially of metaphor. Mullarkey notes that Bergson does not seek a metaphysics without concepts or language, but rather one that uses language, in a sense, against itself and its own conceptual tendencies.[19] He directs us to a passage in *The Creative Mind*, in which Bergson argues that metaphysics

> is strictly itself only when it goes beyond the concept, or at least when it frees itself of the inflexible and ready-made concepts and creates others very different from those we usually handle, I mean flexible, mobile, almost fluid representations, always ready to mold themselves on the fleeting forms of intuition.[20]

The difficulty with this claim asserts itself in the 'at least' Bergson is forced to use; metaphysics is itself when it goes beyond the concept, but an absolute going beyond is not possible in language, in so far as language's 'primordial elements' are themselves conceptual. At best, or 'at least', it can try to 'free itself' from such concepts, by creating 'others very different from those we usually handle'. This implies at least a thread or a tendency within language that links it to the non-conceptual real of real duration.[21] This is consistent with the immanence of the cinematographic to the real that Bergson implies

– it is part of real being, albeit abstracted or drawn from it, and thus cannot be conceived as utterly outside of or disconnected from being. Representation, cinematographic thought, is therefore immanent to being that differs, and thus is not divided from it absolutely, but contingently, in relation to the needs of life. The problem we face in trying to capture this thread is that the more precisely we try to define or determine the difference between conceptual language and flexible or mobile language, the further we move away from the latter: the language we seek is of necessity vague and imprecise, the more so the closer it approaches the reality of being. Even Bergson himself struggles with this difficulty, as the following passage suggests:

> it is easy to see that Butler only uses images, comparisons, etc. to supplement or even simply to decorate the expression of his thought: he could, strictly speaking, do without it. By contrast, in a book like *Creative Evolution* or *The Two Sources*, images are most often introduced because they are indispensable, as none of the existing concepts are able to *express* the thought of the author, and the author is thus obliged to *suggest* it.[22]

Even if one accepts Bergson's contention that language can be forced 'beyond' its 'primordial' conceptual tendency (and it does seem at odds with claims such as 'The intellect is characterized by a natural inability to comprehend life'[23]), the vagueness we are left with remains a barrier, at the very least, to any satisfactory expression of such intuition as we may have of real being or duration. We are left in the paradoxical situation that the more adequately we express it, the less clearly we are able to communicate it to others. For all his remarkable gifts as a writer (he won the 1928 Nobel prize for literature), even Bergson cannot escape this paradox. Paul Douglass notes that Bergson's 'Introduction to Metaphysics'

> tells us that life is like 'the unrolling of a coil', and also like a 'continual rolling up', but actually 'it is neither'. Such cryptic formulations caused understandable annoyance in Bergson's critics. Even friends, like William James, confessed that there is a 'peculiarity of vision' in Bergson's work: 'I have to confess that Bergson's originality is so profuse that many of his ideas baffle me entirely.'[24]

The problem or paradox that gives rise to these 'cryptic', 'baffling' and 'annoying' qualities in Bergson's writing is internal to and thus unavoidable for Bergsonism, inasmuch as it derives from his very conception of both being and beings, and of the cinematographic terms in which the beings must grasp being if they are to live. And given the central place that Deleuze gives to the cinematographic illusion in the critique of external conceptions of difference that sets the scene for his own ontology of difference, it constitutes a problem internal to his own Bergsonism.

A Materialist Practice of Metaphysics

The possibility of a non-cinematographic thought of thought is clearly of some relevance to philosophy. It's obvious, but important to keep in mind, that although philosophy clearly thinks, not all thinking is philosophical. The practice of thought that gives philosophy its specificity, is, for Deleuze, its creation of concepts. This conception of philosophy, and of its difference from science and art as distinct modes of thought, finds its clearest expression in *What is Philosophy?* In that work, Deleuze and Guattari present these three modes as distinct practices of thought, with specific productive and creative outcomes: concepts in philosophy, functions in science and affects in art. They accord no priority to philosophy over these others, only a specificity given in terms of the materials they work with and the relations they construct among those materials. Furthermore, despite their distinctive practices, there is always a 'zone of interference' between or among them, such that they 'intersect or intertwine but without synthesis or identification'.[25]

We may add as a preliminary comment on the relation between this work and the *Cinema* books that, although cinema is certainly an art, Deleuze's treatment of it in the *Cinema* books is strictly philosophical. That is, although cinema, as an art, may be said to think via the creation of affects, the task Deleuze essays in relation to it is to draw on the 'zone of interference' between philosophy and cinema in order to create concepts which nevertheless belong to the cinema. Thus the

> theory of cinema is not 'about' cinema, but about the concepts that cinema gives rise to and which are themselves related to other concepts corresponding to other practices, the practice of concepts in general having no privilege over others . . . Cinema's concepts are not given in the cinema. And yet they are cinema's concepts, not theories about cinema . . . Cinema itself is a new practice of images and signs, whose theory philosophy must produce as a conceptual practice.[26]

The question of philosophy's adequacy to the task of thinking being confronts philosophy with the cinematographic illusion very clearly on two closely related fronts. Firstly, if thought itself is cinematographic, how is it possible for philosophy to think otherwise, to think real movement, real being? Second, even if we were to simply grant philosophy this power by *fiat*, there remains the problem that if one wishes to share such thoughts, they of necessity must be expressed in language, which once again traps them in the realm of the cinematographic. Thus Deleuze must first of all find the means by which to constitute philosophical thought as non-cinematographic thought, and then offer an account of how such thought might evade the cinematographic tendencies of language. And in so far as both are problems arising in and from the Bergsonian foundation of Deleuzian ontology, the responses Deleuze offers are developments of and responses to Bergson's own treatments of them.

Bergson's response to our first problem (that of the means by which philosophy may think being) is simply the notion of intuition itself: 'To think intuitively', he says, 'is to think in duration itself.'[27] Now as I have suggested, to the extent that beings, and thus human beings and their thoughts are an aspect of being, it is at least plausible to argue that their continuity with it affords them the possibility of a participation or relation to it based on that continuity, rather than the cinematographic and practical basis of 'thought, perception and language'. In other words, since we are already 'in' duration, 'all' we need do is overcome our cinematographic grasping of the world and we will recognise the real duration, the real being, which we were always an expression of.

The difficulty, of course, is that to do so we must turn against the constitutively cinematographic character of living beings and thus of human beings. Bergson always emphasises the 'arduous' and ephemeral character of intuition and the 'prodigious' effort required to make this turn.[28] The intuition Bergson speaks of shares little in common with the everyday understanding of intuition as a kind of spontaneous or immediate capacity of thought to grasp things or beings. Indeed, he goes so far as to suggest that to think intuitively 'we must do violence to the mind, go counter to the natural [cinematographic] bent of the intellect. But that is just the function of philosophy.'[29]

Moreover the participation in being, in duration, to which such thought aspires comes at the cost of our capacity to act, inasmuch as it is the cinematographic illusion that affords us that power. Indeed, this passivity appears as characteristic of being. Bergson notes that 'if almost the whole of our past is hidden from us because it is inhibited by the necessities of present action, it will find strength to cross the threshold of consciousness in all cases where we renounce the interests of effective action'.[30] Deleuze, in his turn, points out that this past which we may reach only by abandoning the 'necessities of present action' is, in its purest form, nothing other than being: 'Useless and inactive, impassive, it IS, in the full sense of the word: It is identical with being in itself.'[31] Thus being, and our grasp of being, are given in relation to a fundamental passivity or waiting: as Bergson says, 'the material universe in its entirety *keeps* our consciousness *waiting*; it waits itself'.[32]

Intuition, then, requires the human to turn against itself in something akin to an 'act' of violence, and yet that act is intimately tied to the loss or abandonment or forgoing of the power *to* act. In so far as it offers to the human access to something of being, intuition seems less an act or a power of human thought than a waiting, perhaps interminable, for the arrival of the inhuman, such that we might justly characterise its human experience as a *suffering of time*. As we shall see in the final chapters of this book, this thought of the thought of real being as a 'suffering of time' has an intimate relationship with Deleuze's characterisation of cinema of the time-image.

However, even if this 'suffering of time' is indeed the modality of the human experience of being, it nevertheless offers us no insight into how such intuition might ever be conveyed to another in an act of communication (how can such passivity and waiting be transliterated into action, into words?). Indeed, if we wish to convey precisely what it is that intuition consists of, what it *is*, we are faced with 'the fact that intuition . . . is exactly what excludes, in the words of one commentator, "*the idea itself* of definition"'.[33] Bergson clearly recognises this problem to some degree. He notes, for instance, that 'intuition will be communicated only by the intellect. It is more than idea; nevertheless in order to be transmitted, it will have to use ideas as a conveyance . . . Comparisons and metaphors will here suggest what cannot be expressed.'[34] Nevertheless, this recourse to 'comparisons and metaphors' seems no less vague than the idea of intuition itself, able to be suggested but not expressed. It is hardly surprising then that Bergson's philosophy, and in particular his notion of intuition, have been criticised as 'casual', 'incoherent', 'unsystematic', as an 'analysis against analysis' and as fundamentally irrationalist in its orientation and its outcomes.[35]

Deleuze can be seen to respond indirectly to these charges in *Bergsonism*, in so far as he argues there for an interpretation of intuition as a properly rigorous philosophical method. That is, far from depending on 'a feeling, an inspiration ... [or] a disorderly sympathy',[36] he presents it quite literally as a series of rules which can be applied repeatedly and consistently, irrespective of individual 'vision', to the resolution of philosophical problems.[37] What is important here, for our purposes, is that in so far as intuition is given here as a philosophical method, philosophical thought is itself identified as a *practice* real thought demands, rather than a capacity thought possesses by right.[38] That is, thought must act (and act in a certain way) in order to be philosophical. A paradox then: intuition is a specific act or practice of thought, but an act that thought suffers or undergoes, rather than a power it possesses. As I suggested in the introduction to this chapter, a thought that truly thinks is one for which thought is no longer a power that it holds, but a powerlessness that it suffers. And if this powerlessness has a relation to real being, real duration, it is as the time of an interminable waiting for a thought lacking the power to begin.

Both sides of this problem – that of the means by which thought might grasp being and that of the means by which it might communicate this grasp – can be summed up in terms of the search for precision in philosophy. As we have seen, the fundamental criticism both Bergson and Deleuze direct against cinematographic thought is its abstraction, the 'bagginess' of the concepts it extracts from the becoming of duration and of movement, through which it gains mastery over the living (in so far as it gives us the power to act) at the cost of losing the nuance or specificity of life itself, so that in gaining the power to act, we separate ourselves from the world. What both Bergson and Deleuze seek instead is a true empiricism in philosophy, which is to say, an empiricism capable of grasping things as they are in themselves, rather than as they are constituted relative to the needs of action. As Bergson points out, this empiricism is fundamentally metaphysical: 'a true empiricism is the one which purposes to keep as close to the original itself as possible, to probe more deeply into life, and by a kind of spiritual *auscultation*, to feel its soul palpitate; and this true empiricism is the real metaphysics'.[39] Clearly such an empiricism differs from one in which one simply looks at the world and tries to explain it on that basis. The latter leads inevitably to analyses that reinscribe the cinematographic illusion that makes such 'looking' possible. Nevertheless, metaphysical empiricism and its conventional counterpart do share a commonality, in so far as both assume an objectively real world whose truth is available to us in and through experience, such that Mullarkey argues that Bergsonian philosophy presents us with a 'thoroughly classical . . . realist view of truth as correspondence'.[40]

However, where a conventional empiricism locates this correspondence as one between human perception and the world, Bergson derives it from the character of the world as image in itself, rather than for us. In so far as images are all there is, we ourselves are nothing but images among other images (this is the immanence of beings and being) such that to perceive the world (empirically) is not to perceive some thing, but to plunge into perception itself, into images that move (or movement-images): 'to perceive what can *only* be perceived rather than what is a mixture of abstraction and everyday experience: as such, "metaphysics will then become experience itself"'.[41] Precision in philosophy, then, would consist in a thought that enters into, or rather opens itself up to, the movement of being itself, the movement-images that express being in its duration rather than its abstraction, grasping things in their becoming, so that

> radical empiricism is metaphysical to the extent that it focuses on the individual specificity of its object – the singularity of the individual that can only be sensed [perceived] rather than imagined. Metaphysics is not the contemplation of an alternative reality [a transcendent reality 'above' reality] but the perception of a heightened reality, a perception Bergson eventually calls 'intuition'.[42]

We can see from this why Deleuze insists that philosophy must be a practice, something that itself takes place: if it is to be adequate to the real, it must be real in itself, and not abstract, and thus must be something that itself takes place, takes time, and thus takes place *in* time, because to be precise, to be empirical, it must enter into the movement of being and to do so it too must move.

However, no matter how real the movement of philosophical thought and method, it remains merely solipsistic unless we can convey something of it to someone else. If the practice of philosophical intuition succeeds in opening human thought to the thought of being, it nevertheless must then contend with the cinematographic character of language itself. Mullarkey argues that, in claiming for language the power (however forced) to express or articulate the real movement of being, Bergson nevertheless does not claim for language the power to *represent* this movement (such a representation could only offer a cinematographic illusion of that movement). Just as intuition seeks to place thought within the movement of being, Bergson asks for language and concepts that place themselves within the very movement they seek to express. That is, Bergson's 'aim is not to have thought and language correspond to an immobile thing, but to recreate the movement of things and, by that, render them a part of a process-reality'.[43]

If there is a representation or mimesis in this kind of language and thought, what is mimicked in it is not a thing or static object (an abstraction), but the movement of being itself, or rather, the mobile section of that movement in which a facet or aspect of being is expressed (the flow of a river, the flight of an arrow, the sugar dissolving in a glass of water). Rather than representing an object, philosophical language would seek to trace or retrace the movement of an 'object' (or more properly a 'mobile section of duration') in its becoming, a becoming that is always connected to the being of becoming itself, even if only by the finest thread.

Moreover, both the movement and the language that mimics it are equally real and equally acts of creation. Inasmuch as thought is an aspect of being, it is so in the following sense: everything is an image, so that both the 'object' of a concept and the concept itself are images, and thus movements or constant variations; both the thought and the language Bergson requires are mobile, and must not be confused with the static and abstract concepts and language he criticises. A 'mobile' language does not represent the thing it seeks to account for – it is not an image *of* the thing. Rather, it 'mimics' the movement, the variation that the 'thing' is by recreating that movement, but in its own terms and with its own materials, which *are* its terms. Thus Mullarkey argues that

> if this is mimesis, then it is mimesis with a new meaning: language imitating reality by being real itself, this being achieved by giving language a certain *élan*, a movement of reality ... [it] does not aim, says Bergson, to reproduce either the 'abstract type' or conception of its model, or the 'materiality' of the model: it recreates the 'characteristic movement' that animates its lines.[44]

Nevertheless, it is not immediately clear how this mimesis might work in practice – that is, how it manages to reconcile the cinematographic characterisation Bergson gives of language with the demand for a language that attains the power of a real movement, and thus can 'recreate' the movement of the real in its own terms. It is hardly accidental that what Bergson demands of thought and language seems to describe what we would more commonly attribute to art: a power of creation that causes the (cinematographically) imperceptible to appear to and for the eye or ear or hand. Art is, for Bergson, closely akin to both intuition and image,[45] so much so that he suggests if we were able to experience reality directly (without any cinematographic intermediary), able to 'enter into immediate communication with things and with ourselves [in a pure intuition], I really believe art would be useless, or rather that all of us would be artists, for our soul would vibrate then continually in unison with nature'.[46]

It is hardly surprising, then, that Bergson often invokes the work of art (both in the sense of art as work, as a practice of creation, and of the productions of that practice, that is, artworks themselves) as a model for philosophical intuition and its expression. Indeed he goes so far as to claim that it is the function of artists 'precisely to see and make us see what we do not naturally perceive'.[47] As Mullarkey says, 'Art [for Bergson] is not an act of imagination fancifully creating *ex nihilo*: it is rather a restoration of a world that our normally practical, narrowed and impoverishing perception has destroyed.'[48] That is to say, both philosophical intuition and art constitute acts of creation, not from nothing but *de novo*, and in doing so open our perception to the world in its becoming.[49]

Deleuze's continued interest in and philosophical engagement with the arts, and with literature and cinema in particular, should thus be understood at least partially in terms of the ways in which, as art, they realise or actualise Bergson's demand for a 'forcing' of language beyond its cinematographic tendencies, in order that it create a 'vision' or make visible what is otherwise hidden in and by language's primordial tendencies.[50] Deleuze, however, takes this demand further, by making explicit what is only implied in Bergson: that art not only offers a model for how philosophical intuition might be expressed (non-cinematographically) but that it constitutes a model of a non-cinematographic practice of thought whose 'intuitions' are expressed in and *as* that practice. That is, art shows us not only how to force language or expression beyond its cinematographic tendencies, but also that that forcing is itself *thought thinking* or, more precisely, thought understood as a *practice*. Whether it is a case of affects and percepts (in art) or concepts (in philosophy) the problem of both the intuition of being and the expression of that intuition are resolved as a single problem whose solution is to be found in the notion of (artistic or philosophical) practice.

In the preface to the French edition of *Essays Critical and Clinical*, Deleuze notes that writers, as Proust says, invent a new language within language, a foreign language, as it were. They bring to light new grammatical or syntactic powers. They force language outside its customary furrows, they make it delirious. But the problem of writing is also inseparable from a problem of seeing and hearing ... One must say of every writer: he is a seer, a hearer.[51]

In their 'forcing' of language beyond its limits, such writers place art in intimate contact with the task of philosophy, even though the materials they work with, and the affects and perceptions they create, differ from the concepts philosophy creates in and with its own materials. We find this intimacy figured in Nietzsche's account of both artists and philosophers as '"physicians of culture", for whom phenomena are signs or symptoms that reflect a certain state of forces',[52] a description that in turn evokes Bergson's characterisation of philosophy as a kind of spiritual or metaphysical 'auscultation'.[53] In both cases, art and philosophy are presented as a kind of diagnostic process, a symptomatology or interpretation of the signs of the world which reveal aspects of being that the cinematographic tendencies of life hide from us.[54]

It is hardly surprising, then, that the practice of philosophy that Deleuze and Guattari sum up in *What is Philosophy?* in terms of the creation of concepts bears a striking similarity to the diagnostic power Deleuze attributes to and analyses with regard to literature in his *Essays Critical and Clinical*. But what does it mean to describe artists and philosophers as 'physicians' or 'diagnosticians' of culture? In his introduction to *Essays Critical and Clinical*, Smith notes that a doctor who labels a disease for the first time

> certainly does not 'invent' the disease, but rather is said to 'isolate' it; he or she distinguishes cases that had hitherto been confused by dissociating symptoms that were previously grouped together and by juxtaposing them with others that were previously dissociated. In this way, the doctor constructs an original clinical concept for the disease.[55]

In this sense Parkinson's disease, for example, is certainly real but nevertheless virtual. Its consistency is not given in the individual symptoms actualised across the patient's body, but in the dissociation and juxtaposition of symptoms 'constructed' by the doctor from those symptoms, from those actual states of affairs. The disease is clearly not just in the physician's mind: the patient's suffering certainly exists, whether or not it is recognised or isolated as a distinct condition.

However, the *concept* of the condition is an invention, and is thus a genuine creation, inasmuch as it constitutes a kind of counter-actualisation of the virtual disease into a new form: the symptoms of the disease expressed across the patient's body are both the actualised mode of the virtual disease as well as signs that the physician must dissociate and juxtapose from out of the mass of divergent symptoms that swarm across the body in question, in order that she might counter-actualise the virtual disease into a new form or consistency – that of the clinician's concept rather than the physical symptoms of the patient. The clinician, in a sense, recreates or enters into the movement from virtual (the disease as it exists outside of and separate from any actual symptoms, or the individuals that suffer from it[56]) to actual (the disease *as* the patient's suffering) but 'in reverse', moving from the actual symptoms to the virtual syndrome, and in doing so gives the disease a new, actual, consistency quite distinct from the diverse and apparently disjoined symptoms of the patient's body.

Of course, for Nietzsche or Bergson or Deleuze, the diagnosis in question is not a medical but an artistic or philosophical one: art, literature, cinema, metaphysics as a diagnosis of the signs of the world, such that for Deleuze, 'The whole of philosophy is a symptomatology, and a semiology.'[57] If art and philosophy differ in this regard, it is in terms of the 'materials' in which their diagnoses are expressed: affects and percepts in art, and concepts in philosophy. Nevertheless, the process or method just described is equally applicable to the creation of concepts Deleuze and Guattari use to characterise the specificity of philosophy. Just as Bergson asks for a language that enters into the movement of real being, Deleuze and Guattari insist that a concept that seeks to be adequate to being as creation, as real movement, must also itself be a genuine act of creation itself.[58] A concept that seeks to *represent* being can only do so cinematographically, as a static abstraction. The problem, then, is how a concept that is a creation in itself can relate to or express anything of the movement it seeks to be adequate to if it is not a representation of it.

The answer lies in its relationship to the movement of actualisation and counter-actualisation we have just seen in relation to the physician's construction of the concept of a disease or syndrome, and is a function of the metaphysical or transcendental empiricism Deleuze practices. As we have seen, the actual (the present, the world in which we act) bears no resemblance to the virtual of which it is the actualisation. Moreover, virtual problems are susceptible of a multiplicity of such actualisations or solutions, which will not necessarily resemble each other either: 'While actual forms or products can resemble each other, the movements of production [of actualisation] do not resemble each other, nor do the products resemble the virtuality that they embody [actualise].'[59]

Thus if we merely look to the signs given in actual world around us, after the fashion of a conventional empiricism, we will fail to see the real differences they actualise and our grasp of being will develop only on the basis of 'false' or 'badly stated' problems, that, as Deleuze says in *Bergsonism*, 'arbitrarily group things that differ in kind'.[60] If Deleuze's own 'transcendental empiricism' seems 'unhinged' or unrecognisable as empiricism, it is because rather than basing its grasp of the world simply in what it experiences in it, it instead begins from particular 'cases' and signs in that world, and seeks from them to find the virtual event that is actualised in them, in unrecognisable and superficially unrelated actual states of affairs, or 'symptoms'. This results in classifications based not on resemblances among experiences, but rather according to a virtual problem or differentiation 'dispersed' unrecognisably across these diverse actual elements. And these classifications are concepts, concepts created out of the dissociation and juxtaposition of the actual in order to mimic not the actual, but the virtual becoming that manifests or actualises itself unrecognisably in the world in which we live and act.

Thus when Deleuze and Guattari speak of the concept as a 'counter-effectuation of the event', they describe a properly philosophical concept that enters into the movement of creation, as Bergson sought to do, but in a sense, in reverse. This reversal does not return us to a point of origin: it is neither a mirror image of the actualisation of the virtual nor a representation *of* the virtual, since the concept is a creation in itself, no less than the virtual problem or its actualisations in states of affairs:

> from virtuals we descend to actual states of affairs, and from states of affairs we ascend to virtuals, without being able to isolate one from the other. But we do not ascend and descend in this way on the same line: actualisation and counter-effectuation are not two segments of the same line but rather different lines.[61]

Being and the virtual events or problems it creates are not sensible, cannot be 'seen' just by looking at the actual world. In order to think being or the movement of being, we must create concepts which are movements in themselves, which enter into the movement of being by enacting or mimicking that movement in the other direction, from the actual to the virtual, but by its own means and in its own terms.

> Such a mime neither reproduces the state of affairs [the actual] nor imitates the lived; it does not give an image but constructs the concept. It does not look for the function of what happens but extracts the event from it, or that part that does not let itself be actualised, the reality of the concept.[62]

One cannot represent the virtual, then, which differs from itself at all stages, but one can 'mimic' its movement or its differing from itself, 'extracting' it from and with the (actual) materials at hand. And in doing so, 'We go beyond experience [the actual, the symptoms] toward the conditions of experience [the virtual, the syndrome or concept of the disease].'[63]

If it is the case, then, that artists and philosophers can be understood as 'physicians of culture', it is in the sense that in dividing the apparently similar and joining the apparently diverse they construct concepts that 'counter-actualise' or 'counter-effectuate' the virtual event. In doing so, they create of it a new actual consistency which is nevertheless distinct from its actualisation in actions or functions in the world, from the chains of cause and effect among actual states of affairs (the concept of the disease shares nothing of the patient's suffering). It is in this sense that we can understand Deleuze's comment that Sacher-Masoch may be a better guide to masochism than Freud, since 'a writer can go further in symptomatology, ... the work of art gives him a new means – perhaps because the writer is less concerned with causes'.[64] The clinician (or in this case, psychoanalyst) conducts their symptomatology in order to best know what to *do* (what treatment is best for this patient?) and thus subordinates it to the needs of action that entrap life within the cinematographic illusion. The artist, author or philosopher, on the other hand, who introduces or mimics the movement of real being in the concepts they create, through and in their work instead extract the event from the lived and from the necessities of action and of cause and effect as a concept (for Sacher-Masoch, that of masochism) and in doing so are better able to find a path for thought beyond or outside merely human experience.[65]

We can see in this concept of the concept Deleuze's account of the means by which properly human thought might introduce real movement into its thoughts or, rather, place its thought within the real movement of becoming, 'ascending' from actual to virtual in the counter-actualisation or counter-effectuation of the event of being's differentiation. In this sense it can be understood as a development or extension of Bergson's claims for a use of language that is capable of 'forcing' language beyond its primordial cinematographic tendencies.

At the same time, it can also be traced back to Deleuze's early analysis of Bergsonian intuition as a properly philosophical method, on two levels. Firstly, I would argue that the 'unhinged' empiricism of the method of the 'dissociation of the similar and joining of the diverse' can be read as a development and extension of the 'second rule' of Deleuze's account of the intuitive method. This rule concerns the division of the impure composite of 'fact' (the actual) into its 'qualitative and qualified tendencies', its differences in kind and in degree, so as to 'go beyond experience, towards the conditions of experience'.[66] That is, it provides Deleuzian empiricism with the principle by which the actual should be divided and joined. Secondly, in the movement from the virtual event to its actual manifestations, and then in the movement of counter-effectuation from the actual 'back' towards the virtual, we can find traces of *Bergsonism*'s conception of philosophical intuition as starting from experience and 'diverging' in lines developed according to the recognition of differences in kind, which then converge on 'the virtual image or the distinct reason of the common point' – that image or point corresponding, more or less, to what Deleuze comes to describe as the virtual event or problem.

Thus I would argue that the concept of the concept Deleuze and Guattari present in *What is Philosophy?* has its roots in Deleuze's early response to the problem Bergson faces in attributing to thought the capacity to intuit being, given the cinematographic basis of thought, perception and language. Deleuze and Guattari's concept of the concept is, at one and the same time, a method of both philosophical intuition (in the Bergsonian sense) and the non-cinematographic expression of that intuition, inasmuch as it enters into or mimics the movement of being in precisely the fashion Bergson sought from language. By conceiving of philosophy as a practice, they transform Bergsonian intuition from a mystical sympathy with being into something that might plausibly be called a materialist practice of metaphysics.

Bergson's great problem is that he posits intuition first of all, in terms that make it inexpressible, and then must try to express this in actual language. Deleuze and Guattari, on the other hand, start from the actual, material and cinematographic experience in which the world is given to us first of all, and only then, on the basis of the dissociation and juxtaposition of that actual, material world, move towards the virtual conditions of that experience, or being. From this perspective, we can understand this concept of the concept as a key tool in Deleuze's continuation of the Bergsonian project of developing a philosophy capable of thinking with and in the concrete reality of being, rather than in terms of mere 'baggy' abstractions. That is, it constitutes the grounds of a properly non-cinematographic mode of philosophy and of thought.

However, this is not to say that Deleuze thus banishes the cinematographic illusion from thought (or language or perception). His concept of the concept constitutes a philosophical *method*, a practice of the construction of concepts so as to place them within the movement of being. It is the method *as such* that introduces real movement into thought, and not the concepts it produces and certainly not the language they are expressed in. That is, concepts, in so far as they partake of the real movement of being, have little or nothing to do with communication, or at least retain within them an incommunicable core, which *is* their movement.

We can see in this a significant shift from Bergson's treatment of the problem. Bergson seeks to communicate this incommunicable aspect of being (which is duration, or real movement) by 'forcing' language beyond its limits, but in doing so places himself in conflict with the cinematographic character of language he himself posits. Deleuze, on the other hand, accepts the strictest consequences of the cinematographic illusion, by distinguishing concepts and ideas on the one hand, and communication and information on the other. The 'forcing' of the cinematographic performed by and in artistic and philosophical practice does not result in something that can be transmitted and exchanged as 'data' or information. The latter is the domain of cinematographic language and communication, part of the realm of action and mastery.[67] For Deleuze, the ideas and concepts created by art and philosophy remain incommunicable and are only 'shared' with others, with readers and viewers and listeners, to the extent that those others subject them to a practice of creation in turn.

This has significant consequences for what it means to read Deleuze (or perhaps any author) and in particular for what one does with the concepts one finds in his work. Unless one's reading and thinking and doing with Deleuze constitutes a practice of creation in its own right, his concepts will remain as static, abstract and cinematographic as those of Platonism, mechanism, or indeed of

Hegel, since in so far as we grasp them as actual words on the page or in our ears, all they can do is communicate something other than the incommunicable and virtual movement that constitutes them as concepts. This, it seems to me, is the basis for at least part of Deleuze's hostility to discussion and interpretation in philosophy. Philosophers, he claims,

> have very little time for discussion. Every philosopher runs away when he or she hears someone say, 'Let's discuss this.' ... Of what concern is it to philosophy that someone has such a view, and thinks this or that, if the problems at stake are not stated? And when they are stated, it is no longer a matter of discussing but rather one of creating concepts for the undiscussible problem posed. Communication always comes too early or too late, and when it comes to creating, conversation is always superfluous.[68]

That is, to engage with concepts, with thought, with philosophy, is not to discuss or interpret them, or to 'apply' them as one does a coat of paint. All that one can do with a concept is to create concepts with it in turn, to subject it to the method of dissociation and recombination, of counter-effectuation, and create something of one's own in relation to the virtual and 'undiscussable' problem it poses, not in order to communicate it, but in the hope that someone else will, in their own turn, do the same to one's own concepts. This is the distinction Deleuze poses between a theory of the cinema and the creation of its concepts: a theory one applies, but a concept can only be the material, starting point or provocation for new concepts.

Transcendental Empiricism as Cinematic Philosophy

If, like Bordwell, we look at the *Cinema* books and see what we already know repeating itself under the sign of an arbitrarily imposed theoretical armature ('a new teleology'), we wilfully ignore Deleuze's insistence that these books are precisely *not* a theory of the cinema, a series of baggy concepts draped over an indifferent mass of examples. Alternatively, we might see that 'what we already know' is itself an ill-fitting suit for the cases it clothes, and that Deleuze's 'auteurism' does not consist in a series of static 'illustrations' or 'examples of', but seeks to seeks to think *with* the case, in each case, and not *of* it. Thus Ropars-Wuilleumier says of the *Cinema* books that

> by manipulating fragments that already have an established meaning – hypotheses, ideas, or viewpoints inspired by screening films – Deleuze makes it possible for himself to put them into movement, to make mean-

ings circulate, and to break their initial meanings by inscribing them into his own system of thought.[69]

'To put them into movement' (to put movement into thought, and thus thought into movement), then, is to cause these fragments to differ from themselves, such that what we already know ('fragments that already have an established meaning' – familiar films and directors and authors, familiar historical divisions and progressions) become so many cases of the case which lead us towards the creation of concepts that belong *to* the cinema, but are not given *in* it.[70] The creation of concepts, then, as the introduction of difference into *what we already know* as the introduction of difference into 'ourselves', inasmuch as such ideas are indeed 'our own'. And, therefore, the production of concepts as the production of monsters in ourselves, and for ourselves. Or, to summon up one more difference in difference, and to indicate the directions in which *Cinema 2* will take us, perhaps we could say: the monstrosity of thought outside itself and the unthought in (our) thought.

An understanding of this concept of the concept, then, is integral to any understanding of the *Cinema* books, since they constitute just such a symptomatology in their taxonomy of cinematic signs, which are nothing other than the concepts of the cinema philosophy produces in its encounter with the cinema. Éric Alliez notes that two reproaches have always been made against Deleuze: that 'he is not an author because he comments, but neither is he a commentator because what he writes is always "Deleuzian"'.[71] A 'commentator' because he always begins with the case, sign or symptom, and not a schema into which the case must be placed, so that we are always tempted to think we know what he is talking about ('ah, he's telling me about Spinoza', 'this bit's about Mizoguchi', 'oh look, something on Bazin'). Not a commentator because the necessity of creating the concept of which the case is the actualisation (and not the representation) gives rise to conceptual productions which are not merely 'Deleuzian' in every case, but in which the case becomes to a greater or lesser extent *unrecognisable*, even (or especially) to those who are familiar with the case in question: the creation of the concept as a *'giving birth to monsters'*.[72] Deleuze uses this phrase to describe his work in the history of philosophy, but it is an equally apt description of the *Cinema* books themselves, such that Claire Perkins is able to sum up them up transitively as 'monstrosity as cinephilia as philosophy'.[73]

As a result, to a reader versed in the history of film and film theory, the *Cinema* books can appear, at one level at least, highly familiar: familiar directors and authors, familiar films (albeit hundreds of them), familiar historical divisions and progressions. Thus Rodowick points out that Deleuze's 'knowledge of film history departs little from the general histories that have been so profoundly challenged and revised by the new film history of the past fifteen years',[74] while Bordwell sees him as merely mapping philosophical distinctions onto that same historiographic tradition, such that 'Orthodox historical schemes become ratified by a new teleology. Stylistic development follows not from a law of progress but from the medium's mysterious urge to fill in every square of a vast grid of conceptual possibilities.'[75] However, if one pays attention to Deleuze's treatment of this 'familiar territory', the apparent familiarity can often all but vanish. Even films and filmmakers one feels one knows intimately can appear in nigh-on unrecognisable guises, to the point that Bellour can say that 'it becomes improbable that each auteur would recognize himself in them'.[76]

We need only think of Deleuze's reference (in relation to his taxonomy of cinematic signs) to Borges' 'Chinese' classification of animals that so delighted Foucault ('belonging to the emperor, embalmed, domesticated, edible ... mermaids, and so on'[77]) to start to recognise how this might manifest itself in relation to cinema.

> A classification always involves bringing together things with very different appearances and separating those that are very similar ... a classification is always a symptomatology. What we classify are signs in order to formulate a concept that presents itself as an event rather than an abstract essence.[78]

In so far as a classification or taxonomy (as in the *Cinema* books) is also a symptomatology, it draws together diverse actual elements or symptoms which are visible (the signs of cinema), and constitutes of them a concept 'which marks the meeting place of these symptoms, their point of coincidence or convergence',[79] a point which is itself not actual but virtual.

Deleuze's application of the 'empirical' method of the 'dissociation of the apparently similar and the bringing together of the apparently diverse' accounts for the odd sense of both familiarity and strangeness the reader versed in film and film history often finds within the *Cinema* books. This approach can create some consternation for the reader. Luc Moullet, for example, takes offence at Deleuze's

What Use is Cinema to Deleuze?

aligning the category of the impulse-image with naturalism, and then grouping together under that sign filmmakers who would seem at first glance to share little in common with each other, or with what Moullet understands 'naturalism' to refer to: 'Vidor, Losey, Ray and Fuller', even Stroheim and Buñuel. 'But who is further from naturalism than King Vidor?' he complains.[80] As William D. Routt points out, however, Deleuze's concept of 'naturalism' has little to do with the 'meticulous surface observations' Moullet seems to see as the point of resemblance qualifying a film or filmmaker for the category 'naturalist'. Rather,

> Deleuze claims that cinematic naturalism links surface observation with an invisible system of underlying natural forces which impel characters to act in certain ways. Moreover, some films which are not realistic on the surface are still motivated by 'naturalist' impulses. The visible surface and invisible impulse of a movie are interconnected just like a natural organism appears, to our sight, determined by a specific 'natural' physiology and psychology that we cannot see or hear.[81]

It is the relationship between the visible surface of behaviour and these invisible and unseen impulses that constitutes the virtual problem or event actualised in the works of these apparently diverse and unrelated filmmakers, and whose relation to each other cannot simply be seen, but must be created as a concept (in this case, the concept of the impulse-image[82]).

Thus the unhinged or transcendental empiricism Deleuze practises gives rise to concepts that can make the empirical or actual (film) world around us unrecognisable ('who is further from naturalism than King Vidor?'), despite being constructed with what seem to be the most familiar of materials. And, of course, it provides the organising principle of Deleuze's entire taxonomy of cinematic signs, such that in his treatment of cinema, of films and of film history we find the same practice of 'buggery' Deleuze speaks of in relation to his work in the history of philosophy ('taking an author from behind and giving him a child that would be his own offspring, yet monstrous'[83]). He creates, as something non pre-existent, concepts of the cinema that are not given *in* the cinema, but which are nevertheless 'cinema's concepts, not theories about the cinema',[84] concepts that are cinema's own offspring, but that are nevertheless unrecognisable in it.

We can certainly say, then, that the *Cinema* books constitute an instance of Deleuzian 'conceptology' in practice; but then, one could say that of all of his work, so perhaps this is not saying very much. However, it seems to me that there is a much more intimate or integral connection between the cinema and Deleuze's philosophical practice of the concept, in the following sense. Deleuze's transcendental empiricism extends or develops Bergson's metaphysical empiricism by pushing 'spiritual auscultation' to a veritable symptomatology of being. In doing so he seeks to think by thinking beyond the actual, beyond human experience, on the basis *of* that actual and human experience, but only in so far as that experience is dissociated and juxtaposed such that it can become 'unhinged' or unrecognisable.

We can unpack this a little further. Human experience is constitutively cinematographic, such that what is cut up and reordered, dissociated and juxtaposed, is nothing other than the productive and practical illusions of perception, thought and language that give us the power to act in, and on, the world. Transcendental empiricism, precision in philosophy, the symptomatic method, the creation of concepts all consist in cutting the world up and reordering its pieces: they are nothing other than forms of *montage*. This is a conception of philosophy as a properly cinematic practice that offers thought a non-cinematographic access to being, to real movement and real duration. In other words, *to put real movement into thought is to enter the cinema of the world*. This would be the weight of Jean-Luc Nancy's claim that

> Deleuze's interest in the cinema is not just appended to his work: it is at the centre, in the projective principle of this thought. It is a cinema-thought, in the sense of having its own order and screen, a singular plane of presentation and construction, of displacements and dramatization of concepts (the word 'concept' means this for Deleuze – making cinematic).[85]

But if all of Deleuzian philosophy is already cinematic – already a 'montage thought', we might justly ask why he needs the cinema at all. To ask the question 'what use is cinema to Deleuze?' is to ask after the problem that lies at the core of the *Cinema* books – to ask, in other words, what the stakes of the game are that he puts into play with his discussion of the three theses on movement. As we have seen, this game cannot be separated from the one played throughout most, if not all of Deleuze's work and writing, in so far as the 'monotony' Badiou finds in that work is a function of the Bergsonian ontological foundation that provides Deleuze with the means to escape the dialectical trap set by Hegel. That is, the univocity of this ontological foundation (being which 'speaks' or is 'spoken' always and everywhere in the same and single voice) and the immanence of beings with being that it implies are such that in each and every one of the diverse cases taken up throughout Deleuze's work, it is always the problem of the relation of the actual case to the virtual being it is the actualisation of that is at stake. The significance of the *Cinema* books within the Deleuzian œuvre lies not in the case of cinema, but in the means it offers Deleuze to think through, or think past, the impasse that the cinematographic illusion constitutes for philosophy and philosophical thought.

As we have seen, the cinematographic constitution of living beings, and human beings in particular, enables Deleuze to account for the 'errors' or illusions of thought that manifest themselves in Platonism, mechanism and, at their extreme, Hegelianism, in a strictly positive sense, without any recourse to negation or the negative, and thus in principle as contained and explained in Deleuzian ontology. That is, it allows Deleuze to account for the genesis of negation and the negative as arbitrarily limited or abstract 'moments' within being as becoming. But this cinematographic genesis of the living, of the human being (in the cutting up or abstraction of being in order to gain the power to act), is almost too successful. How can thought, and thus philosophy, think real being, real movement, if that which thinks is necessarily constituted in an illusory relation *to* being – that of the cinematographic illusion? The foundation of any solution to this impasse is the necessity of some kind of relation between beings and being: the cinematographic illusion is nothing but an illusion, no matter how useful or necessary it is for beings that act in the world, such that the barrier it creates to the thought of real being is contingent, and not ontologically necessary or absolute.

Bergson's response to the impasse in question largely stops at this point, in so far as his conception of intuition in thought, and the capacity for 'forcing' or 'stretching' the cinematographic illusion beyond itself in language, in art and in philosophy, are ultimately founded and justified on the necessity of some kind of shared link between beings and being. That this stopping point is premature is demonstrated by the repeated turn or return throughout Deleuze's work to developments or redevelopments within his own thought of the relationship of philosophy, language and art to being, and in particular to the terms in which both the thought of being, and the expression (if not communication) of that thought are possible.

In other words, it is not enough merely to say that beings are part of being, and therefore capable of thinking it and saying it, despite the cinematographic character of human thought and language. The cinematographic illusion may be ontologically contingent, but it is epistemologically constitutive, in so far as it is the basis on which living beings act in and on the world. A thought that seeks to think real being must go beyond (or perhaps behind) its own constitution as thought, and it must do so in particular rather than general or abstract terms, since it is abstraction itself that it must elude in thought, such that we must in each case think the specificity or nuance of the case in question (the 'how, how many, when and where'[86]) by thinking from the actual to the virtual, and not seeking to place ourselves and our thought within that virtual immediately, as if the thought of real being were a power we possess, rather than an 'impower' we suffer. The specificity of the *Cinema* books, the stakes of their game, lie in the case they seek to think, which gathers together or crystallises or is the point of convergence of all the other cases. The case in question is not that of cinema, or of films or film theory, but that of man and his relationship to the world.

To understand the weight this phrase carries in relation to the *Cinema* books, we need to understand the quite specific sense in which each of its terms is used. 'Man' is very simply human being as it is constituted cinematographically: the 'man' of action, the one who acts and reacts, and in these actions seeks mastery and control, the 'man' who communicates, gathers and dispenses information, who construes the world as resource or, at the extremes of action, as battlefield. Deleuze's use of the gendered pronoun is potentially troubling here, unless one reads it not as an obtusely sexist use of language, but rather as an indication that 'man' here is used in the 'molar' or 'majoritarian' sense laid out in *A Thousand Plateaus*: man not as a gender or even a quantitative majority, but as

> a state or standard in relation to which larger quantities, as well as the smallest, can be said to be minoritarian: white-man, adult-male, etc. . . . It is not a question of knowing whether there are more mosquitoes or flies than men, but of knowing how 'man' constituted a standard in the universe in relation to which men necessarily (analytically) form a majority.[87]

'Man', then, is to be understood here as 'the molar entity par excellence',[88] the abstract norm such that becoming-woman is a task for both genders ('Even women must become-woman'[89]) in so far as they would escape the cinematographic conditions of life, and thus of social life. As Brian Massumi points out in the discussion of 'becom-

What Use is Cinema to Deleuze?

ing-woman' in his *User's Guide to Capitalism and Schizophrenia*, within the Deleuzian framework, '"Man" and "Woman" as such have no reality other than that of logical abstractions'[90] – or in the terms of our current discussion, no reality other than that of cinematographic abstractions. Such an interpretation implies that man, as molar, is indeed part of that which must be overcome if thought is to think real difference, to think the world in its reality.

For the sake of clarity, I have chosen to follow Deleuze (and Guattari) in using 'man' in this molar sense, at least in the proximity to the question of the relation of 'man and world' (though I have avoided the use of the gendered pronoun elsewhere). However, it is important to note that the assertion that 'becoming-woman is a task for both genders' is a problematic one. At the very least it risks effacing actually existing women altogether, whether in terms of the molar struggles for women's identities and rights, or in its implications of a symmetry between the molar positions of both male and female identity. As Rosi Braidotti points out, the proposition of such a symmetry 'acts as if sexual differentiation or gender dichotomies did not have as the most immediate and pernicious consequence the positioning of the two sexes in a asymmetrical power relationship to each other'.[91] As such, and notwithstanding Deleuze and Guattari's acknowledgment that it remains 'indispensable for women to conduct a molar politics, with a view to winning back their own organism, their own history, their own subjectivity',[92] the question of 'becoming-woman' and its relation to the politics and theorisation of feminine identity remain contested.[93]

The sense of 'the world' to which this 'man' is related is perhaps more complex. It is undoubtedly 'the world' in its fullest sense, as being in its movement and real difference from itself. But cinematographic human beings both constitute and are constituted in another world in this world: the world of action, limited arbitrary and abstract, to be sure, but no less real or effective for all that (and indeed, for beings and for human beings all the more effective in that, unlike the world of being, it is a world they can live and act in). To speak of the 'relationship between man and the world', then, is to speak of the cinematographic constitution of beings, and of human beings, and of the abstract, limited and arbitrary world grasped in and by this constitution in terms of their genesis on the basis of real being, of the world as necessarily open whole.

In this sense, the philosophical problems that Deleuze says 'compelled' him to look for answers in the cinema might be summed up in terms of the problem of the thought of the world. This phrase too has a dual sense. On the one hand it concerns a strictly human thought or, rather, the means by which human thought thinks the world in which it lives and acts. On the other, in as much as this thought is an aspect of being, it also concerns a strictly inhuman thought to which human thought, human being, must expose itself if it is to think real being, real movement, real difference. This inhuman thought is 'the thought of the world' understood as the world *as* thought, as thinking in itself beyond human thought, in as much as the human thinks it only to the extent that it loses or frees itself from its cinematographic power to act.

More prosaically – and this claim is the hinge on which the argument of this book turns – what Deleuze essays in the *Cinema* books is a genetic account of thought itself and thus of philosophy (and by 'account' I mean both an explanation and a history, or rather, *dramatisation*). And this task can only be addressed in terms of the genesis of beings able to ask such questions of being. To pose it as a question: how does ontological difference give rise to epistemological questioning? What is the genesis of thought? Or as Claire Colebrook puts it, 'why does thought emerge from life?'[94] To answer such questions, Deleuze must first provide an account of the genesis of the cinematographic orientation of human thought on the basis of ontological difference. Then (and this is the hard part) he must be able to show how such cinematographic thought is nevertheless capable of giving rise to a thought and philosophy adequate to being as it is for itself, rather than being as it is given over to human power and action

This is the task of the *Cinema* books themselves. In other words, what Deleuze attempts in them is a vastly more ambitious version of his 'escape' from the dialectic, which adds to that 'escape' the ground and source *of* the errors it exemplifies, in the form of the cinematographic genesis of beings themselves. He thus seeks to provide not just an account, but a genetic account of the entire history of thought and of philosophy (even the most foreign to his own), on the basis of his own philosophy of difference. This is the full meaning of my claim that the proposition the *Cinema* books present us with is a dramatisation of philosophy itself: the history of cinema as the film of philosophy and of the history of philosophy, *as shot from the perspective of being*.

The reasons why Deleuze turns to the cinema in order to achieve this task are mapped out in the analyses of the relations of language, philosophy and thought we have seen in the precursors to the

What Use is Cinema to Deleuze?

Cinema books. Firstly, he finds in cinema a non-linguistic semiotic system that is mobile in itself, and thus is capable of a thought that immediately and already contains real movement: cinema as non-cinematographic thought. Secondly, in so far as Deleuze's method of conceptual production is already cinematic in its method of dissociation and juxtaposition, the cinema *en tout* is already Deleuzian in its mode of thought. Indeed, it is in a sense *more* Deleuzian in its mode of thought than Deleuze himself (who is only human, after all), in so far as it thinks with mobile sections of duration, or movement-images, immediately and first of all.

This, I would suggest, is why Deleuze must turn to cinema in order to find answers to philosophical problems: in its inhuman mode of thought, it is better equipped to think the thought of the world (in both the senses outlined above) than philosophy itself, even Deleuzian philosophy. In this sense, the apparent perversity of writing two volumes on the cinema in the terms of a philosopher who condemns the cinema as the exemplar of a mechanism of thought that divides the human from being reveals itself as the purest pragmatism: Deleuze deploys the cinema to account for and resolve the problems internal to his own Bergsonism, which are simply the problems of the constitution of a thought and a philosophy adequate to being on the basis of the cinematographic genesis of human being and human thought.

These, I would argue, are the stakes of the game, the use that cinema has for Deleuze. The second half of this book will demonstrate how the game is played: how and in what sense the cinema is the correction of the cinematographic illusion (that is to say, how and why it is able to think, and think real being better than human thought); how and why cinematographic thought arises within the cinema on the basis of the cinema's non-cinematographic constitution (the genesis of human thought and of 'abstract' philosophy); and, finally, how this cinematographic thought dramatises the confrontation of human thought with the inhuman thought of being, or thought outside itself, and the unthought in thought.

Notes

1. This is hardly surprising, given that Bergson publishes his account of his cinematographic metaphor in 1907 and says there that he was using this metaphor in his lectures at the *Collège de France* as early as 1902–3. At that point in time, the cinema was clearly still at a very early stage in its

'evolution', its 'conquest of its own essence or novelty' as Deleuze puts it. As Bergson's references to 'the gallop of a horse' in his discussion of the cinematographic illusion of modern science suggest, his conception of the cinema at this point is shaped at least partly by the cinema's pre-history in the form of the experiments of people such as Eadweard Muybridge and Étienne-Jules Marey. Bergson, *Creative Evolution*, 272 n.1; Deleuze, *Cinema 1*, 3; Bergson, *Creative Evolution*, 332.
2. Ménil, 'The Time(s) of the Cinema', 87.
3. Bergson, *Creative Evolution*, 306.
4. Ibid.
5. Deleuze, *Cinema 1*, 2.
6. Ibid.
7. 'In the humblest living being nutrition demands research, then contact, in short a series of efforts which converge toward a center: this center is just what is made into an object – the object which will serve as food.' Bergson, *Matter and Memory*, 198.
8. Ibid.
9. Ibid., 183.
10. Bergson, *Creative Evolution*, 272.
11. Ibid., 273.
12. Ibid., 299.
13. Ibid., 307.
14. Ibid., 303.
15. Ibid. Emphasis in original.
16. Deleuze, *Bergsonism*, 34.
17. The Nietzscheanism such a phrase summons up comes to the surface in *Cinema 2*, where the Bergsonian treatment of the cinema offered in *Cinema 1* comes to take a decidedly Nietzschean turn.
18. Mullarkey, *Bergson and Philosophy*, 150.
19. Ibid., 152–3.
20. Ibid.; Bergson, *The Creative Mind*, 168.
21. This is, I would suggest, the same 'thread' of duration Deleuze describes in *Cinema 1*, which 'descends into the system like a spider' and prevents the set from closing in on itself, maintains it as open to the open whole of duration, and thus introduces 'the transspatial and the spiritual into the system which is never perfectly closed'. Deleuze, *Cinema 1*, 16–17.
22. Bergson, 'Letter to Floris Delattre, 24th December 1935', 369. Emphasis in original. It is to the English essayist and novelist Samuel Butler that he refers. Ansell-Pearson and Mullarkey, *Henri Bergson*, 388 n.57.
23. Bergson, *Creative Evolution*, 165.
24. Douglass, 'Bergson and Cinema: Friends or Foes?', 219.
25. Deleuze and Guattari, *What Is Philosophy?*, 198–9.
26. Deleuze, *Cinema 2*, 280.
27. Bergson, *The Creative Mind*, 34.

28. 'Intuition is arduous and cannot last.' Ibid., 35. As Mullarkey puts it, 'Intuition is clearly distinguished from immediate knowledge, being described [by Bergson] ... as a search requiring prodigious effort.' Mullarkey, *Bergson and Philosophy*, 158.
29. Bergson, *Creative Evolution*, 30.
30. Bergson, *Matter and Memory*, 154.
31. Deleuze, *Bergsonism*, 55.
32. Bergson, *The Creative Mind*, 33. Emphasis in original.
33. Mullarkey, *Bergson and Philosophy*, 159. Emphasis in original. He is citing de Lattre, *Bergson: Une Ontologie de La Perplexité*, 261.
34. Bergson, *The Creative Mind*, 42.
35. For some of the sources of these criticisms, see Mullarkey, 'Introduction', 4–16. A more broadly focused critique that is more contemporary with Bergson's own writing can be found in Benda, *The Treason of the Intellectuals*.
36. Deleuze, *Bergsonism*, 13.
37. Deleuze specifies three rules and two complementary rules in *Bergsonism*'s first chapter, 'Intuition as Method'. Ibid., 15–35.
38. Indeed, if one puts to one side for a moment the question of philosophical method, we can also say that this is true of thought. As Claire Colebrook puts it, for Deleuze 'thinking is not necessary, but only a potential'. Colebrook, *Deleuze: A Guide for the Perplexed*, 2.
39. Bergson, *The Creative Mind*, 175.
40. Mullarkey, *Bergson and Philosophy*, 154.
41. Ibid., 159. Emphasis in original.
42. Ibid., 158.
43. Ibid., 152.
44. Ibid.
45. According to Leonard Lawlor, 'intuition' and 'image' are 'virtually identical in Bergson'. Lawlor, *The Challenge of Bergsonism: Phenomenology, Ontology, Ethics*, 8.
46. Bergson, *Laughter: An Essay on the Meaning of the Comic*, 76.
47. Bergson, *The Creative Mind*, 135.
48. Mullarkey, *Bergson and Philosophy*, 160.
49. As such, the following comment by Bergson in his essay 'The Life and Work of Ravaisson' might equally well be taken to apply to himself: 'The whole philosophy of [Jean Gaspard Felix] Ravaisson springs from the idea that art is a figured metaphysics, that metaphysics is a reflection of art, and that it is the same intuition, variously applied, which makes the profound philosopher and the great artist.' It is clear from the account Bergson offers of Ravaisson that he finds in the latter at the very least a kindred philosophical spirit. 'The Life and Works of Ravaisson', 231.
50. Deleuze suggests something similar in an interview with Bellour and

François Ewald for *Magazine Littéraire* (republished in English in *Negotiations*) where he argues 'Style in philosophy is the movement of concepts. This movement's only present, of course, in the sentences, but the sole point of the sentences is to give it life, a life of its own. Style is a set of variations in language, a modulation, and a straining of one's whole language toward something outside it.' Deleuze, *Negotiations*, 140–1.
51. Deleuze, *Essays Critical and Clinical*, lv. His reference to the 'delirium' of such language points us towards the delirious becomings of language explored in *The Logic of Sense*. We might also note that the reference to the writer as 'seer' or 'hearer' evokes a connection to his account in the first pages of *Cinema 2* of neo-realism as 'a cinema of the seer and no longer of the agent'. Deleuze, *Cinema 2*, 2.
52. Smith, *Essays on Deleuze*, 194; for the source of this account, Smith directs us to Nietzsche, 'The Philosopher as Cultural Physician'.
53. Bergson, *The Creative Mind*, 175.
54. Although in Bergson's case the link between art and philosophy is not immediately present in the quote just cited, but must be 'read into' it via his invocation of the practice of art as a model for the intuitive method, as we have already seen.
55. This introduction has been republished as part of Smith's collection *Essays on Deleuze*. All citations are from the latter. *Essays on Deleuze*, 193.
56. There is a risk here that this description of the virtual disease makes the virtual sound akin to a Platonic Ideal form. This is certainly not the case: the virtual is not abstract, ideal or eternal, but differentiation itself. To illustrate this, we may simply note that diseases evolve, differentiate themselves in and over time, as the tendency for antibiotics to become ineffective with regard to specific diseases over time attests.
57. Deleuze, *Nietzsche and Philosophy*, 3.
58. It should be apparent from this that the definition of philosophy as the creation of concepts is not only, as Paul Patton points out, a 'stipulative definition in which the term "concept" is used to distinguish the object and materials of philosophy from those of science and art', but is also and integrally a response to and development of the problem of thought's relation to being. Patton, *Deleuze and the Political*, 24.
59. Deleuze, *Bergsonism*, 106.
60. Ibid., 18.
61. Deleuze and Guattari, *What Is Philosophy?*, 160.
62. Ibid.
63. Deleuze, *Bergsonism*, 23.
64. In the interview in which this claim is made, Deleuze is asked 'Do you think we may one day speak of kafkaism or beckettism the same way we speak of sadism or masochism?' Although the term 'kafkaism' is

never used in Roberto Calasso's book *K* (which is hardly surprising), it seems to me that in that work Calasso subjects Kafka and his work to a profound symptomatology of precisely the kind Deleuze is describing, quite independently of Deleuze, or Deleuzian terminology or concepts. Deleuze, 'Mysticism and Masochism', 132–3; Calasso, *K*.

65. Bergson makes a very similar set of claims in the first of the two lectures (originally presented at Oxford University) collected and published under the title 'The Perception of Change'. He attributes to artists the capacity to show us a reality we ourselves do not perceive, because the artist 'is less preoccupied than ourselves with the positive and material side of life' whereas our vision is 'narrowed' and 'drained' by 'our attachment to reality, our need for living and acting'. Bergson, *The Creative Mind*, 135–6.

66. Deleuze, *Bergsonism*, 21–9, and 22–3 in particular.

67. Indeed, Deleuze explicitly ties information to questions of power and social control, such that we might say that 'information management' is social management: 'information is exactly the system of control'. The question of the relationship of information and control is also discussed in Deleuze's work in relation to that of Foucault. Deleuze, 'What Is the Creative Act?', 320; *Negotiations*, 177–82.

68. Deleuze and Guattari, *What Is Philosophy?*, 28. Even here we may find a prefiguration of Deleuze's thought in that of Bergson, in so far as, according to Leonard Lawlor, 'Philosophy, for Bergson, cannot be conversation because all conversation or dialectical philosophies merely cut reality up according to the already established divisions of a particular language.' Lawlor, *The Challenge of Bergsonism: Phenomenology, Ontology, Ethics*, 72.

69. Ropars-Wuilleumier, 'The Cinema, Reader of Gilles Deleuze', 259.

70. Deleuze, *Cinema 2*, 280.

71. Alliez, *The Signature of the World*, 102.

72. 'I saw myself as taking an author from behind and giving him a child that would be his own offspring, yet monstrous.' Deleuze, *Negotiations*, 6.

73. Perkins, 'Cinephilia and Monstrosity: The Problem of Cinema in Deleuze's Cinema Books'.

74. Rodowick, *Gilles Deleuze's Time Machine*, x.

75. Bordwell, *On the History of Film Style*, 117.

76. Bellour, 'Thinking, Recounting', 69.

77. Deleuze, 'The Brain Is the Screen', 368. For Foucault's account of Borges' classification, see Foucault, *The Order of Things: An Archaeology of the Human Sciences*, xvi–xxvi. Deleuze leaves out my favourite item of the list: 'animals that from a long way off look like flies'.

78. Deleuze, 'The Brain Is the Screen', 368.

79. Smith, *Essays on Deleuze*, 193.
80. Moullet finds these conjunctions so absurd as to accuse Deleuze of committing 'the kind of astounding error you would have believed him absolutely incapable of and which a schoolboy would never have been guilty of'. Moullet, 'The Green Garbage Bins of Gilles Deleuze'.
81. Routt, 'Poubelle, Ma Belle'.
82. Bellour too notes the risk involved in uniting Stroheim and Buñuel as 'naturalist' under the category of the impulse-image, but resolves that risk for himself in similar terms to Routt. Bellour, 'Thinking, Recounting', 61.
83. Deleuze, *Negotiations*, 6.
84. Deleuze, *Cinema 2*, 280.
85. What is all the more striking about this claim is that Nancy is able to make it in the context of an essay that does not refer to the *Cinema* books at all. Nancy, 'The Deleuzian Fold of Thought', 110.
86. Deleuze, *Bergsonism*, 44.
87. Deleuze and Guattari, *A Thousand Plateaus*, 291.
88. Ibid., 292.
89. Ibid., 291.
90. Massumi goes on to add that 'What they are abstractions of are not the human bodies to which they are applied, but habit-forming whole attractors to which society expects its bodies to be addicted (love, school, family, church, career)' – in other words, the cinematographic abstraction lies as much, if not more so, at the level of the constitution of the social and political as it does at the level of the individual. Massumi, *User's Guide*, 86–7.
91. Braidotti, 'Becoming Woman: Or Sexual Difference Revisited', 51.
92. Deleuze and Guattari, *Thousand Plateaus*, 276.
93. For a sense of this 'contestation' see, for example, Colebrook and Buchanan, *Deleuze and Feminist Theory*; Burchill, 'Becoming-Woman: A Metamorphosis in the Present Relegating Repetition of Gendered Time to the Past', 87; Grosz, *Volatile Bodies: Towards a Corporeal Feminism*, 160–83. The terms of this contestation are, it seems to me, entirely coherent with those of Hallward's critique of Deleuzian philosophy more generally.
94. Colebrook, *Deleuze: A Guide for the Perplexed*, 23.

5

Genesis and Deduction

Cinematic Being

One way of reading the *Cinema* books is to regard them as a kind of counterfactual thought experiment in the history of philosophy in which Deleuze reads *Matter and Memory*, first published in French in 1896, as if it were both a book about, and a prefiguration of, cinema (which was in fact only beginning its birth pangs as Bergson's book was being written). Underwriting this experiment is Deleuze's claim that Bergson, in a move 'startlingly ahead of his time', and ahead of the cinema as such, conceives of the universe as *ontologically cinematic in and of itself*, irrespective of any actual cinema. That is, Bergson offers us a vision of 'the universe as cinema in itself, a metacinema'.[1] Read this way, Deleuze's argument goes well beyond the partial conciliation of cinema and cinematographic illusion implied in his claim that 'Even in his critique of the cinema, [the first chapter of *Matter and Memory* suggests that] Bergson was in agreement with it, to a far greater degree than he thought.'[2]

If the cinema has a privileged access to being, in particular as a mode of thought *of* being, it is because being itself is *already* metacinematic. As we shall see, however, the terms of the genesis of beings (and thus human beings) on the basis of this metacinematic universe are such that human nature is itself constitutively *cinematographic*. To put the argument in its most condensed form, Deleuze draws on Bergson to argue that being itself is nothing but light, and beings arise on that basis as a 'screen' that selectively reflects or reveals that light. Deleuze seeks to demonstrate in the first few chapters of *Cinema 1* that the cinema as such has the capacity to both deduce *and* correct this cinematographic genesis of human being by means of its own strictly formal capacities – its deployment of frame, shot and montage.[3] This double proposition is the basis of the philosophical privilege Deleuze accords the cinema, over and above all other arts and in some sense even over philosophy itself.[4] The cinema has the capacity not only to deduce the genesis of both beings and their abstract grasp of being, but also to articulate or dramatise the relations between them in its own strictly non-human terms. The task of this chapter is to demonstrate how it does so.

Deleuze derives his claims regarding the metacinematic character of being from his reading of the arguments of the first chapter of *Matter and Memory*, in which Bergson sets out to dissolve the philosophical problems arising from both realist and idealist conceptions of the relations between mind and body, or spirit and matter.[5] There Bergson argues that 'both realism and idealism go too far, that it is a mistake to reduce matter to the perception we have of it, a mistake also to make of it a thing able to produce in us perceptions, but in itself of another nature than they'.[6] In this chapter, beginning from a stance of self-consciously quotidian empiricism,[7] Bergson seeks to resolve the excesses of both the realist and idealist positions via the deduction of a strict identity of matter and image, in which

> Matter ... is an aggregate of 'images.' And by 'image' we mean a certain existence which is more than that which the idealist calls a representation, but less than that which the realist calls a thing – an existence placed halfway between the 'thing' and the 'representation'.[8]

Thus for Bergson, an image is neither a representation, more or less flawed, of some externally existent thing (which is, roughly speaking, a realist position) nor the production or projection of a purely mental state (which would correspond broadly to idealism). In their different ways both realism and idealism dissociate the existence of a thing from its appearance, or its appearance from its existence. Realism thus faces the problem of accounting not only for two (real or apparent) modalities of the one 'thing', but also for the mechanism of the relationship (if any) between them, while idealism endows the brain with, as Deleuze puts it, the 'miraculous power' of in some sense producing the order of the universe entirely within itself.[9]

This complicates a state of affairs that may be dealt with far more easily if we begin from a position based in everyday experience. Thus, argues Bergson, 'a mind unaware of the disputes between philosophers ... would naturally believe that matter exists just as it is perceived; and, since it is perceived as an image, the mind would make of it, in itself, an image'.[10] An image so understood is neither the production nor reproduction of some other thing, but is rather the thing itself, existing where and as it is perceived: that which *is*, is image, such that the materiality of being must be understood as consisting of images, and nothing but images. What things are and what we perceive – matter and image – are one and the same thing. In so far as being moves, and thus differs from itself, these images are movement-images. Thus, as Deleuze puts it

> we find ourselves in fact faced with the exposition of a world where IMAGE = MOVEMENT ... There is no moving body which is distinct from executed movement. There is nothing moved which is distinct from the received movement. Every thing, that is to say every image, is indistinguishable from its actions and reactions: this is universal variation.[11]

This world of image = movement is in a sense 'prior' to or, rather, the condition *for* perception, since images so conceived are not functions of perception (as they are in different ways for both realism and idealism). For Bergson perception is, in a very specific manner, both an aspect of this 'image-world' *and* an image in itself. Considered in its priority and thus for itself, the world of universal variation is nothing but light itself, such that to *be* is to be image = movement = matter = light. Being is thus constituted as an 'infinite set of all images', a 'plane of immanence' without orientation or ordering[12] in which these images exist in themselves, but not for anyone or anything else, and 'every image is "merely a road by which pass, in every direction, the modifications propagated throughout the immensity of the universe"'.[13]

> This in-itself of the image is matter: not something hidden behind the image, but on the contrary the absolute identity of the image and movement. The identity of image and movement leads us to conclude immediately that the movement-image and matter are identical ... The material universe, the plane of immanence, is the *machine assemblage of movement-images*.[14]

If this 'in-itself' of the image is cinema, or cinematic in its being, however, it is so in a very particular and peculiar fashion: it is a cinema without a screen, an appearing without an eye, 'the virtual perception of all things'[15] in which 'an image may be without being perceived ... [and] may be present without being represented'.[16] These virtual images in themselves are simply 'lines or figures of light' diffusing or propagating unopposed throughout the plane of immanence, figures that do not appear as such in the absence of something that would capture or reflect or stop them. This is the distinction Deleuze makes when he describes Bergson's imagistic ontology in terms of the universe understood as cinema *in itself* (and not *for* anyone). It is a *Meta*cinema, rather than cinema as such: it is the condition *for* cinema, without yet being cinema.

In this I must disagree with Paola Marrati's claim that Deleuze 'sees Bergson's universe as a perfect *metacinema* but only when it has given rise to "living images" and to everything that our ordinary perception sees and names: actions, affects, bodies'.[17] The universe, or being, is precisely a metacinema in so far as it is grasped *without* reference to 'living images', whereas it is those living images or beings themselves which are to be compared with the cinema properly speaking. This is not merely a 'point of order' – the distinction between the metacinematic *conditions* for cinema and the cinema as such goes to the heart of the tension between ontology and epistemology that I argue motivates Deleuze's engagement with cinema. The first step towards recognising this lies in noting that the universe as metacinema constitutes the conditions for cinema in precisely the same sense, and for the same reasons, that the perception-for-itself of Bergson's image-universe constitutes the condition for perception-for-someone: to speak of a metacinema is to speak of the 'virtual perception of all things' without the appearance of any image that would itself be perceived, that is, without the images that make up cinema as such.

Perception in its everyday sense – the perception of an actual, rather than virtual, image for someone or something – does not arise within this image-world without a screen to stop or reflect the luminous figures of being which would otherwise continue to flow unseen and uninterrupted. Thus although the image-universe may be constituted as a *meta*cinema, it is perception *for* someone that is constituted in properly *cinematic* terms, that is, in terms of a screen on which images finally 'appear'. What Bergson proposes as his candidate for this screen is consciousness or 'living beings': as Deleuze puts it, 'the brain is the screen'.[18] Perception for someone, the image that appears, arises with consciousness and *as* consciousness.[19]

With this proposition, Deleuze poses an account of the genesis of thought not only in terms of its virtual metacinematic conditions, but also in terms of a properly cinematic actualisation of images-for-someone as a function of the brain/screen that reflects them. In other words, both thought and the image-for-someone share the same genesis. Bergson offers us an image of things as luminous in themselves: things *are* light, are image. Rather than illuminating being from a position somehow external to being, consciousness is merely an image among others, whose only privilege is to obscure or subtract from the universal light of things that which does not concern it – the brain is the screen on which the luminosity of the

Genesis and Deduction

world reveals itself in and as actual things for someone. These are the terms of Bergson's model of perception: the thing as image-in-itself, enfolded in and continuous with the 'virtual perception of all things' and the appearing of that image *for* someone or something as a screening or filtering of that 'virtual perception'. Thus the consciousness of living beings will

> allow to pass through them, so to speak, those external influences which are indifferent to them; the others isolated, become 'perceptions' by their very isolation. Everything thus happens for us as though we reflected back to surfaces the light which emanates from them, the light which, had it passed on unopposed, would never have been revealed. The images which surround us will appear to turn towards our body the side, emphasized by the light upon it, which interests our body.[20]

It is important to note that it is in relation to the body as a centre of *action* within the world that this limitation takes place; only those images that are of concern to the body and its needs are actualised, selected for 'reflection'. For the time being, however, we can say that rather than continuing to divide spirit and matter, image and thing, as far as Bergson is concerned, 'there is for images merely a difference of degree, and not of kind, between being and being consciously perceived'.[21]

What is most radical here is that, in so far as the brain/screen and the interval it imposes between action and reaction are one and the same thing, we find ourselves with a definition of the brain in strictly univocal and materialist terms: there is nothing in the brain that is not in the world, no 'interior life' or mental representation or thought that is different in nature from the world. Thus, as Frédéric Worms points out, 'Bergson defends, in an apparently extreme form, the thesis of an "exteriority of the mind".'[22] What then are the terms in which consciousness-in-fact (the opaque screen or cinema of thought) 'appears' within the consciousness-by-right of being (the unbroken luminosity of movement-images or 'flowing-matter')? As we have seen, it is neither something other than an image itself, nor adds anything to the image-world, image-universe: 'There is nothing positive here, nothing added to the image, nothing new.'[23] Consciousness-in-fact differs from consciousness-by-right only in its power of limitation or subtraction: the screen or living being retains from the unbroken continuity of the image in itself only that which concerns its own interests, and what is thus retained is the image as it exists *for* someone. What does not concern us simply passes through unopposed, such that our perception of the world is given as a function of our action within it: 'Our representation of matter is the measure of our possible action upon bodies: it results from the discarding of what has no interest for our needs, or more generally, for our functions.'[24] It is, Deleuze says, 'an operation which is exactly described as a *framing*: certain actions undergone are isolated by the frame'.[25]

The brain/screen does not just reflect, it selects, and this selection constitutes our power of action on and in the world; our thought is *in* the world and is a thought *of* the world, in so far as it acts *on* the world. In other words, our knowledge of the world derives from the action of our bodies as part of that world: representation or the image as it exists for us, and thus consciousness, is strictly speaking a function of action: 'the brain is nothing but this – an interval, a gap between action and reaction'.[26] Bergson's cinematic ontology thus dissolves the philosophical problem of the relation between matter and spirit, mind and body by posing them as one and the same thing; it is a monist, or as Deleuze might say, univocal conception of both being and beings as image, and nothing more than image (indeed, where beings are concerned, we might say that they are, if not 'less' than image, then certainly a limited or 'framed' subset of the open set of images).

In his discussion of Bergson's materialist model of consciousness – the 'special image' of the brain/screen – in the interval it imposes between action and reaction, Deleuze follows his observation that 'All Bergson asks for are movements and intervals between movements which serve as units' with the aside that this 'is also exactly what Dziga Vertov asked for, in his materialist conception of the cinema'.[27] It seems to me that this comparison makes sense only if we take it to suggest that the minimal components required to constitute the materiality of cinema can be characterised in exactly the same terms as those required to constitute the materiality of consciousness. Cinema thus understood can rightly be considered as a mode of thought, or at least of consciousness, in precisely the same material terms as that of living beings (indeed, Deleuze proposes that we turn to the 'biology' of the brain for the principles by which we might seek to understand films, rather than to psychoanalysis or linguistics[28]).

As we have seen, the basis on which Deleuze accords a philosophical privilege to the cinema goes well beyond the metacinematic nature of being itself (Bergson's positing of being as a universe of light = movement = matter = image). Not only is consciousness-by-right identical to being understood as image-in-itself (such that consciousness-by-right must also be said to be metacinematic) but both the image-in-fact (the image *for* someone) and consciousness-in-fact (the consciousness *of* someone, however elementary that 'someone' may be) are actualised cinematically. Thus an actual consciousness is defined in terms of a screen which reflects and thus actualises the image-for-itself in and as an image *for* someone, and thus as the consciousness *of* someone. Furthermore, the mechanism by which this actualisation takes place is no more than a subtraction or exclusion of those aspects of image/matter that are of no interest to that living being; the screen that reflects is also a *frame* that selects and excludes.

Deleuze assigns the task of the *Cinema* books neither in relation to Bergson nor even to philosophical problems more generally. It is, rather, the production of 'a taxonomy, an attempt at the classification of images and signs'.[29] What is vital here, and rarely noted, is that he introduces the taxonomic distinction between action, affection and perception-images in relation not to cinema, but to the dual system of reference which accounts for both the objective existence of images and our subjective apprehension of them. The acentred universal variation of the universe = image constitutes the first system of reference of images; images as they appear for and in relation to the brain/screen as a centre of action constitutes the second.

As such this 'cinematic' taxonomy must be understood as arising from a distinction belonging not to the cinema, but to the limitation imposed on the 'pure' movement-image of being by the necessity of our action within it. That is, the avatars of the movement-image that Deleuze deduces arise as a necessary consequence of the same terms in which living beings and consciousness (the terms are interchangeable for Bergson) arise within the world. In other words, these images constitute the 'material moments of subjectivity'[30] such that 'each one of us, the special image or the contingent centre, is nothing but an assemblage [*agencement*] of three images, a consolidate [*consolidé*] of perception-image, action-images and affection-images'.[31] In other words, the task Deleuze essays in the *Cinema* books *is a taxonomy of the signs of consciousness and subjectivity first of all*, before it is a taxonomy of the signs of cinema. This taxonomy is on the one hand a categorisation of signs that are the material moments of human thought itself and on the other the elementary terms of the cinema in so far as it constitutes a spiritual automaton, a machine for the production of thought.[32]

The pure movement-image from which these image/signs are extracted or subtracted exists only for itself (as do the image-for-itself and consciousness-for-itself of the image-universe), but perception, action and affection-images exist only *for* someone and in a sense *as* someone (they are not signs that represent *to* a consciousness, they *are* that consciousness). That is to say, they constitute and express the relation between the two 'poles' of the double system of reference of images. Things or images exist in and for themselves at one pole, but at the other appear *for* us as bodies determined in relation to their possible action *on* us, and our potential action or reaction to them. The effect of this is a distinction between the way movement exists for itself, and how it exists for us.[33] The movement-image in itself (that is, the image grasped from within the first system of reference) is not the movement of some thing; it is a movement in and for itself, a difference that differs from itself first of all. Grasped in relation to the needs of action (the second system of reference), however, movement-images in themselves now appear *for* someone in terms of bodies that move and are moved within space, such that

> actions, in precisely this sense, have already replaced movement with the idea of a provisional place towards which it is directed or that of a result it secures. Quality has replaced movement with the idea of a state which persists while waiting for another to replace it. Body has replaced movement with the idea of a subject which would carry it out or of an object which would submit to it, of a vehicle which would carry it. We will see that such images are formed in the universe (action-images, affection-images, perception-images).[34]

Perception-images thus arise inasmuch as the special image that is a brain/screen constitutes a centre within the acentred variability of the image-universe, thus orienting the latter as a horizon of possible actions for and by that centre: 'If the world is incurved around the perceptive centre, this is already from the point of view of action, from which perception is inseparable.'[35] The perception-image constitutes the image-universe in terms of bodies in relation to their possible action on us, thus preparing for our possible response to and on them.

> Distance is in fact a radius which goes from the periphery to the centre: perceiving things where they are, I grasp the 'virtual action' they have on me, and simultaneously the 'possible action' that I have on them, in order to associate me with them or avoid them, by diminishing or increasing the distance. It is thus the same phenomenon of the gap which is expressed in terms of time in my action and in terms of space in my perception.[36]

Perception is already part way to action, and an indispensable aspect of it, as one side of the interval or delay the brain/screen imposes on the causal chains of being. On the other side of the interval, the action-image relates movement not to things, but to actions: 'Just as perception relates movement to "bodies" (nouns), that is to rigid objects which will serve as moving bodies or as things moved, action relates movement to "acts" (verbs) which will be the design for an assumed end or result.'[37]

In between perception-images on one side of the gap and action-images on the other, the interval itself is occupied by affection, the 'coincidence of subject and object, or the way in which the subject perceives itself, or rather experiences itself or feels itself "from the inside"'.[38] The aspect of the image-universe that the brain/screen selects and reflects may manifest itself as things at a distance (perception-images) or actions in response to them (action-images), but there is also some part which 'we "absorb", that we refract, and which does not transform itself into either objects of perception or acts of the subject; rather they mark the coincidence of the subject and the object in a pure quality'.[39]

Affection is the 'internalisation' of the object as quality by and for the subject, and it is this quality that the subject acts in response to, rather than acting 'directly' on perception. Things are not just 'near' or 'far', but may be 'sharp', 'fast', 'threatening' and so on, such that action acts on perception mediately, *through* affection, through the qualities of perceived things as they are internalised within the subject. In so far as affection marks the coincidence of subject and object, the affection-image is to be found in the subject as much as in the thing perceived, in an image 'expressed' in or across the perceiving being as 'a kind of motor tendency in a sensory nerve'.[40] Affect thus constitutes a kind of action by the powerless, a movement of the immobile. It remains an action in response to perception, like the action-image, but one expressed through an immobile organ incapable of acting directly on anything else – which is why Deleuze relates the affection-image in cinema to the face, and more generally to 'what Blanchot calls "the aspect of the event that its accomplishment cannot realise"'.[41]

The quality expressed by the affection-image belongs not to the thing perceived nor to the consciousness that perceives it but somewhere 'between' them, in the *relation* between the two that marks their coincidence. It is not merely a quality of 'sharpness', 'speed' or 'threat', but also the 'concern', 'anxiety' or 'fear' expressing the internalisation of the object in the subject. It is thus affection that maintains the connection between perception and action – if the gap imposed by the brain/screen were truly an 'empty' interval, if there were no means of 'crossing' or relating 'received movement' and 'executed movement', they would remain 'incommensurable'.[42] Thus Deleuze notes that where the perception-image relates movement to 'nouns' and the action-image to 'verbs', the affection-image relates it to '"quality" as a lived state' – to 'adjectives'.[43] It is perhaps worth emphasising the *lived* aspect of the affect image; affect is no less physical or concrete, no less bodily and active, than perception or action, for all that it is expressed through a body that cannot move, and an action that cannot act on another directly.

Most important for my argument here are the terms by which Deleuze derives perception, action and affection-images from the 'pure' movement-image or pure perception for-itself, and in particular the centred, stabilising and action-oriented character of those images. As both the 'material moments of subjectivity' and the primary categories of the spiritual automata of the cinema, perception, action and affection-images articulate the relation of thought to being in terms of a centred, stable and active perspective on the acentred variation of being-for-itself. In other words, from within the world of action, there is no direct access to 'pure' movement as differing difference, which is the province of the movement-image as it exists for itself (*the* movement-image). Perception, action and affection-images are movement-images, and thus open in some sense onto the infinite variation or movement of *the* movement-image (the open whole, or being itself), but they are nevertheless limited and selective perspectives on that whole, on that absolute movement.

Deleuze explicitly identifies these avatars with the equivalent of the basic constituent elements of language: action replaces pure movement with a place or goal towards which it is aimed – *verb*; quality or affection has replaced movement with a state which persists – *adjective*; perception has replaced movement with things which move or are moved – *noun*. This attribution of grammatical correlates to the three basic kinds of movement-images[44] mirrors precisely the passage in *Creative Evolution* where Bergson uses the same grammatical correlates to characterise human beings' tendency to grasp movement in abstract and ultimately static terms.[45]

In other words, Deleuze characterises perception, action and affection-images in precisely the same terms in which Bergson chooses to characterise the cinematographic illusion: before they constitute the elementary forms of a taxonomy of cinema, they mark the ways in which 'the mind manages to take stable views of . . . instability'[46] as a necessary result of the terms in which living beings come into being. Thus the taxonomy of the signs of the movement-image is in no sense at odds with the cinematographic illusion: these signs are an alternative way of describing or analysing the terms in which the limits of thought that Bergson calls 'cinematographic' continue to afflict consciousness, even when that consciousness finds its genesis within the pure variation of the image-universe, of perception-for-itself, of being as differing difference.

What we can see, then, is that the passage in which Deleuze presents his characterisation of perception, action and affection-images is itself a paraphrase of the arguments in *Creative Evolution* whereby Bergson lays the groundwork for his introduction of the cinematographic metaphor for the centred, stable and active character of the grasp that consciousness has of being and of movement.[47] The aim of Bergson's argument in this passage is not merely the conclusion that *'the mechanism of our ordinary knowledge is of a cinematographical kind'* but that 'The cinematographical method . . . consists in making the general character of knowledge form itself on that of action.'[48]

That this is so is a direct function of the genesis of conscious beings in fact within the consciousness-by-right of the image-universe. The criterion for the selection and reflection of images to actualise out of the pure virtuality of the image-universe by the brain/screen is action; consciousness, as the imposition of a delay or gap in the unbroken propagation of images, has as its only function the possibility of an active, rather than passive, relation to images and their impact on us. The more reflective possibilities of thought, up to and including philosophy, are built on or derived from this active basis, and oriented by it: 'We are made in order to act as much as, and more than, in order to think – or rather, when we follow the bent of our nature, it is in order to act that we think.'[49] Bergson's analysis of the cinematographic basis of classical philosophy (which is valid for any philosophical system premised on an abstract conception of movement) and of modern science is presented as an explicit demonstration of how the genetic orientation of consciousness towards action has shaped the tendencies of philosophical thought.[50] Moreover, the results of this demonstration bear directly on Deleuze's philosophical reasons for engaging with cinema.

What this indicates is that the relationship Deleuze in fact proposes between the movement-image and cinematographic illusion is more complex than it may at first seem. At the very least, the avatars of the movement-image that arise in relation to the brain/screen (the second 'system of reference of images') cannot be treated as simply 'opposed' to the cinematographic illusion, or strictly separated from it, any more than the 'cinematic' philosophy of *Matter and Memory* can be simply divorced from the cinematographic critique of *Creative Evolution*. Deleuze's analysis of the relation between the movement-image and the cinematographic illusion is less a critique of the latter by means of the former than it is a reformulation of that illusion in terms *of* the movement-image.

Broadly speaking, the tendency of the secondary literature is to either explicitly or implicitly interpret Deleuze's claim that cinema operates in terms of movement-images rather than static frames as the claim that cinema corrects the cinematographic illusion *because* it operates in terms of movement-images. By my reading, this is precisely not the case. Deleuze's aim in defining cinema in terms of movement-images is not to show how it 'corrects' the cinematographic illusion – as we shall see later in this chapter, his demonstration of this correction takes place in quite different terms.

This of course leaves open the question of why he reformulates the cinematographic illusion in this way and what this achieves. The clue lies in Deleuze's observation that

> on the basis of this state of things [being as acentred universal variation of the image-for-itself] it would be necessary to show how, at any point, centres can be formed which would impose fixed instantaneous views. It would therefore be a question of 'deducing' conscious, natural *or* cinematographic perception ... Even in his critique of the cinema, Bergson was in agreement with it, to a far greater degree than he thought. We see this in the brilliant first chapter of *Matter and Memory*.[51]

As I read it, in this passage Deleuze is implicitly criticising Bergson's formulation of the cinematographic metaphor because it describes the *effects* of that illusion without showing how it can be derived or deduced on the basis of duration as real difference. As a result, it remains something external to and arbitrarily imposed on Bergson's own model of being as pure variation – it cuts thought off from being absolutely, as if thought were somehow separate from being or external to it. Hence Deleuze's preference for the more complex model offered in *Matter and Memory*; there, centres of perception are derived or deduced directly from this universal variation, without the need to 'introduce a different factor, a factor of another nature'.[52]

Genesis and Deduction

From this 'internal' perspective, the genesis of 'conscious, natural or cinematographic perception' can all be deduced in precisely the same terms, and it is on that common basis that Deleuze is able to justify his extraordinary intertwining of thought, philosophy and cinema.[53]

The attention given by commentators to the apparent conflict between cinema and cinematographic illusion in their analyses of the *Cinema* books is perhaps understandable, since it does at least initially seem to be mapped out by Deleuze himself. In the opening pages of *Cinema 1*, he argues that

> cinema does not give us an image to which movement is added, it immediately gives us a movement-image ... Now what is again very odd is that Bergson was perfectly aware of the existence of mobile sections or movement-images. This happened before *Creative Evolution*, before the official birth of cinema: it was set out in *Matter and Memory* in 1896. The discovery of the movement-image, beyond the conditions of natural perception, was the extraordinary invention of the first chapter of *Matter and Memory*. Had Bergson forgotten it ten years later?[54]

However, the question 'Had he forgotten it ten years later?' is not a proposal, however tentative, for how one might explain the apparent tension between the arguments Bergson presents in 1896 and those of 1907. It is the first half of a rhetorical figure, rather than an attempted rationalisation, allowing Deleuze to immediately propose as its counterpart the explanation for these differences that he genuinely holds: 'Or did he fall victim to another illusion which affects everything in its initial stages?'[55] Deleuze suggests that anything that is genuinely new (in this case, the concept of movement-images created in *Matter and Memory*), as opposed to a merely incremental change, is in a very real sense unprecedented – it comes into being 'out of place', at odds with the world within which it appears. Thus, he argues, such creations are forced to conceal their novelty to begin with:

> in order not to be rejected [they] have to project the characteristics which they retain in common with the set [of the determined elements of the world into which they enter]. The essence of a thing never appears at the outset, but in the middle, in the course of its development. Having transformed philosophy by posing the question of the 'new' instead of that of eternity (how are the production and appearance of the new possible?), Bergson knew this better than anyone.[56]

His point, I think, is that *Matter and Memory* was too radical for its time and that Bergson's reformulation of the genesis of consciousness in cinematographic terms, rather than those of movement-images, should be understood as an attempt to simplify his arguments, to reduce their 'novelty' in order for it to be better grasped by the unready world it had thrust itself into. Thus the metaphor of the cinematographic illusion presents a simplified abstraction of the relation between movement-for-itself (the pure movement-image) and movement-for-someone (the avatars of the movement-image when it is related to a centre or subject). In order to communicate this relation clearly and directly, Bergson is forced to simplify and abstract it from the more complex but more concrete terms in which it is implicit within *Matter and Memory*: he brings the *effect* of the centred nature of movement-for-someone into clear focus (the cinematographic illusion), but in doing so obscures the terms of its *genesis* within the acentred universe of movement-for-itself.

In both the movement-images of *Matter and Memory* and the static photogrammes of *Creative Evolution* it is images that are at stake – but what has been abstracted from Bergson's treatment of images in the latter is precisely movement itself. The irony here, of course, is that Bergson is forced to abstract from his own account of the relation between real or concrete movement and human thought in order to communicate it. But, as we have already seen, this is an irony that afflicts Bergsonian philosophy *en tout*: the very premises he reasons from require that the closer his thought comes to real movement, the less it is able to communicate it, and the greater the clarity with which he is able to express it the further he moves away from it, and the more abstract his account becomes.

Weak Reasoning, Perversity and Grasping at Threads

As we have seen, Deleuze's preference for grasping the cinema in terms of the movement-images of *Matter and Memory* rather than those of the cinematographic illusion of *Creative Evolution* does not on its own constitute either a rejection or a correction of Bergson's characterisation of living beings and of human thought in terms of their genesis as centred, active and stable perspectives on the pure variation of being itself. The metaphor of the cinematograph is merely a simplified and abstracted presentation of arguments already present in *Matter and Memory* in terms of movement-images; movement-images as they appear for someone rather than in themselves – perception, action and affection-images both as avatars of the movement-image for itself and as the material moments of subjectivity – are nothing other than limited, centred and stable perspectives on the unceasing variation of being, derived directly from the needs of action. If the cinema offers Deleuze a means of 'correcting' the cinematographic illusion, this correction is nevertheless not provided directly by the characterisation of the cinema in terms of movement-images, and neither does that correction (whatever form it takes) constitute a rejection of the philosophical critique that is that metaphor's primary aim.

However, by interpreting Bergson's ontological arguments as the proposition of a being which is metacinematic in character, and deducing the genesis of living beings on the basis of that metacinema in terms of cinema as such, Deleuze is able to reformulate Bergson's characterisation of the cinematographic illusion in terms of movement-images, rather than the static frames of a film strip – that is, in the terms provided by *Matter and Memory*, rather than those proposed in *Creative Evolution*. Doing so offers Deleuze two advantages. Firstly, it provides him with the means to bridge the chasm between ontology and epistemology that Bergson's model of the cinematographic illusion opens up (and in a sense to bridge the gap between *Matter and Memory* and *Creative Evolution* he identifies in the opening pages of *Cinema 1*). Secondly, in doing so, it provides Deleuze with the tools to account for the history of philosophy itself, including the philosophies of identity and representation that he rejects – as philosophies of transcendence – in strictly differential terms, in the following sense.

The dominant tradition of Western philosophy that both Bergson and Deleuze critique is characterised by the abstract concept of movement it directly or indirectly relies on. Such philosophies are thus deduced (at least in principle) on the basis of the genesis of the cinematographic illusion, while that illusion is in turn deduced in terms of its genesis as the centred and stable perspective on the acentred variation of being constituted by living beings. That is to say, by accounting for the effects of the cinematographic illusion in terms of movement-images, Deleuze shows how abstract movement can be deduced in terms of real movement – in precisely the same sense and in the same terms that he is able to deduce negation and Hegelian dialectics in terms of Bergson's ontological conception of difference (the former demonstration is in fact implicit within the latter).

In other words, across the two volumes of the *Cinema* books, Deleuze will ultimately be able show how and why thought, and philosophy, can go so far astray by conceiving of movement abstractly, even though they arise within and as part of the real movement and real difference of the being itself. More than this, it allows him demonstrate the terms in which they come to confront this barrier to thought within thought, in relation to a 'thought outside itself, and the unthought within thought' as an ahistorical moment that both belongs to and unfounds the historical as the mode of human thought and being.

The recapitulation of the history of philosophy, and particularly of the Kantian reversal of the relation of movement and time, that Deleuze finds in the history of cinema *is* this account: the history of cinema as the dramatisation of the history of philosophy told in and by movement-images, rather than via the (Bergsonian) cinematographic illusions of properly human thought and language. To understand *how* this dramatisation operates (which is the task of the final chapters of this book), however, we need first of all to understand the precise terms in which Deleuze demonstrates how the cinema can surpass the centred and stable perspective of natural perception as a function of its own formal properties, and thus escape the illusions of thought that derive from that perspective. In other words, we need to know how cinema escapes the cinematographic illusion, even when that illusion is grasped in the more complex terms implicit in *Matter and Memory*.

Deleuze's account of the relationship between the cinema and the cinematographic illusion – the reasoning by which he absolves the cinema from Bergson's philosophical critique of the cinematographic illusion – has been a point of contention for some of his commentators. Rodowick, for example, finds Deleuze's reasoning on this point 'weak',[57] while Douglass describes his account as 'wonderfully perverse' in its reconfiguration of the premises of Bergson's argument.[58] One of the complicating factors here is that Deleuze appears to offer not one, but two sets of arguments for why the cinema is not subject to the cinematographic illusion. Rodowick's concerns are with the first of these arguments, in which Deleuze responds to the most literal application of Bergson's metaphor to actual cinema in terms of the distinction between the conditions of natural and cinematic perception. Douglass' concerns are with the second argument, in which, as he puts it

> Deleuze cleverly exploits the terminological ambiguities in Bergson's attack on cinematic illusion, transferring the definition of Bergson's term 'cuttings' from the frame to the shot . . . Grasping, then, at threads trail-

ing from this supposed terminological misunderstanding, Deleuze proceeds to claim that Bergson was 'startlingly ahead of his time' in defining the universe as 'cinema in itself, a metacinema'.[59]

As his references to 'exploiting terminological ambiguities' and 'grasping at threads' suggest, Douglass, like Rodowick, is unconvinced by Deleuze's justifications for engaging with the cinema in Bergsonian terms – not because Deleuze's reasoning is 'weak' but because he regards Deleuze's treatment of Bergson as something of a philosophical shell game in which he 'makes us believe that perhaps he understood Bergson better than the philosopher understood himself'.[60]

As we shall see, however, the apparently distinct arguments that Rodowick and Douglass concern themselves with are in fact two faces of the same argument, which, far from 'perverting' Bergson's account of cinematographic illusion, returns it to its origins. Deleuze does so by demonstrating how this illusion is not only already implicit within the arguments of *Matter and Memory*, but that in using the cinematograph as a metaphor, Bergson has oversimplified or abstracted his own ontological insight in a manner that 'traps' him epistemologically. In doing so, Deleuze sets up the terms in which it is cinema itself that allows both Bergson and himself to escape this philosophical trap and provide the philosophical terms in which thought can be 'reunited' with the real movement, or real being, that it arises out of. In order to recognise this, however, we must first deal with Rodowick's criticisms.

Given the terms in which Bergson poses the cinematographic illusion, it seems difficult to avoid the conclusion that the cinema must itself 'illustrate' this illusion. Since the film strip does indeed consist of immobile sections artificially put into motion by the strictly external movement of the projector – static 'photogrammes' running through the projector at twenty-four frames a second – how can cinema *not* reproduce this error of thought? Taken in isolation, Deleuze's response to this question does indeed seem underdeveloped, even perfunctory, given that his entire *Cinema* project rests on this point (it occupies a mere paragraph slightly more than half a page long). Indeed, it seems to rest largely on the assertion that what we experience when watching a movie is not twenty-four static frames a second, but an image that moves of itself.

> Cinema proceeds with photogrammes – that is with immobile sections . . . But it has often been noted that what it gives us is not the photogramme:

it is an intermediate image, to which movement is not appended or added; the movement on the contrary belongs to the intermediate image as immediate given.[61]

The obvious rejoinder to this claim is that the *appearance* of movement created out of static images is precisely the illusion that Bergson condemns – and is the very reason he chooses our experience of movement in the movies as the metaphorical exemplar of this generalised error of thought, perception and language. As Rodowick puts it, 'It is hard to say that movement is truly immanent to the film image when, on the one hand, it is artificially produced below the image by the automated passage of still images, and, on the other it is corrected cognitively "above" the image by mental processes that are still not thoroughly understood.'[62]

What Rodowick fails to take into account here is the distinction Deleuze makes between 'natural' and 'cinematic' perception. Where natural perception is concerned, 'the illusion is corrected "above" perception by the conditions that make perception possible in the subject. In the cinema, however, it is corrected at the same time as the image appears for a spectator without conditions.'[63] What appears perfunctory, or 'weak' in Deleuze's reasoning here, it seems to me, is the lack of detail this paragraph offers regarding both the nature of the 'correction' Deleuze has in mind and the 'conditions' or lack thereof that differentiate natural and cinematic perception. This lack of detail seems all the more culpable given that, without it, his assertion of the difference between natural and cinematic perception amounts to nothing less than the assertion that cinema does not suffer from the cinematographic illusion – which does rather appear to beg the question in question.

However, what Rodowick appears to overlook here is that Deleuze immediately goes on to set up the terms in which he will in fact elaborate on the 'conditions' or lack thereof in question in the very next paragraph. He does so via the distinction he makes between cinema's beginnings in its 'primitive' state (the single shot *actualité* filmed with a static camera, as exemplified in the films of the Lumière brothers) and 'the conquest of its [the cinema's] own essence or novelty ... through montage, the mobile camera and the emancipation of the view point, which became separate from projection'.[64] For Deleuze, in its 'primitive' state the cinema *is* precisely cinematographic in the terms of Bergson's metaphor, but the introduction of montage and the mobility of the camera free it from this illusion. In other words, the condition of natural perception that condemns it to the cinematographic illusion is simply that our point of view is always our own: our perception is always centred and stabilised in relation to the distinct image that our body/brain constitutes for itself within the universal variation of images that constitutes being. Sitting in the cinema, our point of view and that of the projector behind our heads coincide, such that it replaces our point of view with its own. While the point of view of the camera that has shot the images is presented through (and thus tied to) that of the projector that presents them for us (and which substitutes its point of view for our own) we remain under the conditions of natural perception, irrespective of the fact that the images we see on screen are the products of technology rather than nature.

But while the projector of necessity always remains in the one place[65], so that its point of view always coincides with our own, the camera does not *have* to stay static. It is always *possible* for the point of view of the camera to move with respect to that of the projector, either within a shot via a literal camera move, or across shots via montage – and the history of post-primitive cinema is shaped by the realisation of this possibility in its various forms. As soon as the camera takes up this option, its point of view no longer coincides with that of the projector (and thus of the spectator) and the centring and stabilising conditions of natural perception that are at the heart of the cinematographic illusion are broken. In other words, the special privilege of the cinema is its potential or 'tendency' (which is not *necessarily* realised) to free both itself and the spectator from the conditions of natural perception.[66] The movement the spectator is given to experience once freed from these conditions is then no longer the mere reanimation of static sections produced by the external motor of the projector, but rather presents a real movement expressing the properly internal difference of being.

Until the cinema emancipates its viewpoint from that of the projector (until it surpasses its primitive state) it merely reproduces this same condition – it *is* cinematographic. But once the viewpoint of camera and projector no longer coincide – once cinematic perception becomes decentred – rather than reproducing the conditions of natural perception, the cinema corrects the constitutive illusions of such perception, in so far as the images of, and in, the cinema appear 'for a spectator *without* conditions' (that is to say, for a spectator separated or freed from the conditions of natural perception). Far from being perfunctory, the full elaboration of the arguments

Deleuze derives from the terms of this distinction is developed in detail across the first four chapters of *Cinema 1*, and indeed, is the basis on which his entire project rests.

From the perspective of cinema studies, Deleuze's distinction between 'primitive' cinema and the 'conquest of its [cinema's] own essence'[67] has often seemed problematic, since it in effect suggests that cinema properly speaking does not 'begin' until well after its apparent origins in the Grand Café in 1895 (an implication reinforced by the fact that the history of cinema Deleuze appears to present in the *Cinema* books chooses 1914 as its starting point, in the form of the work of D.W. Griffith). Rodowick, in particular, argues that 'Deleuze's historical understanding of primitive cinema is terribly remiss'.[68] He sees Deleuze's approach as beholden to an (implicitly outdated) paradigm adopted from classical film theory, particularly with regard to the importance placed on montage as the differentiating feature of the primitive and post-primitive cinemas.

It seems worth noting, however, that the distinction Deleuze offers between these two 'origins' is contingent, rather than necessary. The 'primitive state' he refers to always remains as a possibility even in the most modern of films (the camera, after all, can always not move, and within the confines of each individual shot there is no montage). That is to say, the boundary between primitive and post-primitive cinema is more permeable than it may at first seem, and the 'essence' of cinema Deleuze finds in montage and the mobility of the camera is already present in the primitive cinema as a power or potential waiting for its chance to appear (as the tale of Georges Méliès' 'accidental' discovery of the power of montage aptly demonstrates[69]). Thus,

> this movement [the concrete movement of the movement-image] was already characteristic of the cinema, and demanded a kind of emancipation, incapable of being satisfied within the limits set by the primitive conditions – so that the so-called primitive image, the image in movement, was defined less by its state than by its tendency.[70]

In other words, the cinematographic is given univocally with the cinematic, such that both the cinematographic illusion and its correction *coexist* as tendencies within the cinema at all times. More precisely, this illusion is merely a function of the arbitrary (non-necessary in the philosophical sense) limitation of the movement-images that Deleuze posits as the essence of the cinema – an essence which nevertheless only reveals itself as such once the point of view of the camera begins to diverge from that of the projector.[71]

Genesis and Deduction

Once we recognise Deleuze's discussion of the state of the primitive cinema as an elaboration of his distinction between the conditions of natural and cinematic perception, it becomes apparent that it plays a genuinely pivotal role in negotiating the relation between philosophy and cinema that both Bergson and Deleuze propose in their different ways. The implications of this distinction extend towards philosophy on one side and towards the cinema on the other. Where philosophy per se is concerned, Deleuze reformulates the account of the cinematographic illusion Bergson offers in *Creative Evolution* in terms of the movement-image proposed in *Matter and Memory*. In doing so, he merely foregrounds what is already implicit within the latter – that the essential limitation placed on living beings' grasp of being by the illusion Bergson later comes to call cinematographic is a function of the need for the living to act. In order to live, such beings must first of all distinguish themselves as a 'centre of action' within the acentred variation of being, and distinguish other beings as distinct elements in relation to that centre (especially those that might count as 'food').

One of the consequences of this is that the movement of the elements (or beings) thus extracted from being can then only be grasped abstractly and spatially, as a movement *of* those elements through space, and thus in terms divided from the concrete movement-for-itself of being. More succinctly, the cinematographic illusion is a function of the centring and stabilising character of natural perception, and the conditions of such perception are a function of the necessities of action. It is this necessity, then, that orients not only perception, but also language and thought, and thus philosophy. As Bergson puts it, 'Before we speculate we must live.'[72]

Having shown how natural perception can be both a product and function of movement-images *and* nevertheless subject to the cinematographic illusion at the same time (and thus having reconciled the apparent disjunction between the arguments of *Matter and Memory* and those of *Creative Evolution*), Deleuze is free to demonstrate how the cinema can also 'correct' this illusion without rejecting or denying its role in natural perception. This demonstration is simply the other face of the same argument, turned this time towards cinema rather than philosophy: if the conditions of natural perception orient it in terms of the centring and stabilising tendencies at the heart of the cinematographic illusion, it is precisely the *lack* of these conditions for cinematic perception that free it from this illusion. Deleuze points us towards the French filmmaker and film theorist Jean Epstein, who was perhaps the first to focus theoretically on this point, which viewers in the cinema experienced practically: not only speeded up, slowed down and reversed sequences, but the non-distancing of the moving body ('a deserter was going flat out, and yet remained face to face with us'), constant changes in scale and proportion ('with no possible common denominator') and false continuities of movement.[73]

The experiences Epstein describes are those of the viewer confronted in the cinema with the impossible (from the human perspective) perceptions of the camera, and with a movement that is aberrant because its image is no longer oriented in relation to a fixed centre (the camera is free to move as it wishes), all the while appearing for the viewer *as if* those images were given with reference to the viewer *as a centre*, since those images are projected from a point of view apparently identical with the viewer's own (that of the projector behind them in the cinema). In other words, the break between the points of view of camera and projector decentres perception for the viewer, despite retaining the appearance or form of natural perception (in so far as the aberrant images given to the viewer's perception nevertheless appear to come from the viewer's own centre of perception).

This is the basis of the cinema's capacity to decentre natural perception; in doing so it frees the viewer's perception from its cinematographic blinkers, and exposes it to a 'profoundly aberrant and abnormal movement' that opens onto the movement-image for itself, rather than the movement-image as grasped for themselves.[74] In short, if the cinematographic character of human nature is a function of the living being or brain/screen as a centred perspective on the acentred variation of being, the cinema offers a correction to that cinematographic perspective not because it is made of movement-images (such images make up the 'material moments of subjectivity' – they're what human cinematographic consciousness is made of too) but because it has the capacity to decentre perception, and to that extent open our 'human nature' to a genuine intuition of real being, real duration in its acentred variability.[75]

As I've noted, Douglass regards Deleuze's treatment of the relationship between the cinema and Bergson's own account of the cinematographic illusion as 'perverse', on quite specific grounds. Deleuze, he argues, completely transforms the nature and intent of Bergson's treatment of it by 'transferring the definition of Bergson's term "cuttings" from the frame to the shot'.[76] Although Douglass presents this observation as a criticism, it seems to me a graceful, succinct and accurate summation of Deleuze's argumentative manoeuvres around the relation of cinema to the cinematographic illusion, and one that is entirely consistent with my arguments so far. Rather than conceiving of cinematic movement as a function of the gap between *frames*, or static 'cuttings' of movement, Deleuze reformulates it in terms of the gap between *shots*, such that cinematic movement is properly understood as the movement of the camera in relation to the stasis of the projector, and not the movement of objects on screen (whose movement does remain cinematographic in precisely Bergson's sense).

By characterising the difference between natural and cinematic perception in terms of the difference between 'primitive' cinema and the essence revealed by the introduction of montage and the mobile camera, Deleuze does not, as Douglass suggests, 'perversely' redefine the cinematographic illusion in order to present Bergsonian philosophy as cinematic in essence. Far from erasing or 'overwriting' Bergson's own account, Deleuze's version retains the cinematographic illusion precisely as the former characterises it, and extends the logic of his argument to include elements that Bergson himself, writing in the 'primitive' phase of the cinema, would have had difficulty foreseeing – to be specific, the elements of montage and the mobility of the camera.[77] Moreover, Deleuze not only deals with these new elements in strictly Bergsonian terms (albeit those of *Matter and Memory* rather than *Creative Evolution*), he does so without replacing or distorting the terms in which Bergson himself does explicitly treat the cinema.

From 'Primitive' Cinema to Real Movement

Deleuze makes it clear that the cinematographic illusion *as Bergson describes it* does indeed describe the conditions of the 'primitive' cinema and remains at the very least implicit within *all* cinema – the film strip and its static frames are not conjured away by an argumentative sleight of hand on Deleuze's part. Rather, the attention Deleuze gives to the role of montage in breaking cinema from the conditions of natural perception reproduced in the primitive cinema enables him to define the terms of a cinematic thought which is non-human in principle – a thought which is no longer constitutively separated from being – on the very same basis by which Bergson accounts for the epistemological limits of all-too-human thought.

In other words, he shows that the cinematographic illusion, far from proffering a critique of the cinema, is deduced on the basis *of* the cinema in strictly Bergsonian terms, without that illusion defining the possibilities the cinema offers to philosophy. And Deleuze does so in terms that apply equally to both Bergson's characterisation of the cinematographic illusion in *Creative Evolution* and to Deleuze's own 'reformulation' of that illusion in the more complex terms implied in *Matter and Memory*. The capacity of the cinema to separate the point of view of the camera from that of the projector (and thus of the viewer) offers cinematic thought the means to overcome or escape those limits and illusions in both cases. I would argue that Bergson's use of the cinematograph to illustrate the illusion in question has been something of a red herring and has led commentators astray when exploring the relation between cinema and that illusion, since within the cinema itself (whether primitive or post-primitive) it arises and is overcome in terms not of the still frames of the film strip, but in those of the identity or disjunction of the point of view of camera and projector. And it's worth noting that Bergson coins his cinematographic metaphor at a time when the cinema was largely characterised by the coincidence and identity of camera and projector as one and the same piece of equipment. Had the mobile camera been commonplace earlier, he may have framed his metaphor differently.

One of the consequences of Deleuze's argument is that the cinema is in a sense both cinematographic and cinematic *at the same time* – both abstract and real movement may 'appear' on screen simultaneously, because they are produced by distinct means that nevertheless both belong to the cinema. The 'correction' the cinema offers of the cinematographic illusion does not take the form of a replacement, effacement or even negation of that illusion. Rather, the cinema presents us with both illusory and real movement at the same time. As we have seen, Bergson accounts for both the objective character of being and our subjective experience of it in terms of a double system of articulation of one and the same reality: the objective reality of the movement-for-itself of being on the one hand, and on the other the subjective reality of that same movement when it is grasped in relation to a centred perspective that arises in the same terms as being itself (that is, as an image). In so far as it begins in its primitive state with a reproduction of the conditions of natural perception (it starts with and from a 'human' or centred perspective) the cinema traces this passage 'in reverse'. It starts from the centre (the subjective and relative movement-for-someone given in terms of the camera/projector that replaces the viewer's own point of view), and from this starting point, the cinema then 'returns' such perception to the absolute or objective reality of movement-for-itself. It thereby opens this centred perception to the acentred universal variation of being – that is to say, to the pure perception-for-itself of Bergson's first system of articulation. As we have seen, it does this by virtue of the aberrant movement of the camera (via montage or the camera's own mobility) in relation to the static point of view of the viewer/projector.

Bergson thus *accounts* for or deduces movement-for-someone in abstract terms as an arbitrary limitation of the movement-for-itself of being. But through the introduction of montage and the mobile camera, the cinematographic movement presented in the cinema's primitive state is revealed as an arbitrary limitation of the real movement that is always implicit in the cinema, as its potential or essence. Thus the cinema 'overcomes' the cinematographic conditions of the viewer's natural perception (overcomes the human) to reveal beyond it the movement-image as a mobile section of movement-for-itself, which opens onto the indefinite elsewhere of the open whole of being. It traces in reverse the 'descent' of beings from being – and as such it has at least the potential to open up or reveal to thought and to philosophy their limits with regard to the thought of being.

Consider, for example, the most obvious and familiar type of movement the cinema offers us, which is the movement of bodies across the screen – a train pulling into a station, workers leaving a factory and so on – a movement that is 'still attached to people or things'[78] rather than movement in and for itself. All that we see in such movement is the reordering of the elements of the set defined by the boundaries of the shot. This is what Deleuze calls 'relative' movement:[79] cinematographic movement, abstract movement, movement understood as equivalent to the line drawn by the passage of a body from A to B. Such movement is an aspect of any film in which people or things act within the world and on each other – which is to say, it is to be found in the vast majority of the cinema.[80]

Bergson sees only this sort of movement in the cinema, but Deleuze, looking beyond the cinema's 'primitive' state, sees coexisting with it another type of movement given not in terms of the translation of elements in space, but rather by the *transformation of relations* between those elements effected in terms of montage and the mobile camera. The essence of the movement-image, he says, 'lies in extracting from vehicles or moving bodies the movement which is their common substance, or extracting from movements [the

movement still attached to things] the mobility that is their essence
... pure movement extracted from bodies or moving things'.[81]

Such movement is absolute, rather than relative, and expresses the universal variation of being itself – but it is worth emphasising that this movement is something that cinema must *extract* from moving bodies by means of its own formal capacities.[82] In other words, it is the formal operation of the cinema that reveals the absolute movement (the essence of movement) of which the merely relative movement the translation of bodies in space presents to us is a mere abstraction.

What Deleuze proposes is not a choice between these two options, between relative and absolute movement, but rather a recognition that the former is merely a limited case of the latter, derived or deduced from rather than opposed to it.[83] We might understand this in practical terms as follows: irrespective of any montage or camera mobility, whenever we focus on the movement of bodies on screen in terms of their translation in space (on the 'content' of the shot) – whenever we emphasise the similarity between our own natural perception and what we see at the movies – we emphasise a properly cinematographic and abstract movement which is *always* there in the cinema as a possibility (and most often as an actuality), whether that cinema is 'primitive' or not. At the very least we can say that this kind of cinematographic movement is given to us whenever the camera is static and we consider the individual shot in 'isolation' from the other shots that make up the film in question. This may seem an overly qualified set of conditions on which to base the claim that it appears throughout all cinema, but I would argue that under most circumstances this relative movement tends to be what we habitually notice and keep *first of all*, irrespective of any other type of movement that may also be present. Such movement – the movement 'attached to people or things' – is 'familiar' because it resembles the movement given to us under the conditions of natural perception.

If our attention is drawn to this, rather than to the absolute movement Deleuze argues is also given in 'post-primitive' cinema, this is because our natural habits of perception make it easier to see and recognise – more 'obvious'. However, if this is all we see, we neglect the real or concrete movement that always coexists with it (although produced by distinct means) at the level of film form itself. Nevertheless, to recognise this real movement, beyond the habits of natural perception, requires a genuine break with the conditions that shape our properly human experience of the world (and not just cinema) and to that extent at least, a break with the human or human nature. This is of course exactly what attracts Deleuze to the cinema, but it seems worth acknowledging that for all that cinema may invite or even demand this break, it cannot require that we recognise and *acknowledge* it.

Were it to be otherwise – were cinema in fact able to *require* that we see and recognise real movement against our own 'human nature' – we would, after all, be left with the tricky task of explaining why it took nearly a hundred years of cinema for someone (Deleuze) to notice this, and write an account of how and why it might be so. Of course, part of Deleuze's argument throughout the *Cinema* books is that certain filmmakers and thinkers have indeed to some degree or other recognised this power of cinema, offered various partial, overlapping and conflicting accounts of its sources and exploited aspects of it in their work.[84] But if they have recognised and expressed it to some degree or other, it has been left to Deleuze to 'extract' it from their work and express it conceptually.

The distinction between relative (or abstract) and absolute (or real) movement is integral to *Cinema 1*'s second chapter, 'Frame and Shot, Framing and Cutting',[85] in which Deleuze seems to shift his focus from Bergson's theses on movement to the analysis of the formal elements of cinema itself. However, this is in fact a continuation of Deleuze's response to the philosophical problems posed or implied in his discussion of Bergson's three theses on movement. And as we shall see, this analysis ultimately offers us an answer to the conundrum of how an image that moves can nevertheless 'impose fixed instantaneous views' while also expressing movement as real duration. The most obvious feature of this chapter is the definition and analysis of the basic elements of film form: frame, shot and montage. However, embedded in this account of features proper to the cinema are the details of his philosophical argument demonstrating the univocity of qualitative and quantitative difference, and of the cinematographic illusion and cinema.

If we consider the simplest example, that of the static shot where frame and shot are identical, such a shot defines the contents of a set – the set of the elements within it, the people, bodies, that appear on screen within the frame. Considered in itself, such a set is closed, in so far as it contains a definite number of distinct elements. These elements – the people and things that occupy the shot – may certainly change their position within the space of the frame, but such change is merely relative, a reordering of elements expressing a difference of degree rather than a difference in kind.[86] If one considers such a shot/set in relation to that which exists 'beyond' its borders (either in terms of the shots which come before or after, or of the 'out of field' of the frame – that which does not appear on screen, but is 'implied' above or below or to either side of the frame), its relation to the next shot (and the next and the next) may be considered strictly additive – the contents of each shot/set merely combine to form a larger set, including more and more elements, equivalent to a simple expansion of the frame to contain what was previously 'out of field'.

From this perspective, the 'out of field' and the shots that come before and after are in principle of the same order: they merely add to the set defined by the shot without changing it qualitatively. Whether this addition takes place through a direct expansion of that shot (by the widening of the frame to incorporate more and more of what was formerly out of field) or by adding a new set or sets to it (each of the shots before and after), 'when a set is framed, therefore seen, there is always a larger set, or another set with which the first forms a larger one, and which in turn can be seen, on condition that it forms a new out-of-field, etc.'[87] This expansion is potentially infinite, but as Deleuze points out, however far it goes it can never constitute a whole, or rather *the* whole. To do so would define the whole itself as a set and thereby set in motion Russell's paradox of the set of all sets. Such a set must either include itself (thus constituting a new set which must be included in the set of all sets, which also must be included and so on *ad infinitum*) or not (in which case it does not contain all sets). In either case the set of all sets fails to define its own contents, and thus fails to be identical to itself, fails to be the set of all sets.

This in turn allows Deleuze to provide a properly ontological characterisation of the whole as the open, which is not a spatial determination, but 'relates back to time or even to spirit rather than to content and to space'.[88] Given the paradoxical character of the concept of the set of all sets, Deleuze concludes that the whole is therefore 'not a set and does not have parts. It is rather that which prevents each set, however big it is, from closing in on itself.'[89] In other words, sets contain only actual elements, distinct things, bodies, people – quantities of things which can be subdivided or multiplied to infinity without changing in kind – but the whole is *qualitatively* different from those contents. It neither constitutes nor can be considered as a totality, either in principle or in fact, since it has no determinable contents (it is not a set). It is neither numerically nor spatially finite *or* infinite (the infinitely large can always be reached spatially or numerically, at least in principle, by the continuous addition of one thing to another).

The whole is never 'present' or visible in any given shot or combination of shots. It does not exist as such, but rather subsists or insists as 'a more radical Elsewhere, outside homogeneous space and time . . . [whose function] is that of introducing the transspatial and the spiritual into a system which is never perfectly closed'.[90] The whole, then, is properly virtual, rather than actual. Having no actual elements or terms to differ from each other, it is rather the continuous variation of being itself, the unlimited universe of light 'before' the arbitrary and cinematographic limitation that the interval of the brain/screen imposes on it. In other words, the whole Deleuze refers to here is simply being in its difference from itself: 'The whole is that which changes – it is the open or duration.'[91] The relation of the shot to that which is 'beyond' it thus has

> two qualitatively different aspects: a relative aspect by means of which a closed system refers in space to a set which is not seen, and which can in turn be seen, even if this gives rise to a new unseen set, on to infinity; and an absolute aspect by which the closed system opens onto a duration which is immanent to the whole universe, which is no longer a set and does not belong to the order of the visible.[92]

Thus although these two aspects of movement are qualitatively different, neither are they separate or distinct. Once again, this is a function of the difference between the two kinds of difference in question here. Relative movement is a function of quantitative and spatial difference, or difference in degree. But as we have seen, no matter how far such a difference is extended (no matter how large the set becomes), it can never give rise to a difference capable of accounting for the differences in difference itself. That is, quantitative difference can never extend itself all the way to a qualitative difference – no matter how far the frame is expanded, it can never become or attain the whole.

The reverse, however, is not true. Because qualitative difference is not given in terms of difference in degree, but rather manifests all the degrees of difference itself, it differs from itself *all the way to difference in degree*. In other words, the absolute movement expressed in the transformation of the open whole differs from itself all the way to the relative movement manifest in the translation of elements within a set. Taken on its own, relative movement is merely spatial and cinematographic; understood in relation to the whole that subtends it, it expresses an aspect of the change in that whole, and thus is a 'mobile section of duration'. Absolute movement as qualitative difference thus 'bridges the gap' between the relative and the absolute by means of its own difference from itself. As Deleuze puts it,

> the whole is therefore that which prevents each set, however big it is, from closing in on itself, and that which forces it to extend itself into a larger set. The whole is therefore like a thread which traverses sets [without ever being a member of them] and gives each one the possibility, which is necessarily realised, of communicating with another, to infinity.[93]

This 'thread' is the concrete expression of the univocity of being itself (of the univocity of relative with absolute movement; of the cinematographic with the cinematic; of identity with difference) and thus of the procedure by which identity and negation (which are characteristics or derived in terms of sets and their elements, but not of the whole) can be accounted for in the purely positive terms of difference. The openness of the whole – its difference from itself – allows it to 'descend' all the way into the merely relative difference found in closed systems or sets. It thereby forces those sets to remain open, both relatively and spatially in terms of their capacity to extend themselves into larger and larger sets, onto infinity, *and* absolutely and temporally as an expression of an aspect of the duration or change of the whole: 'a closed system [a set] is never absolutely closed; but on the one hand it is connected in space to other systems [sets] by a more or less "fine" thread, and on the other hand it is integrated or reintegrated into a whole which transmits a duration to it along this thread'.[94]

Given the 'everyday' character of the relative movement described within the frame, there is no difficulty in translating Deleuze's abstract description of the 'modification' of the respective positions of the elements of a set into terms immediately recognisable to someone sitting in the local multiplex: on screen in front of us a car pulls up and someone gets out, a plane flies overhead, a can rolls down the hill ... This sort of movement is all too familiar, since it simply mirrors the cinematographic tendencies of our own natural perception. But what of the absolute movement that subtends these relative movements? How is it made manifest in the cinema itself – how can we 'see' it – given that it 'does not belong to the order of the visible' and belongs properly to a whole that is never present as such?

The answer turns on the dual character of the shot, in so far as the relation between relative and absolute movement is expressed formally within the cinema via the 'intermediate' status of the shot between the two poles of framing and montage.[95] Facing 'inwards' towards the frame, the shot delimits the contents of a determinate set and manifests a movement which is only relative; facing outwards towards the cut between itself and the shots that come before or after, it follows the 'thread' of duration that links it to the whole, such that 'The shot is movement considered from this dual point of view: the translation of the parts of a set which spreads out in space, the change of a whole which is transformed in duration.'[96] In other words, absolute movement, the non-cinematographic movement that attracts Deleuze to the cinema, is a function of montage.[97]

Thus the dual face of the shot, turned on one side towards both the set, and on the other towards montage, also mirrors in reverse the 'double régime of reference of images' through which Bergson accounts for the objective reality of movement and our subjective abstraction of it. Turned towards the set, the shot defines the elements that constitute that set *as* elements, as images-for-someone, but turned towards montage, the shot opens onto the whole, the universal variation of being itself, and thus links the abstract movement of those elements to the movement-in-itself, or duration, of being.

But *how* does montage express a transformation in the whole as duration itself, rather than a mere translation of elements in space? If absolute movement is not the movement attached to elements, things, people, bodies on screen, if it is neither visible nor present, then how is it given to us to *experience* in the cinema? Although the movement of the elements present on screen may be spatial and visible, the *relations* between those elements are not. As Deleuze reminds us, 'Relation is not a property of objects, it is always external to its terms.'[98] In other words, relations between actual things can never be reduced to an attribute of one thing or another, but exist 'between' them. Since it can never be distinguished as an element in itself, or as an attribute of an element on its own, this relation must be understood as strictly virtual rather than actual, and as dynamic rather than static (it has no 'identity'). It is in terms of relations that things, as elements of a closed set, nevertheless remain connected to the open whole or being.

Imagine a herd of hungry cattle standing in a field denuded of grass;[99] it moves to the next field, where the grass is lush and green, to feed. The path beaten by the cattle's hooves traces their movement in space as a line on the ground, but if this is all we grasp of it, we comprehend movement only in its relative, spatial and abstract aspects. In the movement of the herd from one field to the next, the relations expressed between these elements are also transformed, from (say) hunger and desire where there is no grass, to satiety where there is. These qualities are not attributes of the herd, or of the presence or absence of grass, but rather are an expression of the relations of these elements to each other and to their environment, to the whole that they exist within. If the world of the herd consisted simply of the farm on which they live, with its several fields (if they lived within a closed set), their movement from one patch of grass to the next would be mere translation in space; but on the other side of the fence, that farm opens onto the world, onto the whole, which is not a set, which cannot be given in advance, because its being is transformation itself, a constant creation of the new: 'if the whole is not giveable, it is because it is the open, and because its nature is to change constantly, or to give rise to something new, in short, to endure'.[100] The transformation in relations in question is a function of the herd's movement only in so far as that movement expresses an aspect of change in the whole – movement grasped as a mobile section of duration, rather than in terms of a line beaten on the earth.

Nancy (glossing Deleuze) draws out this tension between translation and transformation in cinematic movement in his discussion of the films of Abbas Kiarostami.

> But what is the motion that, in this way, is cinema (and neither its object nor what it represents or restores, as goes the belief of those who see cinema wholly as an 'animated feature')? Motion is that which 'only occurs if the whole is neither given nor giveable.' Motion is not a displacing or a transferring, which may occur between given places in a totality that is itself given. On the contrary, it is what takes place when a body is in a situation and a state that compel it to find its place, a place it consequently has not had or no longer has. I move (in matter or mind) when I am not – ontologically – where I am – locally. Motion carries me elsewhere but the 'elsewhere' is not given beforehand: my coming will make of it the 'there' where I will have come from 'here.'[101]

Movement as transformation is an act of creation, of 'myself' and of the world, in the transformation of relations between 'elements' that open those elements onto the unceasing variation and creation of being itself. Relation thus manifests the 'thread' of duration that links the cinematographic to the cinematic, abstract movement to real movement, the actual to the virtual, the set to the whole. In other words, it is in terms of relations that Deleuze is able to demonstrate, rather than merely assert, the immanence of the first term of each of these dyads to the second, and it is in terms of relation that we must understand the whole.

> If one had to define the whole, it would be defined by Relation ... It [relation] is also inseparable from the open, and displays a spiritual or mental existence ... Relations do not belong to objects, but to the whole, on condition that this is not confused with a closed set of objects. By movement in space, the objects of a set change their respective positions. But, through relations, the whole is transformed or changes qualitatively. We can say of duration itself or of time, that it is the whole of relations.[102]

Montage (as the aspect of the shot turned 'outwards' towards the whole) thus expresses a *transformation* in the state of the whole rather than the *translation* of elements in space. It is 'the operation which bears on the movement-images to release the whole from them, that is, the image *of* time. It is a necessarily indirect image, since it is deduced from movement-images and their relationships'.[103] Take, for example, a scene of conversation between two people presented in a shot-reverse-shot structure, in which the alternation of shots (that is to say, the movement of the camera position) expresses something like the change from 'looking' to 'being looked at', or 'seeing' to 'being seen'. Although it is rare for such a scene to be filmed so that the alternating perspectives of the camera are tied *directly* to the subjective point of view of the characters themselves, it is very common for the camera to 'side' more or less with the perspective of one character, and then the other, by shooting over their shoulder (often with them partially in frame).[104] Although such a sequence is properly speaking indirect and objective in style, it nevertheless offers an alternating alignment of emphasis from each character's point of view, and variations in the angle of alignment, framing and length of shot can all be used to articulate the internal dynamics of this relationship, all the while placing them within a world whose movement their relationship is inextricably tied to, expresses and is an aspect of. The change in relations expressed here is literally the change in the protagonists relationship that takes place throughout the conversation (they fall in love, betray each other, plan a murder. . .).

Alternatively, consider a scene which opens with a wide shot of the locale in which the action will take place (the 'establishing shot') then moves to a closer but still objective and indirect shot which draws our attention to a specific character within that environment, and then cuts to a subjective and direct shot from that character's point of view, and thus as it relates to or impacts on the character and their goals or actions. The variability of perspective imposed on the viewer by montage means that, rather than their status as a centre of perception providing the common denominator according to which the elements of world are composed or divided into sets, the viewer is subject to a

> pure movement [that] varies the elements of the set by dividing them up into fractions with different denominators [different perspectives or points of view] – because it decomposes and recomposes the set – that it also relates to a fundamentally open whole, whose essence is to 'become' or to change . . . [Jean] Epstein comes closest to the concept of the shot: it is a mobile section, that is, a temporal perspective or a modulation.[105]

It is the composition of these variable temporal perspectives in montage that brings pure movement to light, by varying the relations between the elements of the world, dividing and joining, decomposing and recomposing them according to 'different denominators', rather than according to the common denominator imposed by the centred point of view of natural perception.

The mobile camera perhaps presents a more complex case, since both persons and camera can move, and thus change their perspective – why, in this case, would the cinema offer anything that natural perception cannot? It is not enough to merely note that cameras may move in ways persons generally do not – for example, the technical apparatus that allows such camera moves could, at least in principle, be adapted to move a person in similar ways (on a dolly, a crane, a helicopter and so on). What we must keep in mind is that it is not the camera's movement in space (no matter how unusual it might be from a human perspective) that underlies its capacity to show real rather than abstract movement. Rather, it is the disjunction between the point of view of the camera and that of the viewer/projector in the cinema that constitutes the decisive breach in the conditions of natural perception for the viewer, and thus surpasses the cinematographic limits of human perception and thought: it is not the mobility of the camera with respect to the objects it captures that gives us real movement, *but its mobility with respect to the point of view of the projector.*

If we consider montage from the perspective of the transformation of relations that it effects, we can see why Deleuze aligns it with the mobility of the camera, even though the latter produces a movement that strictly speaking takes place within the confines of the shot itself, rather than between shots. A mobile shot, rather than simply

Genesis and Deduction

determining the elements of a set, effects a transformation in the relations between those elements rather than a mere translation in space, and thus expresses an aspect of duration itself – or at least has the capacity to do so. Deleuze offers the example of such a shot from Alfred Hitchcock's *Frenzy* (1972):

> the camera follows a man and a woman who climb a staircase and arrive at a door that the man opens; then the camera leaves them, and draws back in a single shot. It runs along the external wall of the apartment, comes back to the staircase that it descends backward, coming out on to the pavement, and rises up the exterior up to the opaque window of the apartment seen from outside. This movement, which modifies the relative position of immobile sets, is only necessary if it expresses something in the course of happening, a change in the whole which it itself transmitted through these modifications: the woman is being murdered. She went in free, but cannot expect any help – the murder is inexorable.[106]

The implicit distinction Deleuze makes here between a camera movement which is 'necessary' and one which is merely arbitrary, tells us that the transformation of relations that surpasses the limits of human perception is not an automatic function of the moving camera, but is simply a potential or power the mobile camera has at its disposal (one need only think of the hyperkinetic, but narratively and conceptually insignificant, camera movement characteristic of much contemporary action cinema to recognise what an 'arbitrary' camera movement of the kind Deleuze hints at might look like in practice). This potential coexistence of arbitrary and necessary camera mobility is merely an aspect of the coexistence of the cinematographic and the cinematic Deleuze proposes.

Nevertheless, if, with Deleuze, we define montage in terms of the transformation of relations effected between shots, then the mobile camera in effect constitutes a kind of montage *internal to the shot itself*, as if there were montage between each single frame of the film strip itself: when the camera itself moves, each individual 'photogramme' presents an imperceptibly different 'angle' on the world, continuously decomposing and recomposing it, 'dividing it into fractions with different denominators' whose cumulative effect across the length of the shot is to make visible a transformation in and of that world, in and of the whole.

If, as Deleuze says, the *Cinema* books are the product of a 'natural' movement from philosophy to cinema, it is not simply because the images of the cinema move. Rather, the ontological speculations of philosophy find themselves reflected in the cinema because being itself is already cinematic in nature, such that the movement we find in the cinema does not reproduce or represent the movement of the world so much as it simply *is* that movement. As Rancière puts it, for Deleuze 'Images, properly speaking, are the things of the world. It follows logically from this that cinema is not the name of an art: it is the name of the world.'[107] The priority that Deleuze gives to the cinema over all other arts, and in some sense over philosophy, stems from this identity not only of cinema and world, but also of world and thought.

Just as importantly, the conditions under which the images of the cinema appear for the viewer break with the conditions of natural perception in a fashion that decentres thought's grasp of those images, and produces an abnormal and aberrant movement. Thus the identity of perception and consciousness both for-itself and for-someone that Deleuze proposes is such that, in breaking with the conditions of natural perception, the cinema breaks with the conditions of human thought in its cinematographic genesis. In doing so, it offers a properly cinematic consciousness in its place – a 'spiritual automaton' that opens onto the real movement, real duration and real thought of being. The 'place' here is literal: the projector re-places the viewer's point of view (their perception, and thus their consciousness) with a perception and consciousness of its own, offering a technical reproduction of the conditions of natural perception. But once the point of view of the camera breaks with that of the projector, these conditions are decentred, and both perception and consciousness become abnormal, aberrant – that is to say, non-cinematographic.

As we can now see, Deleuze's characterisation of the cinematographic illusion in the *Cinema* books is more complex and more subtle than is generally recognised. Likewise, its relevance to and roots within Deleuzian philosophy as a whole are deeper and have greater resonance throughout than it might at first seem. However, what we have seen so far is only the first layer of the full complexity of his treatment of that illusion and of the cinema's relation to it. As we will see in the next chapter, the terms in which Deleuze characterises the cinema's correction of the illusion not only enable the cinema to dramatise its consequences for philosophy and the history of philosophy in the cinema's own non-human terms, but also provide the basis on which the cinema is able to think the relation of the human to being itself as a problem for and of thought.

Notes

1. Deleuze, *Cinema 1*, 59.
2. Ibid., 60.
3. Although the deduction and the correction in question derives from quite distinct operations of these formal capacities.
4. It is privileged over the other arts in so far as it is the only form he deals with as a form (and not in terms of specific works or artists), while also insisting on its imbrication within other fields. And it is privileged over philosophy in the sense that Deleuze is 'compelled' to turn to cinema rather than philosophy to look for answers to philosophical problems. Deleuze, 'The Brain Is the Screen', 367.
5. Keith Ansell-Pearson points out that Bergson's arguments on this point must be understood as a counter to Kant's claim that there are 'only three possibilities for a theory of knowledge: (i) the mind is determined by external things [realism]; (ii) things are determined by the mind itself [idealism]; and (iii) between the mind and things we have a pre-established harmony [Kant's preferred option]. In contrast to these three options, Bergson seeks to demonstrate the need for a double genesis of matter and intellect.' As we shall see, the question of a genetic 'radicalisation' of Kantianism, as initially proposed by Solomon Maimon, has a direct bearing on Deleuze's interest in the cinema. Ansell-Pearson, 'Beyond the Human Condition', 61–2.
6. Bergson, *Matter and Memory*, 9.
7. The first sentence of the book reads: 'We will assume for the moment that we know nothing of theories of matter and theories of spirit, nothing of the discussions as to the reality or ideality of the external world. Here I am in the presence of images, in the vaguest sense of the word, images perceived when my senses are opened to them, unperceived when they are closed.' Ibid., 17.
8. Ibid., 9.
9. Deleuze, *Cinema 1*, 56.
10. Bergson, *Matter and Memory*, 10.
11. Deleuze, *Cinema 1*, 58.
12. Since, as Deleuze puts it, on that plane 'there are neither axes, nor centre, nor left, nor right, nor high, nor low'. Ibid., 58–9.
13. Ibid., 58.
14. Ibid., 59. Emphasis in original.
15. Bergson, *Matter and Memory*, 39.
16. Ibid., 34.
17. Marrati, *Gilles Deleuze: Cinema and Philosophy*, 32–3. Emphasis in original.
18. Deleuze, 'The Brain Is the Screen', 366.
19. It should be noted that both Bergson and Deleuze afford the term

'consciousness' a broader reference than its common usage, since any form of life at all, even the simplest, is conscious in their terms, such that we must take care not to conflate their references to consciousness with *self*-consciousness.
20. Bergson, *Matter and Memory*, 36.
21. Ibid., 37. We must, however, keep in mind here Deleuze's treatment of the relation of difference in kind and degree such that differences in degree are merely the greatest degree of difference in kind.
22. Worms, '*Matter and Memory* on Mind and Body', 93.
23. Bergson, *Matter and Memory*, 36.
24. Ibid., 38.
25. Deleuze, *Cinema 1*, 62.
26. Ibid.
27. Ibid., 61.
28. Deleuze, *Negotiations*, 60.
29. Deleuze, *Cinema 1*, xvi.
30. Ibid., 63.
31. Ibid., 66.
32. Although as we shall see, cinematic thought differs from human thought in so far as the formal and material capacities of the cinema allow it to overcome the limits of the human, and to produce a non-human account of human thought itself.
33. A distinction best captured in terms of differing of difference in kind all the way to difference in degree.
34. Deleuze, *Cinema 1*, 59–60.
35. Ibid., 64.
36. Ibid., 64–5.
37. Ibid., 65.
38. Ibid.
39. Ibid.
40. Bergson, *Matter and Memory*, 55–6.
41. Deleuze, *Cinema 1*, 102.
42. Ibid., 66.
43. Ibid., 65.
44. But not, it must be emphasised, to *the* movement-image as it exists for itself.
45. Bergson, *Creative Evolution*, 315.
46. Ibid., 303.
47. Ibid., 299–304. Deleuze acknowledges *Creative Evolution* as the source of these arguments in his endnotes. Deleuze, *Cinema 1*, 59–60, 226 n.13.
48. Bergson, *Creative Evolution*, 306–7. Emphasis in original.
49. Ibid., 297.
50. Ibid., 308–28.

Genesis and Deduction

51. Deleuze, *Cinema 1*, 57–8.
52. Ibid., 61.
53. It's important to point out here that Deleuze doesn't make a point of distinguishing between 'cinema' and 'cinematograph' as I have. As such his reference to 'cinematographic perception' in the quote referred to should be read as a reference to cinema itself, and not the cinematographic character of human or natural perception as *opposed* to cinematic perception.
54. Deleuze, *Cinema 1*, 2.
55. Ibid.
56. Ibid., 3.
57. Rodowick, *Gilles Deleuze's Time Machine*, 22 and more extensively, 216 n.2.
58. Douglass, 'Bergson and Cinema: Friends or Foes?', 220.
59. Ibid. Douglass' reference here to the 'cinematic' illusion makes it clear that he does not distinguish between the cinematographic illusion and the cinema as such.
60. Ibid., 221.
61. Deleuze, *Cinema 1*, 2.
62. Rodowick, *Gilles Deleuze's Time Machine*, 216 n.2.
63. Deleuze, *Cinema 1*, 2.
64. Ibid., 3.
65. Experimental installations utilising, for example, a moving projector notwithstanding.
66. Deleuze, *Cinema 1*, 25.
67. Ibid., 3.
68. Rodowick, *Gilles Deleuze's Time Machine*, 214 n.6.
69. Méliès describes shooting at the *Place de l'Opéra* with a very early film camera, which jammed and took a minute to unstick. During that time, he tells us, 'the passerby, a horse trolley, and the vehicles had of course changed positions. In projecting the strip, rejoined at the point of the break, I suddenly saw a Madeline-Bastille trolley change into a hearse, and men changed into women.' Méliès, 'Cinematographic Views', 30.
70. Deleuze, *Cinema 1*, 25.
71. One might usefully compare this 'arbitrary limitation' to the divorcing of the actual from its movement of actualisation, which, as we have seen, is the basis of the 'genesis' of errors of negation and the negative.
72. Bergson, *The Creative Mind*, 38.
73. Deleuze, *Cinema 2*, 36. Deleuze does not comment directly on what seem to me to be significant differences between the examples of 'speeded up, slowed down and reversed' movement, and the 'changes in scale and proportion' that Epstein offers us in this account. Where the latter present a clear case of movement that is aberrant in space, it

seems to me that the former present us with a movement that is aberrant not only in space but in time as well.
74. Ibid.
75. It seems worth noting that this 'decentring' applies equally with or without reference to the viewer. In so far as the projector replaces the audience's point of view with its own, it is the projector's perspective that is decentred no less than that of the audience. In other words, this decentring 'belongs' to the cinema before it 'belongs' to the viewer: for all that cinematic thought has the capacity to decentre the human, its operation is nevertheless autonomous *of* the human.
76. Douglass, 'Bergson and Cinema: Friends or Foes?', 220.
77. As noted, Bergson tells us that he was using the metaphor of the cinematographic illusion in his lectures at least five years before the publication of *Creative Evolution*. Bergson, *Creative Evolution*, 272 n.1.
78. Deleuze, *Cinema 1*, 25.
79. Ibid., 19.
80. Certain modes of experimental cinema might offer examples of exceptions to this dominant 'rule'. Take, for example, Stan Brakhage's hand-painted films or his *Mothlight* (1963), in which the image is the result of actual moth wings pressed between two long strips of tape, which were in turn run through an optical printer to produce the film strip itself. As we shall see in Chapter 6, experimental cinema (and specifically the American experimental cinema as exemplified by Brakhage) holds a quite distinctive place within Deleuze's taxonomy of cinematic signs by virtue of its particular treatment of cinematic movement.
81. Deleuze, *Cinema 1*, 23.
82. Ibid., 19.
83. In the same way and for the same reasons that external difference is deduced or derived from internal difference, the quantitative from the qualitative, or identity from difference.
84. For an example Deleuze doesn't point to, see Routt's argument that not only is the distinction between perception, affection and action-images in the cinema foreshadowed in 1915 in Vachel Lindsay's tripartite distinction between images of 'splendour', 'intimacy' and 'action' (in the latter's *The Art of the Moving Image*) but Lindsay's treatment of the cinema furthermore 'is underpinned by an understanding of existence as a forest of images not unlike that advanced in Henri Bergson's *Matter and Memory*'. Routt, 'The Madness of Images and Thinking Cinema'; Lindsay, *The Art of the Moving Picture*.
85. Deleuze, *Cinema 1*, 12–28.
86. As Bogue puts it, 'if we consider movement within a closed set we tend to see unchanging bodies shifting positions within a space-container'. *Deleuze on Cinema*, 26.

Genesis and Deduction

87. Deleuze, *Cinema 1*, 16.
88. Ibid., 17.
89. Ibid., 16. It seem to me that there is a complementary argument implicit here that Deleuze does not spell out. If the paradox of the set of all sets is that it necessarily fails to be identical to itself, then we could just as aptly say that such a set differs from itself. In other words the paradox inherent in set theory is one of the paradoxes of becoming, and takes us by its own means and in its own terms from distinct and determined elements (of sets) to pure and indeterminate difference as the condition of and for those elements. As counterintuitive as it might at first seem, then, Russell's 'set of all sets', from this perspective, can be read in this light as the equivalent of Bergson's 'open whole'.
90. Ibid., 17. Capitalisation follows original.
91. Ibid., 18.
92. Ibid., 17.
93. Ibid., 16.
94. Ibid., 17.
95. Ibid., 19.
96. Ibid., 20.
97. Ronald Bogue offers an excellent treatment of the relation between relative and absolute movement, closed sets and the open whole that corresponds closely with the one I have given above. However, he treats it in terms of the question of how we might 'see' the latter, or how it 'manifests itself in our commonsense world'. My point is that our 'commonsense world' is constructed precisely by the exclusion of real or absolute movement. Indeed, that is precisely the purpose and function of the cinematographic illusion and why we need the cinema to 'see' beyond it. *Deleuze on Cinema*, 25–8.
98. Deleuze, *Cinema 1*, 10.
99. I have borrowed the cows, but not the precise details of the analogy, from Deleuze, *Cinema 2*, 44–5.
100. Deleuze, *Cinema 1*, 9.
101. Nancy and Kiarostami, *The Evidence of Film*, 28.
102. Deleuze, *Cinema 1*, 10.
103. Ibid., 29.
104. To be more precise, this is done by placing the camera at an angle with respect to the favoured character of less than ninety degrees to the perpendicular of the eye-line running between the protagonists.
105. Deleuze, *Cinema 1*, 23–4.
106. Deleuze, *Cinema 1*, 19.
107. Rancière, *Film Fables*, 109.

6

The Thought of the World

Cinematic Aberration and the 'Great Kantian Reversal'

Whether we consider the 'primitive' cinema from the perspective of Bergson's characterisation of the cinematographic illusion in *Creative Evolution*, or from that of Deleuze's reformulation of that illusion in terms of movement-images, that cinema is strictly cinematographic in its orientation. It is the introduction of the formal resources of montage and camera mobility that propels the cinema into its 'post-primitive' phase and takes it 'beyond' the cinematographic illusion. In doing so, it leads the cinema to 'the conquest of its own essence or novelty',[1] and inaugurates narrative cinema, in so far as narration is, for Deleuze, a product of the combination of movement-images effected by montage.[2]

However, for all that these premises lay the foundations of Deleuze's Bergsonian treatment of the cinema, Deleuze is not yet done with the cinematographic illusion, or its consequences for both cinema and thought. As we shall see, narrative – specifically the narrative mode of the classical, pre-war cinema – reintroduces the effects of the cinematographic illusion at a new level: that of the relations between shots, rather than relations between the still photograms of the film strip. The terms in which narrative does so set the scene for the 'collapse' of the classical cinema itself, and thus for the 'impossible' break between it and the modern cinema (between the movement- and time-image, and between the two volumes of the *Cinema* books). Unfolding the terms of the classical cinema's trajectory towards this collapse, and this impossibility, is the task of this chapter.

Cinematic narration, as the mode of combination of movement-images, articulates the relationship of the arbitrarily closed set determined by the shot to the whole. In doing so, it also sets the terms of the relationship between the cinematographic, abstract and relative movement of the elements of that set, that shot, and the real, concrete and absolute movement of the whole. And given, as we

The Thought of the World

have seen, that the shot as movement-image is the direct cinematic correlate of the material moments of human subjectivity, narrative in these terms dramatises relations between merely human thought and being, in and by the non-human terms of the cinema itself. In other words, if, as Deleuze suggests, the cinema articulates the 'relationship between man and world, nature and thought'[3] *then narrative is the means by which it does so*. And in so far as ontological speculation necessarily takes the form of an exploration *of* being *by* beings from *within* being – philosophy thinking the relation between man and the world starting from its merely human perspective – then narrative, *as the composition of just such a relation*, constitutes its cinematic equivalent.

However, what merely human philosophy lacks, and what the cinema possesses by virtue of the decentring of natural perception effected in montage and the mobile camera, is the capacity to manifest the thread that links the centred perspective offered by movement-images to the acentred variation of *the* movement-image[4] concretely. Moreover, unlike human perception, thought and language, the cinema does this as a function of its own nature or 'essence'. And in so far as it does so, it reveals the univocity of the cinematographic illusion with the real movement and duration of being – the non-human thought of the cinema thinking (articulating, reproducing) the limits of human thought from beyond those limits. Thus if the cinema recapitulates the history of philosophy 'in speeded up form',[5] it is able to do so in so far as there are as many modes of narration as there are modes of composition of movement-images. Different modes of composition of images – of montage – constitute speculative constructions of differing conceptions of the whole and of our relation to it, different ways of thinking the relation between man and the world. As Deleuze puts it 'since the most ancient philosophy, there have been many ways in which time can be conceived as a function of movement, in relation to movement, in various arrangements. We are likely to come across this variety again in the different "schools" of montage.'[6]

It is in this sense that the cinema is an 'experimental brain' or spiritual automaton, and that specific instances of the cinema constitute or enter into different forms of ontological speculation that parallel those found in the history of philosophy. Deleuze does not suggest that there is a one-to-one correlation between the history of philosophy and that of the cinema; the overall trajectory may be same, but the cinema enters into that movement by its own means, and in its own terms. He does on occasion link the films collected under the respective signs of his cinematic taxonomy to particular philosophical approaches and perspectives, and sometimes even identifies specific filmmakers with specific philosophical approaches (most directly in his description of Eisenstein as the 'cinematic Hegel'[7]). However, the passage where Deleuze compares the histories of philosophy and cinema does specify one direct correlation, albeit a pivotal one. While the classical cinema corresponds to philosophical perspectives that subordinate time to movement,

> it is possible that, since the war, a direct time-image has been formed and imposed on the cinema. We do not wish to say that there will no longer be any movement, but that – just as happened a very long time ago in philosophy – a reversal has happened in the movement–time relationship in which it is no longer time which is related to movement, it is the anomalies of movement which are dependent on time.[8]

Where philosophy is concerned, this is what Deleuze refers to in his book on Kant as the 'great Kantian reversal', in which 'it is no longer a question of defining time by succession, nor space by simultaneity, nor permanence by eternity . . . [time] is not an eternal form, but in fact the form of that which is *not* eternal, the immutable form of change and movement'.[9] This reversal plays a central role in Deleuze's resolution of the philosophical problem he turns to the cinema to resolve. We will examine this connection in detail in the next chapter. For now, what is of interest is that this reversal, in so far as it belongs to the cinema, reveals a deep-seated tension in the argument of the *Cinema* books themselves. Specifically, it points towards a conflict in the terms in which the relationship between cinema and the cinematographic illusion is presented *Cinema 1* and in *Cinema 2* respectively.

In the former, while establishing the Bergsonian basis for his treatment of the cinema, he argues that it is the disjunction of camera and projector that provides the cinema with the means or capacity to overcome, to contain and to explain the cinematographic illusion. Specifically, the introduction of montage and the mobile camera produces an aberration of movement that opens the closed set of the shot to the open whole, or duration as unceasing variation. It is on this basis that Deleuze is able to claim that the cinema 'thinks' in terms of real, rather than abstract, movement. This implies that the classical cinema should operate in terms of real movement no less than the modern, since it is montage and the mobile camera that inaugurate the era of the classical cinema. In *Cinema 2*, however, the terms in which the mode of narration of the classical cinema comes to be defined (montage as the composition of movement-image according to sensory-motor schemata), and the relation that is then posited between it and modern cinematic narration, suggest that it is *here* that the cinematographic illusion finds its 'correction' and is revealed as a limited and abstract perspective on being as it exists for itself, as we shall see.

The classical cinema is characterised by what Deleuze calls 'rational' linkages between shots, whose coherence is ensured by the composition of movement-images according to a sensory-motor schema – in other words, perception and action are coordinated according to relations of cause and effect. Rational movement and coherent causality require and imply an ordered and linear passage of time from one moment to the next; this is a spatialised conception of movement in which the passage of time is grasped in terms analogous to the static divisions of a clock face.

Take, for example, a hypothetical sequence of two shots edited together: a static close up of the timer on a bomb counting down towards zero in the basement of an anonymous building, followed by a wide shot of a man running at speed down the middle of a crowded city street. There is no direct or overt link between these shots – the spaces they occupy share no physical connection, there is no cut on movement or graphic match to link them formally, the point of view and scale of each shot are different. In other words, the passage from one to the other ought in principle to produce aberrant movement.

What prevents this from happening is precisely the imposition of a linear progression of time, and a spatialised conception of movement derived from it, marked by the counting down of the timer. The images of the bomb and the running man are linked as cause and effect via the imposition of a linear progression, and thus spatialisation, of time. The man's desperate movement is measured by his progress towards the bomb in space, and the end of its countdown in time: he is running to get to the bomb in time to defuse it. Ordered in this fashion, the two shots constitute a minimal *narrative* in the mode of the classical cinema. What was aberration in relation to montage alone thus becomes rational in so far as montage is ordered according to this sensory-motor schema, and this schema constructs movement in cinematographic terms.[10]

Thus rather than aberrant movement being a function of montage from the earliest moments of the post-primitive cinema (and therefore an aspect of the classical cinema in its entirety), the classical cinema recentres the aberrant movement the cinema itself produces through the imposition of sensory-motor schemata as a principle for the organisation of images. The appearance of aberrant movement then emerges in the cinema as a result of the *collapse* of such schemata, which release or give rise to the 'anomalies of movement which are dependent on time'[11] that are characteristic of the modern cinema of the time-image. This is the 'great Kantian reversal' of the relation between time and movement Deleuze finds in the post-war cinema.

We are thus left with two apparently contradictory and incompatible accounts of the cinema's 'correction' of the cinematographic illusion. On the one hand this illusion is overcome in terms valid for the whole of 'post-primitive' cinema, in the production of aberrant movement via montage. On the other, it is corrected in terms valid for the modern cinema alone, via the anomalies of movement produced by the collapse of the rational and causal linking of images that characterised the classical cinema. How can we account for this conflict while maintaining the validity of both (since to do otherwise would be to put the argument of the *Cinema* books as a whole in disarray)?

Deleuze draws our attention to this problem early in *Cinema 2* when he notes that the characteristic features of the time-image were already apparent in the early stages of the classical cinema. How then, he asks, 'are we to delineate a modern cinema which would be distinct from "classical" cinema or from the indirect representation of time?'[12] His answer is that the aberrations of movement produced by the disjunction of camera and projector were recognised at this stage, but 'warded off' via the introduction of sensory-motor schemata as a principle of composition of images. Although, on the one hand, the decentring effects of this disjunction introduces a 'disproportion' between a received movement and an executed movement (a perception-image and an action-image), on the other, such schemata work to *re*centre the cinema, not at the level of individual images or shots,[13] but at the level of the relationship *between* shots. That is to say, the gap or interval between shots is ordered such that the relationship between perception and action is constrained to causal and coherent linkages from one to the next:

> what was aberration in relation to the movement-image ceases to be so in relation to these two images [perception and action-images]: the interval [between received and executed movement] now plays the role of centre,

and the sensory-motor schema restores the lost proportion, re-establishes it in a new mode between perception and action.[14]

The centred perspective of natural perception disrupted by montage and the mobile camera is thus restored in this 'new mode' in terms of the linkage of perception and action in terms of cause and effect, which ensures the commensurability of relations between shots. Movement is 'saved' from its aberration by becoming relative rather than absolute,[15] by being restored to a translation in space that is also a spatialisation of time – an indirect image of time as a function of movement, rather than a direct image of time, duration, transformation for itself. In other words, while the decentring effects of montage do indeed 'correct' the cinematographic illusion and provide the cinema with the means or capacity to express real movement (to produce the cinematic equivalent of Bergsonian intuition), the organisation of montage in the classical cinema according to sensory-motor schemata 'wards off' this correction by *recentring* cinematic perception, reimposing the cinematographic illusion at the level of the relation between shots, rather than that of the identity of the point of view of camera and projector.

Deleuze notes that in philosophy, 'aberrations of movement were recognised at an early stage . . . [but] were in some sense corrected, normalised, "elevated" and brought in line with laws which . . . maintained the subordination of time'.[16] In the same fashion, sensory-motor schemata suppress aberration and subordinate time to movement by constraining relations between images to rational, causal and linear links, which reimpose a centred and thus cinematographic perspective at the level of montage, rather than the shot. For philosophy, the history of this suppression lasts centuries ('from the Greeks to Kant'[17]). The cinema repeats this trajectory in 'more fast-moving circumstances',[18] such that the 'great Kantian reversal' of the relation between movement and time occurs within the cinema in the collapse of such schemata, allowing real movement to appear once more. However, the relationship between the real movement of being and the merely human and cinematographic thought this reversal articulates is more complex than the simple overcoming or surpassing of the limits of the human that Bergsonian intuition requires. Rather than giving rise to thought as a power adequate to the real movement of being (the thought of the whole as the open), the modern cinema – the cinema of the time-image – gives rise to the confrontation of thought with its own 'inpower' (*impouvoir*),[19] its 'powerlessness to think the whole and to think oneself, thought which is always fossilized, dislocated, collapsed'.[20]

This confrontation is the confrontation of thought with its own inability to think, and with it the cinema offers Deleuze a way to concretely explore the relation between all-too-human cinematographic thought and the unthought which haunts it – real movement, or duration as the being of difference. This relation appears within the *Cinema* books as or in terms of the break between classical and modern cinemas, movement- and time-image, and between the two volumes of *Cinema 1* and *2* – a relation which, as we have seen in Chapter 2, is precisely *impossible*. Where the 'mystical leap' of intuition seeks to overcome or leave the human behind, the *Cinema* books foreground the human in its relation *to* being, in the exposure of human thought to being as the impossibility of thought. In this exposure thought reveals itself as a suffering we undergo, rather than a power we possess, which

> can only think one thing, *the fact that we are not yet thinking*, the powerlessness to think the whole and to think oneself, thought which is always fossilized, dislocated, collapsed ... [such that] what forces us to think is 'the inpower [*impouvoir*] of thought', the figure of nothingness, the inexistence of a whole which could be thought.[21]

Thought as a relation to the outside, thought outside itself and the unthought within thought: all this returns us to the central paradox of the *Cinema* books, in terms of the passage from *Cinema 1* to *Cinema 2* and the shift in the characterisation of the whole from Bergson's 'open' to the 'outside' mapped in the work of Blanchot. Resolving this paradox means accounting for it in Bergsonian terms (we must 'reach' Blanchot on the basis of Bergson). As we shall see, Deleuze's reformulation of the cinematographic illusion in terms of movement-images as mobile sections of duration provides us with the tools to do just that. However, in order to do so, we must pass by way of the paradoxes internal to *Cinema 1*, starting with the tendency of the classical cinema to construct a closed, totalised and transcendent image of the whole on the basis of the movement-image, despite the inherently decentring forces of montage and camera mobility which work to open the closed set of the shot to the openness of the whole, and to the real movement of being.

The Classical Cinema as Totalisation

Rodowick argues that there is an 'inherent tension' within Deleuze's account of the movement-image, one which Deleuze himself does not make clear, between 'the movement-image considered in itself as Image of universal variation',[22] and what Rodowick refers to as 'the cinematic movement-image' – in other words, action, perception and affection-images. The former is the ontological premise that founds the problematic of both Bergsonian and Deleuzian philosophy. Whether we call it the virtual, duration, internal difference, concrete or real movement, the open or the whole of relations, it amounts in each case to a nuance of the same fundamental premise: that being is that which differs from itself first of all. In other words, it is the basic premise of all of Deleuze's work, including the *Cinema* books, even if the terminology may differ from book to book or argument to argument. It is not this ontological premise that is in question in the *Cinema* books, but rather the cinema's capacity to 'think' in terms adequate to it – and 'cinematic movement-images' are the materials by which it seeks to do so. The 'tension' between the two that Rodowick refers to lies in the fact that, although it is the ontological premise of the open whole that grounds the capacity of cinematic movement-images to think in terms of real movement, the sensory-motor composition of cinematic movement-images characteristic of the classical cinema tends towards the construction of an image of the whole as *totality* (or at least as totalisable in principle) – that is to say, as a closed, rather than open, whole. Thus 'the whole history of cinematic movement-images is marked by this paradoxical position: the desire to build an image of organic totality out of a force that assures the openness of the whole, or the inability of any set to close except in a partial way'.[23]

This 'tension' is a direct function of Deleuze's identification of the movement-image with the shot,[24] which in turn is defined as

> the intermediary between the framing of the set and the montage of the whole, sometimes tending towards the pole of framing, sometimes tending towards the pole of montage. The shot is movement considered from this dual point of view: the translation of the parts of a set which spreads out in space, the change of a whole which is transformed in duration.[25]

As I've argued, in so far as the shot tends towards the determination of an arbitrarily closed set, it emphasises the cinematographic aspect of movement (the translation of the elements of the shot in space), but where it tends towards montage, it opens that set to the real movement of being (the transformation of relations between elements as an expression of duration). Moreover, the tendency of a given shot towards one or the other of these two poles emphasises one or the other of two qualitatively different aspects of the out-of-field (that which exists beyond the boundaries of the shot). On the one hand, there is an 'absolute aspect by which the closed system opens on to a duration which is immanent to the whole universe, which is no longer a set and does not belong to the order of the visible'.[26] In this case, the shot opens onto the open whole as the unceasing variation of being. On the other, there is 'a relative aspect by means of which a closed system refers in space to a set which is not seen, and which can in turn be seen, even if this gives rise to a new unseen set, onto infinity'.[27] From this perspective, the whole is simply an infinitely expandable or expanding set, 'a universe or plane of genuinely unlimited content',[28] which nevertheless remains closed in so far as it remains at any given moment a set of determined elements. As Deleuze points out, these two aspects are necessarily intermingled in any given shot, but depending on the nature of the 'thread' of duration which links shot to shot, 'when we consider a framed image as a closed system, we can say that one aspect prevails over the other ... The thicker the thread which links the seen set to other unseen sets the better the out-of-field fulfils its first function, which is the adding of space to space.'[29]

What is central here is that the tendency of cinematic movement-images towards a totalisation of the whole that Rodowick refers to is a direct function of the tendency of the shot towards the determination of the elements of a set on the one hand, and of the tendency of the 'relative' out-of-field such sets imply to construct an image of the whole as an infinitely expandable but nevertheless in principle closed set on the other. Such a set both is 'genuinely unlimited' in so far as it continues to expand, *and* constitutes a closed or totalised whole in so far as, at any given moment, it nevertheless determines the elements of a finite set. If one grasps the whole only in terms of this continual expansion, one is in danger of confusing the whole with this ever-expanding set – a totalised or totalisable whole, closed and in some sense given in advance. It is only the openness of the whole – the fact that it is 'not a set and does not have parts' – which prevents this closure and opens the set/shot onto the real movement of being.

The 'tension' Rodowick refers to thus exists not between the cinematic movement-image and the ontological premise of being as that which differs from itself (this premise necessarily underpins Deleuze's analysis of the cinema as a whole). Rather, it concerns the manner in which the cinema's thought of the whole (its mode of ontological speculation) is pulled between the two poles of the construction of an image of the whole corresponding to that ontological premise (the whole as the open) and an image of the whole as an infinitely expandable, but nevertheless closed and thus totalised or totalisable set.[30]

What the organisation of shots according to sensory-motor schemata does, however, is precisely to limit relations between shots to those that emphasise the simple expansion of the set. Such schemata 'ward off' the decentring power of montage (as an opening onto the universal variation of the whole) by constraining it to a merely additive rather than transformative power. Each shot is 'added' to the next, merely expanding the set of elements acting on each other in a coherent space and in linear time – a set that remains finite, no matter how large it gets. In other words, the mode of narration of the classical cinema tends towards a concept of the whole as a closed or closable totality given in terms of the rule or rules governing the linkage of images, and limiting them to relations of perception and action, cause and effect.

Sensory-motor schemata thus define or construct a cinematic *Idea* of the whole given or giveable to human thought in terms of a rule or rules of action and reaction, of causality, which define the possibilities of the world those rules construct. Deleuze tells us that 'We can say of duration itself or of time, that it is the whole of relations',[31] but the coherence and commensurability of shots imposed by sensory-motor schemata derive from the way in which it restricts possible relations between images to ones which are directly or indirectly ones of cause and effect, action and reaction. As Rodowick puts it:

> throughout this schema, the rational interval is the guarantee of continuity and commensurability, both in the extension of the referent into an image and in the linking of one image to another in causal chains ... While associated images are linked horizontally, they also expand vertically through a dialectic of integration and differentiation. The linked images form an image or concept of the whole (integration), which is extended in turn as part of a set of a higher order (differentiation).[32]

The whole is thus 'given' to thought in terms of causality as a 'rule' for the potentially infinite extension or differentiation of the set (this causes this, causes this, causes this ...). The sensory-motor schema is an 'agent of abstraction' precisely in so far as it constructs a concept or Idea of the whole in spatialised terms, which constrain our grasp of its openness to the unceasing expansion of a set of actual elements, thereby divorcing these elements from the virtual and properly open whole of which they are the actualisation[33] (and in doing so it repeats or dramatises the error philosophy falls into when it divorces the actual from its actualisation – the errors of identity, representation and negation).

For all that this set may be potentially infinite, it nevertheless remains closed in so far as the rule or principle by which it expands is given in or as that Idea. Thus the coherence, commensurability and continuity of images imposed or restored to cinematic movement-images by sensory-motor schemata articulates the reciprocal determination of both an Idea of the world graspable in thought and a mode of relation *to* that world as masterable in action. We derive an Idea of the world on the basis of sensory-motor schemata (integration), and that Idea in turn justifies and assures the coherence and effectiveness of our action in and on the world (differentiation). Thus Deleuze's description of the classical cinema as the articulation of the 'unity of nature and man . . . the sensory-motor relationship between man and world, nature and thought'.[34]

What is vital to note here is that in reimposing the centred perspective of natural or human perception in this new 'mode', via the composition of shots according to the causal and linear principles of a sensory-motor schema, the non-human spiritual automaton of the classical cinema not only restricts its thought to a merely human (cinematographic) perspective, it raises that perspective to the level of a transcendent principle. That is to say, the whole derived by the sensory-motor schemata of the classical cinema constitutes the cinematic equivalent of a transcendent Idea of the world, in the Kantian sense.

As Smith summarises with admirable clarity, such Ideas present us with a concept of an object that goes beyond any possible experience. We cannot perceive or experience the world or the whole as such, but rather derive the Idea of it indirectly

> through the extension of the category of causality: that is through the use of the hypothetical syllogism (if A, then B) – if A causes B, and B causes C, and C causes D, and so on. This series constitutes a kind of *problem* for us. We can continue working through this problem, continuing through the series indefinitely, until we final reach the 'Idea' of the totality of everything that is: the causal nexus of the world, or the Universe. But in fact we can never, ever, have a perception or intuition of the world, or the

totality of what is. To use a famous Kantian distinction, we can *think* the world as if it were real, as if it were an object, but we can *never* know it. Strictly speaking, the world is not an object of our experience; what we actually know is the problematic of causality, a series of causal relations that we can extend indefinitely.[35]

Within the cinema, the 'problematic of causality' that is given to us in experience corresponds to the sensory-motor schemata governing the relation between shots in montage, that is to say, *narrative* (in the terms Deleuze defines it). All films end, of course, but the rules or montage principles governing relations between shots are, like the principle of causality, infinitely extensible and subject to the same hypothetical extension that Kant argues gives rise to an 'Idea of the World'. Thus, as Deleuze puts it, 'what originates from montage, or from the composition of movement-images is the Idea'.[36]

Taken from this perspective, Deleuze's treatment of the classical cinema and of its sensory-motor organisation of images performs or recapitulates in cinematic terms the Kantian critique of the limits of reason's legitimate application. The sensory-motor schemata of the classical cinema are, as Deleuze's choice of terminology suggests, the cinematic equivalent of the schematism whereby the objects of experience are related to and subsumed under the categories of the understanding – most especially, in this case, that of causality. As Deleuze puts in in his book on Kant: 'the schema is a spatio-temporal determination which itself corresponds to the category, everywhere and at all times: it does not consist in an image, but *in spatio-temporal relations which embody or realise relations which are in fact conceptual*'.[37] The operation of such schemata remains legitimate so long as it is applied to the objects of experience, to the phenomenal world of appearance. But the world is not, and cannot be, given to experience in this fashion. By extending its sensory-motor schemata to the construction of an Idea of the world, the cinema thus produces or repeats in its own terms the transcendental illusion that leads thought to conceive the world as an object *of* thought, subject to reason's powers in the same terms as the phenomena given to us in experience.

As Henry Somers-Hall notes, this illusion is not itself fallacious: 'Knowledge requires the Idea of a totality, and the necessity of the Idea of a totality makes it appear as if such a totality could actually be given.'[38] The Idea of the world derived hypothetically in the classical cinema by means of sensory-motor schemata does precisely this: in so far as it offers the whole as a closed totality, it presents that totality as given or giveable *as* an Idea. But as Kant argues, such transcendent Ideas are illegitimate precisely because they posit the world as a definite *object* corresponding to an indefinite causal series, one we might ask questions about as if it were something we could actually experience: 'For instance, did the world have a beginning in time, or is it eternal? Does it have boundaries in space, or does it go on forever?'[39] Such Ideas, Kant argues, lead reason into aporias or 'logical paradoxes', (specifically, the 'antinomy of the world') because they are asked of something that not only does not, but cannot exist as an object of our experience – the noumenal realm of the world as it is in and for itself.

There is, however, a fundamental difference in the ways in which Kant and Deleuze conceive of 'the world as it is for itself'. As Somers-Hall points out, what Kant calls the noumenal serves a limiting and regulative role, 'preventing the pretensions of sensibility from applying beyond their legitimate ground',[40] and remains necessarily undetermined (it is because it is undetermined that it cannot be 'incorporated' into the totality of the Idea of the world[41]). Indeed 'for Kant, the antinomies represent an indirect proof of transcendental idealism, as it is only with the additional assumption of the noumenon, as that which falls outside of appearance, that we are able to resolve the antinomies'.[42] For Deleuze, however, what lies outside things as they appear for us is difference itself. In these terms, the world as it is for itself is simply the being of difference – in the Bergsonian terminology of the *Cinema* books, the openness of the whole. Thus Somers-Hall argues that Kant's antinomies of the world are reconfigured by Deleuze into the antinomy of *representation*, which lies in 'the inability of representation to think difference apart from as purely representational [and thus as strictly external] or as undifferenciated abyss'.[43]

The resolution of this antinomy requires a positive characterisation of the noumenal in non-representational terms, that is to say, in terms of (internal) difference.[44] Both Smith and Somers-Hall present Deleuze's interpretation of the differential calculus as a direct rejoinder to Kant's treatment of transcendental Ideas in these terms, in so far as it allows Deleuze to demonstrate how difference as the undetermined nevertheless constitutes the terms of a reciprocal determination capable of determining specified or actual elements.[45]

To put it in terms more familiar from my argument so far, what Deleuze describes in terms of the calculus can be seen as a develop-

The Thought of the World

ment and variation of the discussion of the passage from the virtual (the undetermined) in its movement of actualisation (determination) to the actual (the determined) that Deleuze presents in *Bergsonism*. As we have seen, this is itself a variation and development of the logic of the relation of internal and external difference he outlines in 'Bergson's Conception of Difference'. In that relation, the strictly external difference of difference in degree (the actual or determined element) is produced by (deduced from) the differing from itself of internal difference (the undetermined), and thus accounted for in strictly positive terms as the greatest (most extreme) degree of difference. Deleuze's interpretation of the calculus allows him to apply this logic to his critique of the limiting and regulative function the noumenal has for thought under Kant, and to reframe it in terms of a positive, generative and creative genesis of thought for which the noumenal must be understood as the difference from itself of being.[46] Thus where for Kant the Idea of the world marks the limits (or the 'off-limits') of the *possible* conditions of experience, for Deleuze it constitutes the ground of a genetic account of the *real* conditions of experience.[47]

Thus the 'thought of the world' constructed by the classical cinema in terms of sensory-motor schemata must ultimately be understood as constituting a transcendental illusion in Deleuzian, rather than Kantian, terms. Such schemata misconstrue the openness of the whole as a function of an infinitely expanding set of actual elements, rather than as that which maintains the openness of the set to the acentred universal variation of the virtual. By construing the world or the whole as an object of thought, they divorce the whole from the openness that is its most essential characteristic and treat it as a 'thing' subject to thought and thought's mastery – a totality that is closed or closable in principle. Moreover, this determination of the whole by and for thought is reflected in the mastery of the whole in action it makes possible, in so far as it justifies and assures action's effectiveness and coherence.

In *Difference and Repetition*, Deleuze puts it this way:

> in effect, the undetermined object, or object as it exists in the Idea [the World in so far as it can never be an object of experience], allows us to represent other objects (those of experience) which it endows with a maximum of systematic unity ... the object of the Idea becomes indirectly determined: it is determined by analogy with those objects of experience upon which it confers unity, but which in return offer it a determination 'analogous' to the relations it entertains with them.[48]

In the terms under consideration here, the world is not given or determined directly (it can never be an object of experience), but rather is determined indirectly (as an Idea) through the hypothetical extension of the sensory-motor schema or 'montage school' governing relations between images in a given film. That Idea in turn endows the objects of experience given in that film (the shots it is composed of) with a 'maximum of systematic unity' (the assurance of rational and coherent relations between those shots) in so far as the montage rules governing their narrative organisation have been raised to the level of a transcendent principle in the form of an Idea of the World. This reciprocal determination is of course premised on a (transcendental) illusion. Its cinematographic basis divorces the thought of the classical cinema from the very openness of the whole that montage offers to open it up to, and constitutes a closed totality, a unity of world and action which separates and isolates it from real movement and real being.

This movement of reciprocal determination has a vital connection to the 'organic' image of thought or 'plane of immanence' that underpins the classical cinema. The plane of immanence, as Deleuze and Guattari describe it, 'has two facets, as Thought and Nature, as *Nous* and as *Physis*'.[49] On the one hand, it is 'always single, being itself pure variation',[50] a chaos of infinite speed in which every determination is lost before it can be found[51] (pure acentred variation). This movement is both the image of thought and the substance of being[52] (the two 'facets' of the plane of immanence as *Nous* and *Physis*). But on the other hand, the plane of immanence is also the multiple 'sections' or planes of consistency that philosophy extracts from that chaos (like a 'sieve') in so far as it attempts to 'acquire a consistency without losing the infinite into which thought plunges'.[53]

The attempt to do so is, according to Deleuze and Guattari, the very problem of philosophy itself, and the history of philosophy can be mapped in terms of its 'solutions' to this problem.[54] The movements philosophy selects, and the consistency it thereby acquires, construct

> varied and distinct planes of immanence that, depending on which infinite movements are selected, succeed and contest each other in history. The plane is certainly not the same in the time of the Greeks, in the seventeenth century, and today ... there is neither the same image of thought or substance of being.[55]

Such planes, however, are neither the philosophies in question nor the concepts those philosophies create. Rather they constitute in

The Thought of the World

each case 'the image thought gives itself of what it means to think, to make use of thought, to find one's bearings in thought'.[56] Such an image is a pre- or non-philosophical 'presupposition' or 'non-conceptual understanding' which nevertheless '*does not exist outside philosophy*',[57] but grounds the concepts which it is philosophy's task to create.

> Philosophy is at once concept creation and instituting of the plane. The concept is the beginning of philosophy, but the plane is its instituting. The plane is clearly not a program, design, end or means: it is a plane of immanence that constitutes the absolute ground of philosophy ... the foundation on which it creates its concepts.[58]

In the *Cinema* books, Deleuze argues that the classical and modern cinemas each constitute their own distinct (pre-philosophical) image of thought. For the classical cinema, thought is a power that we possess, modelled on and derived from our action in the world, which both (indirectly) produces and is justified by the linking of shots according to 'rational divisions, projecting a model of truth in relation to totality', as Rodowick puts it.[59] This image of thought is the target of critique for Bergson for its cinematographic and totalising tendencies, but also for Kant, for its transcendent orientation (and as we will see in a moment, Deleuze's treatment of the cinema brings these two critiques together in a single movement).

By contrast, the modern cinema, by reversing the subordination of time to movement in the classical cinema, disorders and decentres thought via the irrational linkages it constructs between images: 'narration [the organisation of such images in montage] ceases to be truthful, that is, to claim to be true, and becomes fundamentally falsifying ... It is a power of the false which replaces and supersedes the form of the true.'[60] Far from being a power we possess, the time-image of the modern cinema 'affirms a specific power, or rather "impower" of thought: "we are not yet thinking"'.[61]

We will return to this 'impower' of thought in the next chapter. For now, however, what is important is that the image of thought that the classical cinema 'presupposes' is premised on a fundamental illusion: it treats movement as if it were something immanent *to* the whole (as if the whole were a container in which things moved to and fro) rather than recognising real movement (pure variation) as the being of the whole (and movement-images as 'mobile sections' or 'presentations' of the plane of immanence[62]). As Deleuze and Guattari argue:

175

whenever immanence is interpreted as immanence 'to' something a confusion of plane and concept results, so that the concept becomes a transcendent universal and the plane becomes an attribute in the concept. When misunderstood in this way, the plane of immanence revives the transcendent again: it is a simple field of phenomena.[63]

The Idea of the world that the classical cinema derives indirectly via sensory-motor schemata conflates the plane of immanence (the openness of the whole as acentred universal variation) with the infinite expansion of a closed set constructed in terms of the hypothetical syllogism governing its expansion ('if this, then this, then this', and so on to infinity). Such Ideas construct a plane of immanence in terms relative to the human, as a horizon which (in Rodowick's words) is 'terrestrial and human centred ... grounded in a stable, geometric perspective that assures the continuity of vision'.[64] In doing so it raises the effects of the cinematographic illusion to the level of a 'transcendent universal' and reduces the plane of immanence to a world of perception and action played out across a 'simple field of phenomena'.

As Smith points out, it is the 'ruthless critique' of transcendence implied by Kantian philosophy that allows Deleuze to 'align himself with Kant's critical philosophy, despite their obvious differences'.[65] The appearance of such transcendent Ideas in cinematic form within the classical cinema must thus be understood in the context of Deleuze's claim that the cinema 'repeats' the history of philosophy, *including the philosophies of transcendence that are the objects of this 'ruthless critique'*. Deleuze's treatment of the classical cinema is from this perspective an extension and development of the critique of the dominant tendencies of the Western philosophical tradition that is the main target of Bergson's metaphor of the cinematographic illusion.

As Ansell-Pearson notes, this critique is presented by Bergson himself as a development of, response to and correction of the terms of Kant's own critique of the transcendent orientation of this tradition.[66] In this light, the ontological speculation manifest in the classical cinema's articulation of the relation of man and world corresponds to such philosophies in so far as the spatialised conception of movement they both share grasps time indirectly as a function of movement, and in turn seeks to grasp being in strictly transcendent terms.[67]

The collapse of the sensory-motor schemata that underpin the classical cinema and of the image of thought that accompanies them frees the cinematic articulation of time from its subordination to movement and constitutes in turn an explicit recapitulation of the 'first great Kantian reversal [of] the *Critique of Pure Reason*' in which 'Time is no longer related to the movement which it measures, but movement is related to the time which conditions it.'[68] It is important to recognise, however, that the terms in which Kant and Deleuze characterise or 'produce' this reversal are not the same. Most significantly, the difference between their accounts is integral to the critical response to Kant that aligns Deleuze with the post-Kantian tradition inaugurated by Solomon Maimon.

For classical philosophy (as Deleuze glosses it), time is grasped as the order of succession, an ordered series of points in space (this, then this, then this, and so on) such that 'time is fundamentally subordinated to something which happens in it . . . [and there is] a subordination of time to change, to movement, to the course of the world'.[69] The 'great Kantian reversal' of this subordination is a function of the way that Kant treats time and movement as separate and distinct *a priori* conditions for any possible experience, such that time is thus not grasped as the measure of movement but rather as 'the form of everything that changes and moves . . . It is not an eternal form, but in fact the form of that which is not eternal, the immutable form of change and movement'.[70] Deleuze follows Kant in this definition, but where for Kant time and space 'are the forms of appearing, or the forms of presentation of what appears'[71] (the *a priori* forms of being known of phenomena), for Deleuze, the temporalisation of difference he effects in 'Bergson's Conception of Difference'[72] means that time as the form of change is simply the being of difference itself (or, in terms of the *Cinema* books, the openness of the whole). If we accept Somers-Hall's argument that Deleuze replaces the Kantian 'noumenal as undetermined and unknowable' with 'difference as undetermined but determinable' then the significance of the definition of time as the form of change must therefore be decidedly different for Kant and Deleuze. Specifically, where for Kant time constitutes a condition of *possible* experience, for Deleuze it becomes the condition of *real* experience.

Deleuze's reconfiguration of the terms of the reversal of time's subordination of movement thus responds directly to the demands of Maimon's critique of Kant. As Smith points out, Kant's assumption of the 'facts' of reason produces

> a vicious circle that makes the condition (the possible) refer to the conditioned (the real) while reproducing its image. Maimon argues that

Kant cannot simply assume these facts, but has to show that they can be deduced or engendered immanently from reason alone as the necessary modes of its manifestation.[73]

According to Maimon this vicious circle can only be overcome if the genetic condition of thought is located in difference itself – a task that 'reappears like a leitmotif in almost every one of Deleuze's books up through 1969, even if Maimon's name is not always explicitly mentioned'.[74] As Smith points out, while Maimon seeks to meet this demand by incorporating 'elements of Spinoza, Leibniz and Hume ... Deleuze begins to trace out an alternate post-Kantian tradition that will ultimately link up Maimon with later philosophers such as Nietzsche and Bergson'[75] and that it 'is not difficult to trace out the same Maimonian influences in Deleuze's work on Bergson [as one finds in his work on Nietzsche]'.[76] Likewise, Ansell-Pearson notes that Deleuze's 1960 lecture course on Bergson 'indicates precisely where Bergson's importance lies, namely in the effort to radicalise the post-Kantian project commenced by Maimon'.[77]

In this context, I argue that the otherwise startling appearance of Kant at the heart of (and break or crack between) the two volumes of Deleuze's Bergsonian account of the cinema should thus be understood in the context of them as a continuation and nuance of the post-Kantian project of Deleuzian philosophy. The deduction of the brain/screen (and thus of the cinematographic condition of the human on the basis of the metacinematic universal variation of light – being as difference, the open whole) corresponds precisely to the Maimonian demand for a genetic deduction of the conditions of real thought on the basis of difference. In doing so, the limits Kant ascribes to reason are 'repositioned' by Deleuze such that it is not the undetermined and undeterminable character of the noumenal that places it beyond the reach of reason, but rather the cinematographic genesis of human thought on the basis of difference (as undetermined but determinable) that forms the barrier or limit to the human thought of being as it is for itself.

Furthermore, on this basis, Deleuze is able to retain the force of Kant's critique of the transcendental illusions that thought falls into, in so far as thought constructs for itself an Idea of the world on the basis of the problematic of causality. That is, those illusions are accounted for as a consequence of the cinematographic genesis of human thought. They are dramatised in the classical cinema's recapitulation of the errors of transcendence that philosophy falls

The Thought of the World

into when it fails to overcome (or even recognise) that genesis. In other words, the classical cinema dramatises and demonstrates how the transcendental illusion of a world, given to thought as Idea, is constructed in and *for* thought on the basis of difference as the genetic condition *of* thought.

In this context, one might reasonably expect the collapse of the sensory-motor schemata that marks the end of the classical cinema, and the reversal of the subordination of time to movement this collapse marks, to give rise to a cinematic thought free of the cinematographic chains those schemata had imposed, and thus adequate in some sense to the task of thinking the difference of the world, or the world as difference. Instead, we find something quite different. The terms of this reversal are not those of a 'freeing from' or 'correction' of the cinematographic and transcendent illusions of philosophy and of thought, as if it simply put them on the correct footing to proceed henceforth without error. Neither can we speak here of a simple continuation of the cinema's 'recapitulation' of the history of philosophy, if by history we mean the linear and causal passage from one moment to the next. Rather, 'history' and thought too collapse: thought as a power we possess is replaced only by thought as a suffering we undergo, a fundamental powerlessness of thought confronted by being as that which we cannot think.

As we have seen, the 'passage' from the classical to the modern cinema, from movement-image to time-image, and indeed from the first volume of the *Cinema* books to the second, is strictly speaking impossible, disastrous, taking place only as an event which in some sense erases the event of its own 'taking place'. This is the 'great Kantian reversal' as a disaster in and for thought, in so far as the only thought it leaves us with is that we are not yet thinking. It must be said that there is an undeniable oddity about placing Kant's name in proximity with a term drawn from the work of Blanchot. However, as we shall see, it is precisely Deleuze's Bergsonian revision of Kant, and of Kant's treatment of the relation of thought to time, that produces this conjunction in terms of the break between the classical and modern cinemas. And the consequences of this break are articulated in the cinematic dramatisation of the vicissitudes of thought and philosophy.

The consequences of this reversal for cinema, for thought and for the relation between the two, must, however, be put to one side until the next chapter. To get there, we must first of all account for this 'reversal' within the cinema in cinematic terms – that is to say, in terms of film form. The key here lies in the nature of the Idea of the whole that sensory-motor schemata produce. Deleuze is explicit that there is not one sensory-motor schema for the whole of classical cinema, but several, and the difference between them lies fundamentally in the nature of the whole derived from their specific mode of organisation of causal relations between images – that is to say, in the terms of the 'hypothetical syllogism' by means of which they derive their Idea of the world.

Thus we find the 'great organic unity' of the American cinema (represented by Griffith), in which the whole is defined by analogy with the 'unity in diversity' of an organism, expressed in terms of parallel alternating montage;[78] the mathematical and intensive sublime of French Impressionist film and German Expressionism respectively, where 'what constitutes the sublime is that the imagination suffers a shock which pushes it to the limit and forces thought to think the whole as intellectual totality which goes beyond the imagination';[79] and the dialectical unity of the Soviet cinema's montage of opposition 'under the dialectical law of the One which divides itself in order to form the new, higher unity'.[80] In each case, the given montage Idea, or Idea of the world, reciprocally determines the whole as an object of thought through a 'hypothetical syllogism' that in turn constitutes the 'laws of thought' governing the passage from one idea to the next in parallel with the laws of causality governing action in the world (this is the classical cinema's equivalent of Spinoza's spiritual automaton[81]).

Deleuze's concern at this point is not to critique or evaluate these montage Ideas, but simply to demonstrate that the organisation of images via montage in each case 'puts the cinematographic image into a relationship with the whole; that is, with time conceived as the Open. In this way it gives an indirect image of time, simultaneously in the individual movement-image and in the whole of the film.'[82] It's important to note that Deleuze does not foreground the role of sensory-motor schemata in 'closing' the openness of the whole at this point in his argument (early in *Cinema 1*). Indeed, such schemata are not introduced explicitly into his argument until his 'recapitulation of images and signs' in *Cinema 2*. Nevertheless, their effects are implied by the role of these montage principles (organic, extensive and intensive sublime, dialectical) in determining the relationship of the image (the shot) with the whole. In so far as they give us an indirect image of time – an image of time derived from the causal, linear and rational movement determined by those principles – the

The Thought of the World

'relationship with the whole' they articulate can only grasp its openness in closed terms.

Just as ontological speculation which starts from the human (from our cinematographic grasp of actual elements divorced from the virtual) is inadequate to the task of thinking being in its own terms, so the sensory-motor montage principles which govern the classical cinema can only give rise to an image of the whole as an ultimately closed or closeable totality. By limiting relations between images to those of action and reaction (and thus reinstating the cinematographic illusion in a new mode), they lose the capacity montage offers of opening onto the unceasing variation of the whole, and constrain it to the construction of an ever expanding, but always finite and closed, set.

In *Cinema 2*, by introducing the role of sensory-motor schemata in reimposing the cinematographic illusion within the classical cinema (albeit in a new mode), Deleuze reorients and reframes his treatment of the cinema of the movement-image, so much so that Ropars-Wuilleumier is led to argue that 'the very foundations of the first volume tumble down in the second'.[83] This 'tumbling down' is, as I've argued, one of the fundamental interpretative challenges that the reader of the *Cinema* books faces, in so far as the arguments of the second volume derive from and extend those of the first, while simultaneously radically reshaping them. The 'impossibility' of reading the two volumes together (as either coherent *or* incoherent) derives directly from this re-reading (the arguments of *Cinema 1* found those of *Cinema 2*, but at the same time those of *Cinema 2* unseat the earlier arguments they depend on). What we are now in a position to see is that this tension and this 'impossibility' turn on the shift in the characterisation of the classical cinema's relation to the whole announced by *Cinema 2*'s introduction of sensory-motor schemata as the organising principle of montage/narrative within the classical cinema.

The first four chapters of *Cinema 1* in particular focus on setting up the (Bergsonian) terms in which Deleuze approaches the cinema as such, and map out the in-principle power or capacity of the cinema to think in terms of real movement, and its capacity to articulate and explore thought's relation to being (to the whole as the open). These chapters emphasise the role that montage plays in decentring the cinematographic orientation of the primitive cinema (and, in principle, generating disproportions and aberrations of movement), and thus opening the closed set of the shot onto the whole as the open.

Deleuze does not, however, introduce the role sensory-motor schemata play in the organisation of the classical cinema in that volume, such that his analysis of the signs of that cinema (Chapter 5 and onwards) downplays the way in which it suppresses the very aberration of movement that montage makes possible, and so reintroduces the cinematographic illusion into cinematic thought (this time at the level of relations between shots, rather than that of the static frames of the film strip).[84]

Nevertheless, as we progress through these signs and chapters, we do find indications of what is to come. Deleuze briefly introduces the notion of a 'sensory-motor link' between perception and action specific to the 'large form' of the action-image (where the situation leads to action which transforms the situation), but it is not until the final paragraph of the book that he speaks of a new image (in the post-war cinema) that 'discovered' 'a requirement which was enough to smash the whole system, to cut perception off from its motor extension, action, from the thread which joined it to a situation ... The new image would therefore not be a bringing to completion of the cinema, but a mutation of it.'[85]

It is this tension – between 'bringing to completion' and 'mutation' – that is at stake in the impossibility of reading the *Cinema* books as a whole. 'Bringing to completion' posits the post-war cinema as an *end* – both a (teleological) goal and as a completion, finality or closure. But it is this very end or closure which creates the conditions for the 'mutation' Deleuze speaks of, which is not merely that of the 'new' post-war cinema but of the classical cinema as well, whose dreams or goals 'complete' it in terms which retrospectively reveal a completely different cinema to the one we thought we were dealing with throughout *Cinema 1*.

What I want to argue is that the 'mutation' Deleuze speaks of affects not only what comes 'after' (the post-war cinema) but also retrospectively 'mutates' the classical cinema as well, in so far as the break between classical and modern cinemas reveals 'the power or capacity of cinema [to become adequate to the thought of the whole as open] ... to be only a pure or logical possibility'.[86] It is the capacity for the production of aberrant movement implicit in montage[87] that presents this possibility: it is the recentring of movement imposed by sensory-motor schemata that wards it off. At the same time, however, it is the tendency towards totalisation implicit within such schemata that establishes the conditions for the completion or closure of the classical cinema, and in doing so sets up the terms

The Thought of the World

in which the break between the classical and the modern cinemas imposes itself, 'mutating' the cinema in both directions.

Cinema as 'Art of the Masses'

The force of my argument throughout this book has been that the task of the *Cinema* books fundamentally concerns thought and, more precisely, the adequacy (or otherwise) of thought to real movement, and thus to being as real difference. The cinema thus engages the ontological problematic articulated by Heidegger in terms of the adequacy of merely human thought to the thought of being – the question of how, and in what terms, the thought of mere beings might confront the task of grasping or mastering or opening onto being as that which exceeds them in every sense. As Benoît Dillet points out, Deleuze's relationship with this problematic is an ongoing and persistent one throughout his work, figured in his 'constant reference to a phrase from Heidegger's lecture course *What is Called Thinking?*: 'We are not yet thinking.'[88] Dillet notes that Deleuze's appropriation of this Heideggerian theme foregrounds a conception of thought as a practice which is both involuntary *and* political, and that Deleuze's treatment of the cinema in particular explores this relationship in terms of cinema as the 'art of the masses'.[89]

For the casual reader of the *Cinema* books, this claim may come as a surprise, inasmuch as Deleuze does not bring these themes to the fore until deep into the arguments of *Cinema 2*, in the chapter appropriately titled 'Thought and Cinema'.[90] However, in doing so he crystallises arguments and problems which have heretofore remained 'in suspension', implicit but unresolved throughout his treatment of cinematic movement and its relation to the whole (the very arguments I have tried to foreground and extract throughout this book). That chapter is thus, for my purposes at least, the hinge on which the argument of the *Cinema* books turns.

It begins with Deleuze's statement of what he identifies as the goal or dream of the cinema from its very beginnings: 'Those who first made and thought about cinema began from a simple idea: cinema as industrial art achieves self-movement, automatic movement, it makes movement the immediate given of the image.'[91] This is a conception of the cinema as movement-image: not a representation of things that move, but movement as something in itself, movement as the image itself. Such movement is profoundly aberrant in so far as it is no longer merely relative to a centred and human perspective, but absolute: a mobile section of the real movement of being itself.

When we go to the movies, the cinema replaces our head with its own: our point of view or centred perspective is overlaid with that of the projector, and the disjunction of the point of view of the projector that screens from that of the camera that films thereby decentres our own thought, replaces our neurons with shots, our synapses with montage. Our exposure to this mobility 'shocks' thought into movement precisely because it decentres the brain and places it into movement, into variation, and forces thought to think movement itself by opening it onto the acentred universal variation of being: 'Automatic movement gives rise to a spiritual automaton in us, which reacts in turn on movement.'[92]

Thus where Heidegger claims that man possesses the mere logical possibility of thinking, with no guarantee that he actually does so, the cinema claims as its right and power the capacity to shock us into thought, to push our thought into movement. '"It is as if cinema were telling us: with me, with the movement-image, you can't escape the shock which arouses the thinker in you.'[93] Moreover, as Deleuze emphasises, the collective nature of this experience (both in terms of the audience in the cinema together, and in terms of cinema as a popular or mass art) is such that this 'shock', this thought, concerns the people, the masses directly: the cinema constructs 'A subjective and collective automaton for an automatic movement: the art of the "masses".'[94]

Deleuze unpacks these claims through an analysis of Eisenstein's conception of the cinema, because its dialectical formation can be broken down into clearly determined 'moments' while still being 'valid for the classical cinema, the cinema of the movement-image in general'.[95] Eisenstein's cinema (and indeed that of the Soviet school of the 1920s and '30s as a whole) is dominated by a fundamentally dialectical conception of montage. The 'shock' the cinema imposes on thought is conceived in terms of the clash or opposition between shots (which may take many forms) which gives rise to synthesis at a higher level – that of the concept ('"From the shock of two factors a concept is born"'[96]). The dialectical conflict generated by montage forces thought to think – to produce the synthesis of opposites which at its end is the unity of the whole itself: 'The whole is the concept . . . Montage is in thought "the intellectual process" itself, or that which, under the shock, thinks the shock.'[97]

But if this conflict gives rise to the Idea or concept of the dialectical unity of the whole, this Idea in turn governs the relations between

The Thought of the World

images and the terms of passage from one image to the next in a cycle of reciprocal determination: 'The whole is produced by the parts, but also the opposite . . . The whole as dynamic effect is also the presupposition of its cause.'[98] The product of the dialectical synthesis of two shots constitutes one pole or term of the next opposition, the next shock, the next synthesis and so on in turn – this is the 'dialectical circle or spiral' which constitutes the operation of thought in and through images. Thus we go from image to concept or Idea, but also from the Idea to its expression in images. On the one hand we go 'from the movement-image to the clear thinking of the whole that it expresses';[99] on the other 'we go from a thinking of the whole which is presupposed and obscure to the agitated, mixed-up images which express it'.[100]

The former is the montage Idea (the Idea of the world); the latter is the expression or thinking of this Idea in images – 'Internal monologue . . . [which] constitutes the segments or links of a truly collective thought.'[101] The (in this case dialectical) Idea of the world is the indirect product of the 'hypothetical syllogism' implied by the terms in which relations between images are articulated by the specific sensory-motor schema governing a given 'school' of montage, giving the whole to thought as intellectual totality. But at the level of relations between individual shots as we experience them, this Idea is implicit and unconscious. It is given in experience as the affective charge that internalises the passage from perception to action 'giving "emotional fullness" or "passion" back to the intellectual process'.[102] Thus with the Idea of the whole 'we went from the shock image to the formal and conscious concept, but now [we go] from the unconscious concept to the material image, the figure image which embodies it and produces shock in turn'.[103] If internal monologue constitutes a 'truly collective thought' it is because the internalisation of the affective or pathetic charge (the sensory-motor experience of the film as a passage of images) is governed by the Idea of the World that orders and justifies the links that join and relate them. The cinematic brain or thought of the cinema is a thought of the whole which links experience, pathos, affect, to being itself as it is given in and by that Idea.

Thus there is a final moment in Eisenstein's dialectical schema, embedded in the previous two:

> not from image to concept, or from concept to image, but the identity of concept and image. The concept is in itself in the image, and the image is

for itself in the concept. This is no longer organic and pathetic, but dramatic, pragmatic, praxis or action thought. This action thought indicates the relation between man and the world, between man and nature, the sensory-motor unity, but by raising it to a supreme power.[104]

The adequacy of merely human thought to the thought of the whole, of being, is resolved in terms of this sensory-motor unity: man's action expresses and reveals the whole, which in turn governs and unifies man's action, such that individual pathos (the affective internalisation of action as quality) is raised to a truly collective level: 'A subjective and collective automaton for an automatic movement: the art of the "masses".'[105] The thought of the whole is given as the whole *as* thought: it is no longer a question of an individual thinking, but the whole (the masses, the people) as subject in itself: the whole of thought as the thought of the masses.

The 'intellectual montage' of the final sequence of Eisenstein's *Strike* (1925) offers a concrete example of such a schema at work. The sequence cuts between shots of a bull being slaughtered and shots of striking workers fleeing from the forces of their capitalist oppressors, who kill the workers as they run, shooting them in the back and murdering them en masse. There is no narrative or spatial connection between these two elements, such that the conjunction between them created through montage is essentially arbitrary. This is the kino-fist, the punch to the head which forces thought to think, to seek the intellectual connection between the images as a whole which gives their conjunction its meaning: 'the bosses are slaughtering the workers like animals.'

This shock to thought is not enough, however. Merely to introduce the *idea* of capitalist oppression is not enough to revolutionise an audience, to move them into action: cinema must work on the heart and the body as well as the mind. Hence the pathos of the bull's suffering. The shots of its killing are not merely documentary in nature (there is no question that the image is one of a real bull actually being killed), they foreground the violence and suffering of the moment: the hammer blow to the head which stuns it, the repeated slashing of the knife that tears its throat wide open, the blood that gushes, the violent flailing of its body as it dies. There is no avoiding the pure visceral sensation, the affective charge these shots generate. By comparison, the shots of the workers being killed are mere performance; a staged and acted moment all too easy to distance oneself from, even (or especially) if one grasps the political 'message'.

The Thought of the World

The montage of bull and workers together, the cutting back and forth between them, however, pushes the audience beyond the merely intellectual by transferring the affective, visceral charge of the bull's actual slaughter onto the performed massacre of the workers, 'giving "emotional fullness" or "passion" back to the intellectual process'[106] as Deleuze puts it, so that we feel, rather than merely think, the suffering of the workers. From the shock to thought which moves from image to concept, to the affective charge that the image returns to the concept, the suffering of the workers moves from abstract idea to felt suffering which calls for *action*. This is the final movement of Eisenstein's dialectical schema: the identity of concept and image, idea and pathos, as 'action-thought', in which

> there is a sensory-motor unity of nature and man, which means that nature must be named the non-indifferent . . . But it is also man who passes to a new quality, in becoming the collective subject of his own reaction, whilst nature becomes the objective human relation. Action-thought simultaneously posits the unity of nature and man, of the individual and the mass: cinema as art of the masses.[107]

For Eisenstein, this action-thought is nothing other than the revolutionising of the masses – he seeks not to tell the story of the revolution, or to 'raise consciousness', but to shock his audience into a revolutionary thought which is inseparable from revolutionary action. For man to become the 'collective subject of his own reaction' here means to create a class-consciousness inseparable from a class-action, a proletarianising of his audience in which the people become adequate to the revolution as an expression of the dialectical movement of world history, or of being itself. This is the unity of the one and the many, the people as a mass subject whose actions are the material (and materialist) manifestation of a dialectical 'thought of the world'.

Thus for Eisenstein, 'cinema does not have the individual as its subject, nor a plot or history as its object; its object is nature, and its subject the masses, the individuation of mass and not that of a person.'[108] This is the *telos* or finality which orients and governs Eisenstein's dialectical montage: not the mere idealism of the world thinking itself in its movement towards absolute knowledge, but rather a concrete and material action-thought (a properly Marxist dialectical materialism). The end to which this action-thought is directed is not merely revolution, or the overthrow of the bourgeoisie and the institution of the dictatorship of the proletariat, but, rather, the final withering away of the state, and with it the realisation of the people as the collective subject of their own action in or as a 'higher' or fully realised communism.[109] This goal or end orients and determines sensory-motor 'action-thought' as a movement towards ultimate knowledge and/as ultimate unity, which in turn justifies that movement according to the dialectical laws which construct that unity, ordering movement and thought as the rational and coherent (dialectical) passage from one image/thought to the next.[110] It is, as Rodowick says, 'an image of Truth as globalizing or totalizing apperception, linking humanity and the world as commensurable points in a sensorimotor whole'.[111]

Deleuze does not offer any equivalently detailed analysis of the relationship between 'man and world, world and man' articulated by the organic, extensive or intensive sublime montage Ideas governing American, French Impressionist or German Expressionist cinemas respectively. Nevertheless he makes it clear that his analysis of the operation of Eisenstein's dialectical montage Idea is valid for the whole of the classical cinema in general.[112] In each case

> the concept as whole does not become differentiated without externalising itself in a sequence of images, and the images do not associate without being internalised in a concept as the whole which integrates them. Hence the ideal of knowledge as harmonious totality, which sustains this classical representation.[113]

Irrespective of the 'school' of montage in question, the classical cinema seeks to offer the world to us as an object of thought, and as the basis for our action within that world as meaningful, rational and effective: the thought *of* the world as a totalised or totalisable whole which unifies and justifies our action *in* the world. Interiority and exteriority, thought and action, man and world, are reconciled at the level of this Idea, such that the unity of the one and the many, of being and beings, is at hand, even if only in principle or as possibility.

Although the terms in which this 'harmonious totality' is constructed may differ, in each case the classical cinema articulates the same dream, 'from Eisenstein or Gance to Elie Faure': that of 'cinema as a new Art and a new Thought . . . bound up with a metaphysical optimism, a total art for the masses'.[114] For Eisenstein this is the raising of the masses to the status of revolutionary subject adequate to and realising itself in the dialectical movement of being towards complete determination or ultimate self-knowledge: the whole as *telos*, finality, end of history. The American, French and German

The Thought of the World

montage Ideas Deleuze outlines articulate this 'dream' in different terms, but what unifies this vision in its various manifestations is its underlying image of thought as an image of Truth: the adequation of thought to being takes the form of the unity of man and world wherein the correspondence and coherence of our perceptions and actions (the rational interval between them) both reveal and are justified by the Idea of the World as totalised or totalisable whole. As Rodowick puts it, 'The movement-image is defined by an organic will to truth, or a fundamental philosophical belief in the representability of the whole.'[115]

The 'metaphysical optimism' Deleuze refers to is precisely the identification of the thought of being with 'the accession of the masses to the level of true subject'[116] whose unity is given in and realised by its thinking of the whole: the unity of the people as one given in the sensory-motor unity of thought and being, 'the unity of nature and man, of the individual and the mass'.[117] Sadly, however, as Deleuze points out, this dream or idea of the cinema proves itself in the end to be not only naïve, but false. 'Everyone knows that, if an art necessarily imposed the shock or vibration, the world would have changed a long time ago, and men would have been thinking for a long time. So this pretension of the cinema, at least amongst the greatest pioneers, raises a smile today.'[118] The aberrant movement that montage and the mobile camera put at the cinema's disposal reveal themselves in the classical cinema as a mere logical possibility, its power or capacity to produce a shock to thought suppressed or warded off by the imposition of a thought of the whole or thought of the world given as a transcendent totality. By reducing the openness of the whole to an Idea of the World representable in thought and masterable in action the philosophical consequences of the cinematographic illusion are raised to the level of transcendent principle, and the plane of immanence is reduced to a mere field of action.

Worse still, the action-thought or sensory-motor unity of man and world embedded in this image of thought is such that these consequences concern action *in* the world as much as they do the thought *of* the world. Rather than giving rise to an art and a thought of the masses – a 'subjective or collective automaton' shocking the masses into thought – 'the spiritual automaton [of the classical cinema] was in danger of becoming the dummy of every kind of propaganda: the art of the masses was already showing a disquieting face'.[119] The 'metaphysical optimism' attached to the 'unity of man and nature, individual and mass' founders on the recognition that the ontological dimension of this totalisation overlaps with a political dimension tending towards the totalitarian.

> How strangely the great declarations of Eisenstein, of Gance, ring today; we put them to one side like declarations worthy of a museum, all the hopes put into cinema, art of the masses and new thought ... the mass-art, the treatment of the masses, which should not have been separable from an accession of the masses to the status of true subject, has degenerated into state propaganda and manipulation, into a kind fascism which brought together Hitler and Hollywood, Hollywood and Hitler. The spiritual automaton become fascist man.[120]

The disruptive power of cinematic (and philosophical) aberration is warded off precisely because of its capacity to decentre the human, to disturb our mastery of and power over the world, to place our thought and action in question. Such decentring leaves thought, leaves us, in a truly impossible situation: impossibility of thought, impossibility of action, disorientation, disruption, destabilisation of every identity, power, unity (of individual or mass). Who would desire such a fate, if such a fate left it possible to desire at all? Surely better to assert that power, to seek the unity of the people in or as the active expression of the world's thought, or thought of the world – to be as one with each other and the world in thought and action?

What the fate of the classical cinema warns us is that such a dream comes at a cost, that its fundamental underlying premise – the very Idea of the World in terms of which our mastery is granted – realises the unity it promises not in terms of the people raised to the level of mass subject, but rather as the people *subjected* (Eisenstein's dialectical optimism come face to face with Stalin.)

The 'spiritual automaton become fascist man' means simply that a thought governed by an Idea of the World as one (totalised or totalisable whole) in its end or finality thinks *only* the One. The unity of the one and the many, world and man that the classical cinema offers reveals itself as the subsumption of the many *to* the one, the people to the state, the leader, the master: the classical cinema is 'Hitler and Hollywood, Hollywood and Hitler'. In the end, as Deleuze says to, or with, Serge Daney, 'The organic whole [of the classical cinema] was simply totalitarianism',[121] and if the classical cinema 'dies' in the war, it is because the war reveals its 'dream' as horror:

> 'the great political *mises en scène*, state propaganda turning into tableaux vivants, the first mass human detentions' realised cinema's dream, in circumstances where horror penetrated everything, where 'behind' the

image there was nothing to be seen but concentration camps, and the only remaining bodily link was torture.[122]

If this is the 'death' of the classical cinema, it is also its completion and fulfilment. The action-thought articulated in its sensory-motor schemata construes thought as a power we possess, and the whole as a totality or unity within our grasp. The relation between man and world, world and man that it constructs is figured at or in its extremity in terms of absolute knowledge, the adequation of thought to being: *telos* as completion and closure, the end of the world, the Hegelian dead end. Thought as mastery, thought as a power we possess, would be a thought oriented to and by its own end, a thought whose movement is one towards completion, finality, death. If the sensory-motor schemata of the classical cinema produce an image of thought as adequate to being – if they articulate the relation between us and the world as one of our power in and over the world – they are tied in some sense to this finality, this closure, this death.

Thus Deleuze argues that far from raising thought from a mere possibility to a reality, far from imposing a shock to thought and imposing thought on the masses as its early practitioners had hoped, the cinema of the movement-image is from its very beginning linked historically and essentially to the organisation of war, state propaganda and ordinary fascism.[123] War, violence, death as the expression of a fascist totalisation of thought and action; the unity of the one and the many, of man and world, revealed as the subsumption the many *to* the one, the people to the state, a unity whose final image is the mass grave, the gas chamber, the ovens: Hegelian finality, Hegelian fatality.

The bleakness of this conclusion concerns more than simply Deleuze's analysis of the classical cinema and its failed dreams. In so far as that cinema constitutes a recapitulation of the history of philosophies of transcendence – any philosophy whose image of thought is premised on the subordination of time to movement – then its conclusions bear directly on such philosophy as well. As we've seen, Deleuze's analysis of the cinema starts from and with Bergson's critique of finalism and mechanism within philosophy, a critique figured in the metaphor of the cinematographic illusion itself. But for the classical cinema, this illusion has been raised to a new level. It is no longer merely a question of a centred perspective on acentred universal variation (this is 'already' decentred within cinema by the disjunction of camera and projector).

The illusion is reintroduced in a new form and at a new level, through the introduction of sensory-motor schemata that limit relations between shots to causal, linear and coherent links, thereby warding off the aberrant movement that montage and the mobile camera threaten to give rise to. The capacity of montage to both de- and recentre perception is a direct function of Deleuze's reformulation of the cinematographic illusion in terms of relations between movement-images rather than static frames. The shot *is* the movement-image, but the shot has two faces – turned out towards the openness of the whole (power of decentring) and turned inwards towards the determination of a closed set. Sensory-motor schemata serve to link shots based on relations derived from the determination of the shot *as* set, such that montage only serves to expand that set, and not to open it to the acentred variation of the whole (power of recentring). It is in terms of such schemata and the transcendent Idea(s) of the world inferred on their basis that Deleuze is able to analyse and explore the operations of human thought and philosophy 'from without' as it were, using the tools provided by the strictly non-human formal capacities of the cinema (frame, shot and montage).

In other words, the cinematic 'analysis' of human thought embedded in Deleuze's treatment of the classical cinema characterises that thought as cinematographic in its operation and transcendent in its 'natural' metaphysics ('natural' in so far as such metaphysics are derived on the basis of the cinematographic genesis of the human and of human thought). The transcendent character of the Idea of the World derived from this orientation towards action (the 'hypothetical syllogism' of causality) grasps being as a totality or totalisable whole. And in so far as the Idea of the World as a totalisable whole (whatever form it takes) returns in a movement of reciprocal determination to organise and give justification, coherence and unity to our action in the world, the politics of totality and of totalitarianism are never far away: totalitarianism as the political correlate of ontological totalisation. Deleuze's analysis of the cinema thus raises Bergson's critique of the cinematographic errors of philosophy to the level of a political critique of the metaphysical orientation of human nature.

This is not quite the same as saying we are totalitarian by nature or doomed to fascism. Deleuze does not regard the work of Eisenstein, or Gance or Griffith or Lang as totalitarian; neither are the philosophies of transcendence necessarily precursors for or justifications of political repression and violence (although some – including Bergson himself – have suggested something along

The Thought of the World

these lines[124]). Nevertheless, if thought and deed are shaped by and oriented towards the demands of action, they are always already on a trajectory towards such political and actual violence (even if that violence is never realised). Action demands the power *to*, and if thought is power we possess, it is a power that seeks mastery. And in so far as it seeks to master the world, action exists within a tendency that at its extreme finds its realisation in or as death. When Daney tells us that in the end, behind the image of the classical cinema 'there is nothing to be seen but concentration camps', it is because this horror is the point towards which the action-thought of the classical cinema flows – and this action-thought models nothing other than the natural metaphysics of human thought. The 'spiritual automaton become fascist man' is not a divergence or error in thought, but the end towards which thought as power points us, even if that end may sometimes seem far away.

The entanglement of ontological and political critique embedded in Deleuze's treatment of the cinema offers an interesting riposte of sorts to Hallward's claim that Deleuzian philosophy defines itself through its attempt to escape *from* the human, and is thus 'essentially indifferent to the politics of this world ... [offering] only the most immaterial and evanescent grip on the mechanisms of exploitation and domination that continue to condition so much of what happens in our world'.[125] *Contra* Hallward, Deleuze identifies the human as that which must be escaped *from* in order to respond adequately *to* the politics of this world. If the 'spiritual automaton become fascist man' is the ultimate trajectory of the cinematographic orientation of human thought and action, and that orientation is nothing other than the genesis of our human nature, then the 'mechanisms of exploitation and domination' Hallward refers to are so entwined with that nature that to correct them in human terms is simply to risk recreating them in another form. The intolerability of the world demands our action, but it is our action that paves the path on which the intolerable treads.

Nevertheless, the force of Hallward's critique remains: even if our attempts to alter the politics of this world in this world are doomed by our nature, freedom *from* the human still seems to offer little to the problem of the freedom *of* the human. What is at stake here is precisely the question of the relation between human being and being itself: if the cinematographic nature of the human condemns it to a politics of violence, and 'freedom' lies only in the realm of the creative self-differing of being, then the freedom *of* the human rests on the possibility of a relation to being *as it is for itself*, and not for us. This relation cannot be built on the overcoming of the human (there can be no relation if one of the two terms is dissolved): it can only be constructed in terms of the human experience *of* being. This is, of course, the problem that drives Deleuze to the cinema and is articulated directly in the *Cinema* books through the relationship they articulate between the classical and the modern cinemas, and between their respective images of thought.

However, as we saw in Chapter 2, this relationship is, in a very specific sense, impossible. The relationship between *Cinema 1* and *Cinema 2*, and thus between the world as it is for us and as it is for itself, is figured as a gap or break which is simultaneously historical (between pre- and post-war cinema), formal (between rational and irrational modes of montage) and conceptual (between their respective images of thought). But to grasp the break between these terms in terms of either side is to erase the other and so lose the gap, the relationship that is to be accounted for. The impossibility of this relation, then, *is* that relationship. *The human experience of being is the experience of impossibility itself.*

Here the problem that Deleuze turns to the cinema to resolve dovetails with the interpretive challenge posed by the impossible relation between the two volumes of the *Cinema* books. In Chapter 1 I argued that this challenge could only be resolved by accounting for the passage and break between those volumes on the basis of the same Bergsonian foundations that *Cinema 2* seems to turn against – a displacement figured in the shift in the characterisation of the whole from the Bergsonian open to Blanchot's 'outside'. What should now be apparent is that this difficulty is in fact the formal expression (in and as the break or gap between the *Cinema* books themselves) of the problem that drives Deleuze to the cinema in the first place: how or in what sense can we think the relation of the human, and of human experience, to being as it is for itself, and not for us? So if we want to know how the cinema allows him to resolve this problem, we need to map the path he follows in order to get from Bergson to Blanchot, on the basis of the same Bergsonian principles that underpin both *Cinema 1* and 2. This is the task of the next chapter.

Notes

1. Deleuze, *Cinema 1*, 3.
2. This is at least part of what Deleuze means when he agrees with Metz

that 'The historical fact is that cinema was constituted as such by becoming narrative.' Narrative, in so far as it is a function of montage, is the essence of cinema itself. Deleuze, *Cinema 2*, 25.
3. Ibid., 163.
4. That is to say, the movement-image as it exists for itself, before its differentiation into perception, action and affection-images in relation to a centre of perception.
5. As Flaxman and Kerslake respectively both gloss Deleuze's comments in the latter's introduction to *Cinema 1*. Flaxman, 'Introduction', 4; Kerslake, 'Transcendental Cinema', 7.
6. Deleuze, *Cinema 1*, 30. He identifies these 'schools' as those of American 'organic' montage, French Impressionist and German Expressionist montage (associated with the Kantian extensive and intensive sublime respectively) and Soviet dialectical montage. Ibid., 29–55.
7. Deleuze, *Cinema 2*, 156–64 and 210.
8. Deleuze, *Cinema 1*, ix.
9. Deleuze, *Kant's Critical Philosophy*, vii–viii. Deleuze's discussion of the way in which the history of the cinema repeats that of philosophy in *Cinema 1* is a clear paraphrase of this passage. *Cinema 1*, 1.
10. It should be noted that this example is partial at best, since the relation of two shots taken on their own does not serve to determine a scheme. The 'rules' governing the organisation of relations between shots within the classical cinema only become apparent across a series of shots, and only fully so across a film in its entirety.
11. Deleuze, *Cinema 1*, ix.
12. Deleuze, *Cinema 2*, 39.
13. Which would be equivalent to natural perception as reflected in the conditions of the 'primitive' cinema.
14. Deleuze, *Cinema 2*, 40.
15. Ibid.
16. Ibid., 39.
17. Ibid., ix. One might argue that the 'minor tradition' Deleuze articulates in his work on the history of philosophy represents his attempts to foreground and connect diverse, fragmentary or partial attempts to subvert this suppression from within philosophy itself.
18. Ibid.
19. Ibid., 168.
20. Ibid., 167.
21. Ibid., 167–8.
22. Rodowick, *Gilles Deleuze's Time Machine*, 73.
23. Ibid.
24. 'The shot is the movement-image.' Deleuze, *Cinema 1*, 22.
25. Ibid., 19–20.

26. Ibid., 17.
27. Ibid.
28. Ibid., 16.
29. Ibid., 17.
30. Deleuze suggests that the 'signature' of a cinematic auteur, and even of entire 'schools' of montage can be analysed in terms of an examination of how the relevant films negotiate the tension between these two poles and between the conception of movement and of the whole thus implied. Such movements, he suggests, express 'genuine Ideas in the "filmic space"'. Ibid., 21–3.
31. Ibid., 10.
32. Rodowick, *Gilles Deleuze's Time Machine*, 184.
33. And to the extent that it does so, it runs the risk of reintroducing the error of defining the whole as the set of all sets.
34. Deleuze, *Cinema 2*, 163.
35. Smith, *Essays on Deleuze*, 108–9.
36. Deleuze, *Cinema 1*, 32.
37. Deleuze, *Kant's Critical Philosophy*, 18. Emphasis in original.
38. Somers-Hall, 'Transcendental Illusion and Antinomy', 135.
39. Smith, *Essays on Deleuze*, 109.
40. Somers-Hall, 'Transcendental Illusion and Antinomy', 146.
41. Ibid., 144.
42. Ibid., 128.
43. Ibid.
44. Ibid., 144.
45. A very condensed version of this argument might look like this: in so far as Deleuze identifies the noumenal with difference-in-itself, it is characterised as the relation of difference to itself in so far as it differs from itself (put in terms of the calculus, the relation of the independent variables dx and dy – the relation between the change in x and the change in y). These terms are undetermined except in so far as they enter into this relation. In other words, the relation itself, although external to its terms, is constitutive of those terms. Moreover, the reciprocal determination of the terms of this relation allows us to determine in turn the complete set of values of dx/dy. Smith, *Essays on Deleuze*, 115; Somers-Hall, 'Transcendental Illusion and Antinomy', 145–7.
46. In other words, his critique of Kant's treatment of transcendental Ideas via the calculus is a nuance or differing from itself of the logic of the relation of internal and external difference Deleuze presents in 'Bergson's Conception of Difference'.
47. As Smith points out, in this Deleuze fulfils the demands of Maimon's critique of Kant: 'the search for the genetic elements of real experience (and not merely the conditions of possible experience), and the

positing of a principle of difference as the fulfilment of this condition'. Smith, *Essays on Deleuze*, 111.
48. Deleuze, *Difference and Repetition*, 169.
49. Deleuze and Guattari, *What Is Philosophy?*, 38.
50. Ibid., 39.
51. Ibid., 42.
52. Ibid., 38.
53. Ibid., 42.
54. Ibid. Much of this chapter of *What is Philosophy?* can be read as sketching the outline of just such a history.
55. Ibid., 39.
56. Ibid., 37.
57. Ibid., 41. Emphasis in original.
58. Ibid., 40–1.
59. Rodowick, *Gilles Deleuze's Time Machine*, 12.
60. Deleuze, *Cinema 2*, 131.
61. Rodowick, *Gilles Deleuze's Time Machine*, 177.
62. Deleuze, *Cinema 1*, 59.
63. Deleuze and Guattari, *What Is Philosophy?*, 44–5.
64. Rodowick, *Gilles Deleuze's Time Machine*, 181.
65. Smith, *Essays on Deleuze*, 109.
66. Ansell-Pearson, 'Beyond the Human Condition', 63 in particular and 61-5 more generally.
67. To be precise, the 'hypothetical syllogism' implied by the causal coordination of images in the classical cinema gives rise to an 'Idea of the world' derived in strictly cinematographic terms, as a function of the spatialised conception of movement that linear causality entails.
68. Deleuze, *Kant's Critical Philosophy*, vii.
69. Deleuze, 'Cours Vincennes, 21/3/1978'.
70. Deleuze, *Kant's Critical Philosophy*, viii.
71. Deleuze, 'Cours Vincennes: Synthesis and Time, 14/3/1978'.
72. This temporalisation of difference is, according to Giovanna Borradori, one of the key outcomes of Deleuze's interpretation of Bergson in 'Bergson's Conception of Difference'. Borradori, 'The Temporalization of Difference', 10–12.
73. Smith, *Essays on Deleuze*, 67.
74. Ibid., 66.
75. Ibid., 68. It should be easy to see how Bergson's critique of the possible and the real (and Deleuze's appropriation thereof) bears directly on this project.
76. Ibid., 68–9.
77. Ansell-Pearson, 'Beyond the Human Condition', 58.
78. Deleuze, *Cinema 1*, 30.
79. Deleuze, *Cinema 2*, 157. As Deleuze puts it in *Cinema 1*: 'In the

mathematical sublime, the extensive unit of measurement changes so much that the imagination is no longer able to comprehend it, runs up against its own limit and is annihilated; but it gives way to a thinking faculty which forces us to conceive the immense or the measureless as whole. In the dynamic sublime, it is intensity which is raised to such a power that it dazzles or annihilates our organic being, strikes terror into it, but arouses a thinking faculty by which we feel superior to that which annihilates us, to discover in us a supra-organic spirit which dominates the whole inorganic life of things: then we lose our fear, knowing that our spiritual "destination" is truly invincible.' As Rodowick glosses it (in terms applicable to the whole of the classical cinema), the sublime 'augments our powers of thought through a totality that expands in contemplation of the infinite'. Deleuze, *Cinema 1*, 153; Rodowick, *Gilles Deleuze's Time Machine*, 181.
80. Deleuze, *Cinema 1*, 34.
81. 'Ideas . . . have no cause save in the attributes of thought that unfold as spiritual automata according to certain laws.' Rodowick, *Gilles Deleuze's Time Machine*, 174.
82. Deleuze, *Cinema 1*, 55.
83. Ropars-Wuilleumier, 'The Cinema, Reader of Gilles Deleuze', 257–8.
84. Although it remains implicit within those analyses and discernible in retrospect.
85. Deleuze, *Cinema 1*, 215.
86. Deleuze, *Cinema 2*, 157.
87. Through which the shot appears as a mobile section of the unceasing variation of the open whole.
88. Dillet, 'What Is Called Thinking?', 250.
89. Ibid.
90. Deleuze, *Cinema 2*, 156–88.
91. Ibid., 156.
92. Ibid.
93. Ibid.
94. Ibid., 156–7.
95. Ibid., 157. Why does Deleuze choose to analyse Eisenstein's 'dialectical' montage as an exemplar applicable in general terms to all classical modes of montage? On the one hand, he characterises Eisenstein later in *Cinema 2* as a 'cinematographic Hegel'. On the other, as we saw with regard to 'Bergson's Conception of Difference', Deleuze regards the Hegelian dialectic as the most extreme expression of a thought based on external difference. From these two together we can infer that, for Deleuze, Eisenstein's films offer the most extreme – and thus clearest and most easily analysed – example of the totalising orientation that characterises *all* of the modes of montage in the classical cinema. Ibid., 210.

96. Ibid., 158.
97. Ibid.
98. Ibid., 158–9.
99. Ibid., 159.
100. Ibid.
101. Ibid.
102. Ibid., 158.
103. Ibid., 159.
104. Ibid., 161.
105. Ibid., 156–7.
106. Deleuze, *Cinema 2*, 158.
107. Ibid., 162.
108. Ibid.
109. In the sense Marx outlines in his 'Critique of the Gotha Program': '*In a higher phase of communist society, after the enslaving subordination of the individual to the division of labor, and therewith also the antithesis between mental and physical labor, has vanished; after labor has become not only a means of life but life's prime want; after the productive forces have also increased with the all-around development of the individual, and all the springs of co-operative wealth flow more abundantly – only then can the narrow horizon of bourgeois right be crossed in its entirety and society inscribe on its banners: From each according to his ability, to each according to his needs!*' Marx, 'Critique of the Gotha Program', 154–5. Emphasis in original.
110. It is on this basis that Deleuze is able to call Eisenstein a 'cinematographic Hegel'. *Cinema 2*, 210.
111. Rodowick, *Gilles Deleuze's Time Machine*, 184.
112. Deleuze, *Cinema 2*, 157.
113. Ibid., 210.
114. Deleuze, *Negotiations*, 70–1.
115. Rodowick, *Gilles Deleuze's Time Machine*, 185.
116. Deleuze, *Cinema 2*, 164.
117. Ibid., 162.
118. Ibid., 157.
119. Ibid.
120. Ibid., 164.
121. Deleuze, *Negotiations*, 69.
122. Ibid. Deleuze reiterates these points almost verbatim in *Cinema 2*, 164.
123. Deleuze, *Cinema 2*, 165.
124. Bergson identifies Hegel as a source of theoretical justification for German militarism 'after the fact' in an address given to the *Académie des Sciences Morale et Politiques* in late 1914, published as *The Meaning of War*, 6. Karl Popper in his turn lays the responsibility for

the rise of fascism in Germany and for twentieth-century totalitarian political thought more broadly, firmly at the feet of what he calls 'irrationalist' philosophy in general, and of Hegelianism in particular, in Popper, *The Open Society and Its Enemies*. For my own account of Popper's critique and its bearing on Deleuze's own Bergsonism, see Thomas, 'Fascism, Irrationalism and Creative Evolution, or Deleuze, Running Away'.
125. Hallward, *Out of This World*, 162.

7

The Night, the Rain

Film, Death (the 'Reverse Proof')

A key point that the arguments of the previous chapter imply, but do not state directly, is that there are not two conceptions of the whole at work in the *Cinema* books (one for each volume), but three: not only the whole as the open and the whole as the outside, but 'between' them, the whole as a closed totality. The addition of this totalised conception of the whole provides us with the key to understanding the transition from Bergson to Blanchot, and thus from the Open to the outside: it is the totalised whole that provides us with the terms in which to understand how cinematographic thought gives rise to the conditions of its own collapse, in its confrontation with its own limits. As such, it seems worth offering a summary account of the articulation of these concepts and their relation to each other, precisely because in this form they offer an outline or sketch of how Deleuze is able to move from Bergson to Blanchot on the basis of strictly Bergsonian principles.

The whole as the open is a Bergsonian characterisation of the fundamental proposition of Deleuzian thought: that being is that which differs from itself first of all. The cinematographic character of human thought is such that it can only grasp the whole in this sense to the extent that the human condition itself is overcome. However, by characterising the cinematographic illusion in terms derived from *Matter and Memory*, rather than those of *Creative Evolution*, Deleuze is able to deduce the cinematographic genesis of the human from and on the basis of this open whole, rather than presenting it as a given (as Bergson does). He is able to bring the formal resources of the cinema to bear on the analysis of this illusion and its consequences because this deduction of the material moments of human subjectivity is also and on the same basis the deduction of the primary divisions of his taxonomy of cinematic signs. Thus in so far as the cinema offers a correction to the cinematographic illusion, this correction is not a function of movement-images (on their own they remain strictly cinematographic), but rather of the disjunction of projector and camera effected by montage and the mobile camera, and the aberration of movement this disjunction produces.

However, although the classical cinema arises with the introduction of this power, the products of that cinema are nevertheless characterised by their rejection or warding off *of* that power, that aberration. By ordering montage according to sensory-motor schemata, the classical cinema reintroduces the effects of the cinematographic illusion at the level of the relations between movement-images (rather than those between individual frames of the film strip, as in Bergson's original metaphor). Such schemata give rise in turn to an Idea of the world as a closed totality. In doing so they raise the cinematographic illusion to the level of a transcendent principle. By limiting relations between images to linear, causal and rational connections, the classical cinema is able to construct in strictly cinematic and non-human terms the cinematographic orientation of human thought and the products thereof. It is on this basis that the classical cinema can be said to recapitulate the history of philosophies of transcendence, identity and representation. Where Bergson merely critiques the cinematographic orientation of Western philosophy, Deleuze is thus able to deduce that orientation and its philosophical consequences on the basis of Bergsonian principles (the open whole as self-differing difference).

If this tendency towards totalisation and closure thus represents the natural metaphysics of human thought, it also confronts that thought with its own limits. The totality it constructs assures the coherence and unity of our actions in the world so construed, but the unity it offers is ultimately the stillness and silence of death, by way of the violence that underpins our own action and power. We 'reach' the intolerable, the impossible, the disaster, on the basis of our very own powers of thought and action: it is our cinematographic nature itself that orients the human towards and by the intolerable, violence and death. The historical dynamic of Deleuze's account of the cinema correlates the experience of the war, of fascism and the revelations of the camps with the break between the classical and modern cinemas. The sensory-motor schemata governing the cinema of the movement-image collapse here as a consequence of cinematographic thought's exposure to those limits. In its confrontation with those horrors, with the intolerable as the product of its own powers, thought collapses, unable to comprehend that horror in thought, or to act in response to it in any adequate or meaningful way. Thought becomes powerless,

The Night, the Rain

disastrous, impossible, and with this impossibility, a third concept or image of the whole comes to the fore: the whole as the outside.

Something very important has happened here that provides a solution to the paradox posed by the break and the relation between the two volumes of the *Cinema* books. The gap between the two volumes appeared impossible to bridge because the two images of thought that governed them seemed irreconcilable. On the one hand, to treat this gap in terms of classical cinema risked reducing the modern cinema to a consequence and extension of the causal logic of the former, thus reducing the time-image to another instance and variation of the movement-image. On the other hand, to grasp that gap in terms of the time-image risked disrupting the very chains of causality that defined the classical cinema and erasing it in turn. But, in so far as the totalisation of the whole is a reciprocal consequence and ground of the causal logic of the classical cinema, *it is the classical cinema itself that produces the conditions of its own disruption.* The consequences of the totalisation of the whole that the classical cinema 'adds' to the division between the whole as the open and as the outside are such that it bridges the gap between the open and the outside, in the sense that the gap between them is no longer impossible, *but has taken the form of impossibility itself as the terms of the human relation to being.*

The human is not 'overcome' in this relation: it does not ascend to being in being's own terms, but remains human. Rather, the cinematographic orientation of the human is exposed to its own impossibility: the experience is that of the exposure of the human and of human thought to being as the outside, of thought outside itself and the outside of thought. This experience is that of the modern cinema itself: the disjunctive linkage of shots according to irrational montage we find therein is the formal expression in cinematic terms of the experience of cinematographic (and thus human) thought exposed to its own limits. What we can see, then, is that the passage between *Cinema 1* and *2*, between the open and the outside, between Bergson and Blanchot, passes by way of the totalisation of the whole constructed by the cinematographic orientation of human thought. It is this totalisation that thereby creates the conditions for the exposure of human thought to its own limits, and to the impossibility those limits open onto. The image of thought that governs both the modern cinema and the account thereof in *Cinema 2* is given directly in that impossibility: thought as the outside, thought as disaster, thought as the confrontation with the impossible itself.

This outline offers a sketch of how we might account for the impossibility that attends the break or gap between the *Cinema* books, and how this break bears on the question of the human relation to being. However, the limitations of this account should be clear. The exposure of thought to its limits mapped out here relies on historical events that are strictly external to thought, and to cinema itself: the war, fascism, the death camps as the 'cause' of thought's exposure to the intolerable and to thought's own impossibility. Even if thought as power orients human life towards action, violence and death, this cannot account for the particular form this violence takes at any given moment. The specific historical events in question cannot, and should not, be regarded as something that could be deduced or accounted for on the basis of either the conditions of human thought or the cinema's articulation thereof – not least because it would be morally repugnant to do so.

The task of this chapter, then, is to show how the exposure of human thought to its own limits, to impossibility and to death can be derived on the basis of thought's own cinematographic genesis, and how the cinema is able to think these limits in its own non-cinematographic terms. Moreover, the terms in which this is done must also account for how the historical events surrounding the break between classical and modern cinemas can be approached in non-historical terms without denying or dismissing the moral significance of their historical reality.

Deleuze offers us the initial key to these tasks early in *Cinema 1*, at the end of his deduction of cinematic perception, action and affection-images (which is equally a deduction of the material moments of human subjectivity) on the basis of the acentred universal variation of being. He concludes this deduction with what he calls a 'reverse proof', in which he attempts to

> retrace the lines of differentiation of these three types of images, and try to discover the matrix or the movement-image as it is in itself, and in its acentred purity, in its primary regime of variation, in its heat and light, while it is still untroubled by any centre of variation.[1]

The terms in which he poses the question of how to effect this 'retracing' reinforce the point that the product of the differentiation he has mapped out is nothing other than human subjectivity and thought: 'How can we rid ourselves of ourselves, and demolish ourselves?'[2] In other words, having 'descended' from the universal variation and difference from itself of being to the differentiated movement-images (perception, action and affection-images) that constitute the material moments of human subjectivity (the centred perspective of a brain/screen), he now seeks to reverse this movement and 'ascend' once more towards the acentred variation of *the* movement-image, via the dissolution of man, of ourselves as a centre of perception on an acentred universal movement-image.

As if to emphasise the identity of his taxonomy of cinematic movement-images with his deduction of those images as the material moments of human subjectivity, this 'reverse proof' is offered in terms derived not from philosophy, but from cinema. More specifically, it is presented through an analysis of Samuel Beckett's *Film* (1965).[3] Despite being released well after the break Deleuze posits between the classical and the modern cinemas, his account of *Film* positions it firmly in the classical mode, in so far as it organises perception, action and affection-images according to a sensory-motor schema – even if its goal is ultimately to bring this schema to an end, to its end.

Beckett's project presents itself under the banner of Bishop Berkeley's 'formula of the image',[4] *esse est percipi* – to be is to be perceived. Deleuze argues that the 'demolishing of self' undertaken according to this formula takes the form of a series of conventions governing the relation of camera and subject, the goal of which is to dramatise the escape of the protagonist (played by Buster Keaton) from existence by progressively escaping the tyranny of perception itself.[5] The film ends with him immobile in a stilled rocking chair (exclusion of action and the perception of action), having masked or excluded anything in his room which might 'perceive' him – animals, mirrors, even pictures (exclusion of perception and the perception of perception) and leaving only the perception of the camera itself. Having by various conventions remained out of his (and our) view, behind his back, until now, the camera finally comes face to face with the protagonist – and is revealed as the protagonist himself, with the only exception that one eye is covered with a patch (mirroring the monocular vision of the camera). Here, Deleuze says, 'we are in the domain of the perception of affection, the most terrifying, that which still survives when all the others have been destroyed: it is the perception of self by self, the *affection-image*'.[6]

Deleuze reads the progressive extinction of action and perception-images throughout *Film* as taking us from the world given to us in experience towards the conditions of that experience: 'Beckett ascends once more towards the luminous plane of immanence, the plane of matter ... he traces the three varieties of image back to the mother movement-image.'[7] But what is most striking about the reascension Beckett effects, this reverse movement towards the conditions of experience *starting from the world as experience, and as experienced*, is that what it returns us to is not light, movement and the creative vitality of difference differing from itself, but rather what appears as its opposite. Deleuze projects the trajectory of *Film* beyond its end, beyond the subjective finality of a world reduced to a centre of perception perceiving only itself, towards the extinction of even this final image: 'Will it die out and will everything stop, even the rocking of the rocking chair, when the double face [of camera/ protagonist] slips into nothingness? This is what the end suggests – death, immobility, blackness.'[8] 'Death, immobility, blackness': a 'proof' then, that in its reversal seems to return it to the antithesis of its luminous origin.

Deleuze does go on to argue that even the darkness and death Beckett points towards in his elimination of the human is merely a 'subjective finality', a 'means in relation to a more profound end', that of

> attaining once more the world before man, before our dawn, the position where movement was, on the contrary, under the regime of universal variation, and where light, always propagating itself, had no need to be revealed . . . the luminous plane of immanence, the plane of matter and its cosmic eddying of movement-images.[9]

However, the gap between this 'subjective finality' and 'the world before man', and more particularly the leap Deleuze makes across this gap, seem to me in need of a fuller account than he offers here, not least because it remains unclear how 'death, immobility, darkness' can serve as a means towards an end given in terms of a 'cosmic eddying' of movement = light. Deleuze does give the fuller account this gap demands, I think, but only in so far as it lies at the heart of the *Cinema* books, and of philosophy itself.

To be precise, I think that the *Cinema* books as a whole *are* that account, manifested concretely in the (impossible) gap between those books, and that the gap in question is ultimately the gap between the cinematographic character of human nature and the universal variation of being as it exists for itself. If Beckett's *Film* speaks to this gap, it is because the elimination of the human Deleuze finds therein, and the 'death, immobility, blackness' to be found at or beyond its end, constitute the finality towards and by which the classical cinema is oriented. This finality reveals itself in or as the

The Night, the Rain

impossible gap between the *Cinema* books, between the classical and modern cinemas, between the movement-image and the time-image, the open and the outside. As such an examination of the 'reverse proof' Deleuze finds in Beckett's *Film* can offer us an entry point into understanding the impossible relation that exists between its two volumes as a reflection or expression of the philosophical problems that Deleuze turns to the cinema in order to explore.

The comparison between the analysis Deleuze offers of Beckett's *Film* and the analysis he offers of experimental cinema is instructive in this regard. Where Beckett's path to the 'world before man' must travel by way of the dark, by Deleuze's account, experimental cinema seeks to establish itself in that world directly.[10] This difference is a direct product of the different formal techniques that each deploys, and how these techniques bear on the status of the human therein. Beckett starts with a strictly classical organisation of perception, action and affection-images organised by a sensory-motor schema and then proceeds to eliminate those images step by step, and in doing so collapses the sensory-motor schema which orders them (he removes both the sensory = perception-images and the motor = action-images, leaving only the affection of self by self). By this elimination he seeks to reascend to a world before man.

By Deleuze's account, experimental cinema on the other hand (especially as exemplified in the American tradition represented by the work of Stan Brakhage or Michael Snow) imposes no sensory-motor constraint on its images. It draws immediately and directly on the capacity of montage and the mobile camera to produce aberrant movement by correlating images that are 'incommensurable from the viewpoint of our human perception'.[11] This non-human perception abandons the presentation of perception as it is *for* someone, in order 'to reach "another" perception which is also the genetic element of all perception'.[12] This 'genetic element of all perception' is simply the movement-image for itself, as that from which perception, action and affection-images (and thus the cinematographic human condition) are deduced.

In so far as it seeks to install itself directly in a world before man, experimental cinema understood in this fashion fulfils in an immediate sense what Bergson demands of intuition: it grasps being in being's own terms.[13] But where intuition must overcome the human to do so, the cinema's non-human thought shares no such barrier. It need neither 'descend' nor 'reascend', but has the capacity to install itself directly in the real movement of being, since montage and the mobile camera, and thus aberrant movement, are (for Deleuze) the very essence of the cinema. Thus

> if from the point of view of the human eye, montage is undoubtedly a construction, from the point of view of another eye, it ceases to be one; it is the pure vision of a non-human eye, of an eye which would be in things. Universal variation, universal interaction (*modulation*) is what Cézanne had already called the world before man, 'dawn of ourselves', 'iridescent chaos', 'virginity of the world'. It is not surprising that we have to construct it since it is given only to the eye which we do not have.[14]

The 'non-human eye' which would be 'in things' is perception-for-itself, the unrevealed luminosity of being. That is, the aberrant movement that montage constructs enters directly into the movement of being as it is for itself. It is for this reason that experimental cinema, under the sign of the *gramme*, constitutes the 'degree zero' of Deleuze's taxonomy of cinematic signs: 'the genetic element of all possible perception, that is, the point which changes, and which makes perception change, the differential of perception itself'.[15] Just as beings, and human beings, 'descend' from the unrevealed luminosity of being into and as a world of action and reaction, Deleuze's taxonomy descends from this aberrant genesis into the signs of classical cinema, into the realm of perception, action and affection-images constrained by sensory-motor schemata to a cinematographic construction of the world as a closed totality (and this 'descent' is the cinematic dramatisation or enactment of the genesis of beings, and human beings, immanent to being).

Thus where the classical cinema constructs an Idea of the whole as a closed totality, and the modern presents the whole as the outside, experimental cinema alone seeks to grasp the whole in and as the real differing from itself of the Open. However, there is no doubt where Deleuze's interests lie in the *Cinema* books: his treatment of experimental cinema constitutes a handful of pages in several hundred devoted to the classical cinema. The dramatisation or construction of the human by the latter is of more interest to him here than 'the world before man'. It is here that the contrast of experimental cinema with Beckett's *Film* becomes significant. If the classical cinema marks the 'descent' of cinema from the 'world before man' to the world *for* man, Beckett's film marks a conscious attempt to reverse that descent, to reascend to the world before man by the elimination *of* man.

But this ascent is more challenging that it might at first seem.

The Night, the Rain

To treat this relation as transitive – as if 'to ascend' were a simple reversal of 'to descend' – would amount to mistaking a transformation in duration for a translation in space, treating time itself as if it were reversible, and thus both abstract and unreal. If to ascend were merely the reverse of to descend, then at the conclusion of this double movement things would be precisely as they were: in effect, *nothing would have happened*, nothing would have *moved*. If, rather, movement expresses a transformation in the whole, then in the descent from acentred variation to a centred perspective on that variation – in the actualisation of the virtual – we must recognise that the whole itself is transformed, real duration is expressed. To reascend the path is not to return to a point of departure which remains 'in place', as it were, but to attempt to decentre a properly human perspective in order to open onto being as that which is never what it is, but rather only the becoming other of difference differing from itself. It is to expose the human to the in- or non-human, beings to being, from the perspective *of* beings, which is not identical to a being 'before' beings, since what has been added is, precisely, beings themselves (even if the task at hand is to 'eliminate' them).

Thus if the gap between the 'more profound end' of acentred universal variation and the 'subjective finality' of 'death, immobility, blackness' bears further exploration, it is because it marks the difference between a 'world *before* man' and man's attempt to *regain* this world – the difference between the descent from the unrevealed luminosity of the image-for-itself into distinct images-for-someone, and the attempt to reascend from the position of a centred perspective on variation towards the pure variation for itself. What returns, or seeks to return, in this reascension is man, that is to say, the very element that must be eliminated in order *to* return, and this is precisely the paradox of Bergsonian intuition.[16]

Beckett's reverse proof suggests that for all that the plenitude of *the* movement-image, or being-for-itself, 'descends' into the signs that constitute the material moments of human subjectivity (the avatars of the movement-image), retracing this path from the centred perspective of all-too-human thought does not return us to this plenitude 'as it is in itself', but rather to the 'subjective finality' of death, stillness, the dark *as the human experience of the in- or non-human*, that is, of being. Being as it is for itself is not deathly: it is creation, acentred universal variation, unrevealed luminosity of the world. Neither is being as it exists for someone deathly as such (although death no doubt bears heavily on the living): human beings 'screen' the light of being only in order to reveal it, to construct a world of beings on which to act and so live. But having descended into this world, to reverse this genesis is to abandon action, power, and the world as it is for us. It is, in this sense, to turn towards death.

This reversal is nothing other than the attempt to abandon the human condition and, in so far as this can be an experience, it is one in which thought and action fail us, our power no longer serves, in which the world of things withdraws itself from us leaving only silence and the dark. For the human as human, the unrevealed luminosity of being is simply the absence of light, the absence of things: to reascend towards being is to expose oneself to the absence of beings, to an existence without existents. Such an experience would be akin to what Emmanuel Levinas, drawing on Blanchot, calls the *il y a*, the 'there is': what there is when there is nothing, presence of absence, the silent murmuring of insomniac night.[17]

This is precisely the movement of Beckett's *Film*: the reascension of beings towards being in the elimination of the material moments of human subjectivity and thus the elimination of the world as it is for that subjectivity, leaving only the experience of the absence of the world. Levinas unfolds this experience for us in the following terms: 'let us imagine all beings, things and persons, reverting to nothingness. One cannot put this return to nothingness outside of all events. But what of this nothingness itself? Something would happen, if only the night and the silence of nothingness.'[18]

The asymmetry we see here between the luminous creativity that 'descends' into or as beings, and the deathly stillness that comes to meet those beings if and as they seek to reascend is an expression or nuance of the underlying logic that runs throughout and grounds all of Deleuze's thinking. That is to say, it is isomorphic with the asymmetry between internal and external difference he unpacks in 'Bergson's Conception of Difference'. Internal difference differs with itself all the way to external difference, and can thus account for, or perhaps descend all the way to, external difference. But since external difference can only differ from some other thing, some other determined identity, it cannot account for internal difference, cannot 'reascend' to that difference without finding some means to overcome or cease being itself, and so differ *from* itself (the human cannot reverse its cinematographic genesis without ceasing to be human).

This kind of asymmetrical binary, where one of the two terms nevertheless provides for the genesis or deduction of the other, appears repeatedly throughout Deleuze's work. For instance, the virtual grounds, produces and accounts for the actual, likewise the active for the reactive, the schizophrenic for the paranoid, non-sense for sense, active force for reactive force, the molecular for the molar, deterritorialisation for reterritorialisation and so on.[19] We must be careful to note, however, that repetition produces difference, not identity: although the logical topography of the argument may be the same, the case in question is not. The heterogenesis of Deleuzian philosophy is such that what is deduced in each case is a nuance (and thus difference) of the differing from itself *of* difference (all the way to identity), and what might be counter-actualised of or in each case likewise cannot be considered the 'same' concept.

What is distinctive in *this* case, in Deleuze's treatment of the cinema, is the focus on the *human* within this ascent. Whether we look at Bergsonian intuition, or Deleuze's development of it into his cinematic practice of concept creation, the ascent towards being (the concept as counter-actualisation of the event, montage thought, symptomatology) requires the overcoming, the elimination, the decentring of the human. It is the ascent to being and the techniques or means by which this might be achieved that is the focal point in these cases: the human is present only as that which must be overcome or discarded for in order to make the ascent.[20] Experimental cinema constitutes a kind of 'ideal' form of this attempt, in so far its construction of a 'world without man' need not even overcome the human but merely draws on the resources laid up by the already non-human aberration of movement produced by montage and the mobile camera.

It is this aberration that Deleuzian philosophy, in so far as it is cinematic, seeks to emulate in order to free itself from the lures of representation and identity, of the cinematographic illusion raised to the level of transcendent Idea. But it is *not* what Deleuze seeks to explore in the *Cinema* books, which is why experimental cinema occupies only a few pages therein.[21] The nuance that Deleuze draws out of Beckett's *Film* is the focus it places on the human experience *of* this overcoming: the attempt by the human to reascend to a 'world before man' *in human terms*, and thus the foregrounding of the impossibility of such an ascent *as* an experience, such that experience is given *as* impossibility. To reascend to a world before man is to expose the very identity that would think the difference of the world to its own absence.

'To be exposed to one's own absence' is a paradoxical formation, to be sure, but the terms in which Beckett's *Film* constructs this experience *as* an experience enable us to construct a precise characterisation of it, and of the terms in which it takes place. Perception, action and affection-images are the material moments of subjectivity, and it is their organisation and correlation that puts a world at our disposal. As the 'coincidence of subject and object', affect internalises perception as pure quality, and it is this quality that we act in response to, such that perception 'extends into action through the intermediary of affections'.[22]

But if perception is internalised as affection, and that affection is externalised as action, having eliminated both perception and action, *Film* removes both the world and any possible response to it, and leaves us with only the affection of self by self, 'the most terrifying'. This is where the film ends, but this is not yet 'death, immobility, blackness'. To get there Deleuze must project the trajectory Beckett has described beyond its end, beyond the end of the film ('Will it die out, will everything stop ... when the double face slips into nothingness?'[23]). The reason for this is perhaps obvious: where there is darkness there is no image; where there is stillness there is no movement; there where my death is I am not. This is what I would say: what Beckett's *Film* offers us in the end, as its end, is neither darkness nor stillness nor death, but the exposure (or the experience of the exposure) of experience *to* them. In the absence of world and movement, perception and action, all that is left to the affection of self by self is the experience of the absence of the world, which must include the absence of self in so far as the self is an agent of action. The only perception that could be internalised as affect, the only affect that could be extended into action under these circumstances, is the interminable experience of absence, of nothing happening, endlessly.

In his discussion of the affect-image in *Cinema 1*, Deleuze notes that

> Maine de Biran had already spoken of pure affections, unplaceable because they have no relation to determinate space, present in the sole form of a 'there is' ... because they have no relations to an ego [*moi*] ... The affect is impersonal and is distinct from every individuated state of things.[24]

If there is more than an accident of terminology connecting de Biran's 'there is' and Levinas' *il y a*, it would be the invocation of an experience which subsists even in or perhaps *as* the absence of any *moi*, any 'determined space' or 'individuated state of things'. What

The Night, the Rain

is essential here is that it *is* an experience: the presence of absence as the exposure of experience to the impossibility *of* experience. In the reascent towards being and the conditions of its own genesis, what the human comes face to face with is the exposure to one's own absence as the experience of the impossibility of possibility (since in this relation the possibility that is 'my own' death is taken away too, since where my death is I *am* not). The human experience of this absence can only take one form: not death (there is no experience to be had there) but the relationship *to* death.

The treatment of this relation within Deleuze's account of the cinema locates that account within one of the fundamental recurring themes of philosophy. Death, and man's relation to death, is one of the primordial figures of philosophical thought, and of thought in so far as it is philosophical, although the manner in which that relation is itself thought no doubt takes many forms. As Ullrich Haase and William Large summarise the historical recurrence of this figure, for Plato, death is the realm of the 'never changing essence of things'[25] such that it is in our relation to death that we grasp the eternal. For Hegel, it is the sovereign power of the negative by which 'consciousness "vanquishes" the destructive power of death' (negativity as 'creative destruction').[26] For Heidegger, this relation presents itself as 'being towards death' and thus as the possibility of impossibility, which offers the authenticity of *Dasein* as individuation.[27] Deleuze invokes this relation between philosophy and death directly in *Cinema 2* when he notes that 'the philosopher is someone who believes he has returned from the dead, rightly or wrongly, and who returns to the dead in full consciousness. The philosopher has returned from the dead and goes back there. This has been the living formulation of philosophy since Plato.'[28]

If the cinema dramatises the history of philosophy by its own means, it should hardly be surprising that this figure should find its place there too, or that its passage throughout the *Cinema* books should bear on the question of thought and thought's adequacy to being. Thus the Idea of the whole as a totality echoes in its own terms the most 'classical' formulation of thought's relation to death, in the following terms. The whole as totality, as end or completion (as closed set), is that which corrects or stabilises the potential for aberration inherent in montage, 'donates' a determinate content (and thus identity) to being as the discrete and actual elements which make up the closed set. This totality (the Idea of the whole or world) is what ensures the coherence of the relations between the elements of its set in terms of their causal linkages. For man as a centre of perception and action within this world, the closed totality within which action is possible is circumscribed by the figure of death as a border or boundary, that which completes one's life, finishes it or brings it to an end, but also delimits it and so gives it a determinate content such that its meaning finally reveals itself, for good or ill. This donation of coherence, identity and significance is what the ancient Greeks express with admirable clarity in the injunction to 'call no man happy until he dies' (which perhaps belongs as much to drama as it does to philosophy[29]).

However, as Jacques Derrida points out, the figure of death as a border or boundary also constitutes an *aporia*, in so far as it marks or extends itself as a line which cannot be crossed, and which in a sense has only one side (there is no 'beyond' of death for the one who dies). Travelling from the Greeks 'towards' a questioning or interrogation of Heidegger by way of Levinas and Blanchot, Derrida notes that although 'my death' certainly concerns me in the most personal of ways, and even if it imposes on my being a 'being towards death' as the possibility of impossibility (the authenticity of *Dasein* as individuation), it is nevertheless precisely that which I cannot experience as such. I cannot die as or for myself, for there where my death is *I* am not.

Death thus constitutes a boundary that can neither be found nor crossed for oneself or as oneself, such that any determination or authenticity it might offer is immediately taken away in or as the same gesture by which it is imposed.[30] This is, Derrida says, Blanchot's constant theme: 'the impossible dying, the impossibility, alas, of dying',[31] the 'impossibility of possibility' in which (as Haase and Large put it) '"my" death ... exposes me to the dissipation of myself, to an experience of insufferable anonymity'.[32] The experience of the exposure to death that Beckett constructs through his elimination or reduction of the material moments of subjectivity is, I think, precisely the experience of this non-border or non-passage. The 'terror' of the affection of self by self that Beckett leaves us with is precisely that of man's exposure to impossibility as the ungrounding ground of his possibility.[33] This is no longer thought as mastery, but rather as its own impossibility.

The Suspension of the World

If Deleuze's treatment of Beckett's *Film* offers us a coherent account of what it might mean to understand the human relation to being

The Night, the Rain

in terms of man's relation to death, that account is and can only be valid for *Film* itself, and not for the cinema as a whole. It turns on the very specific means by which Beckett seeks to eliminate perception and action-images in order to reduce human experience to the affection of self by self: the experience of the presence of absence as the terms of the relation of human being to death. It is thus particular to this case, and this case only. In order to bring the analysis unfolded in it to bear on the whole of cinema, we must therefore be able to locate the 'affection of self by self' that Beckett constructs in *Film* in relation to the condition of the cinema as a whole.

The key to doing so lies in the collapse of the sensory-motor schemata that constrain the classical cinema to a cinematographic and totalising grasp of the world. In so far as such schemata constitute the cinematic articulation of human (and thus cinematographic) thought, we must understand the collapse of such schemata as the fragmentation or failure of the human itself. Where Beckett sets out consciously and deliberately to eliminate the human, the collapse of such schemata cannot be regarded as an individual aesthetic or creative choice. Rather, it concerns the whole of the classical cinema, and is entwined with something like a generalised loss of faith in the capacity of perception to apprehend the horrors it sees, all unwilling, or of action to respond adequately to a world in which such things are possible. Nevertheless, the consequences of this collapse are the same as Beckett's conscious elimination of the human. That is to say, the trajectory is the same in both cases: it draws the image towards silence and the dark, the exposure of the human to the absence of the human. As such, for the cinema as a whole, the exposure of human being to being, to death, is marked by the break or gap between the classical and modern cinemas.

Here we can return to Deleuze's identification of this break with the 'great reversal' Kant effects within philosophy, in which 'Time is no longer related to the movement which it measures, but movement is related to the time which conditions it.'[34] Kant's appearance at this pivotal point in Deleuze's argument has a startling and potentially arbitrary quality to it, in so far as Kant appears to play no significant role elsewhere in the argument of the *Cinema* books.[35] As such, one might justly wonder 'why Kant? And why here?' As we shall see, however, this is less a case of a sudden and unwarranted appearance by Kant in the middle of a Bergsonian treatise on the cinema than it is an instance of Deleuze effecting a strictly Bergsonian revision of Kant by means *of* the cinema.

The first step in demonstrating this is to note that the correlation I am proposing here of the 'affection of self by self' with the break between classical and modern cinemas can only be fully justified through and in terms of Deleuze's identification of that break with the Kantian reversal in philosophy. Most importantly, this reversal is articulated not in Kantian terms as such, but in those of a properly Bergsonian account or revision *of* Kant. With Kant's reversal, time is no longer grasped indirectly as a function of movement (time grasped in terms of the linear and unidirectional succession of cause and effect), but rather appears directly as 'the immutable form of change and movement'.[36] The Bergsonian parallels here are clear. On the one hand, the latter's critique of the cinematographic orientation of Western philosophy is precisely a critique of its subordination of time to movement. On the other, movement grasped as a 'mobile section of duration' is simply movement understood as an expression of time, or in Kantian terms, time as 'the form of everything that changes and moves'.[37]

In other words, the reversal that Kant effects in philosophy is precisely what Bergson calls for in his critique of the cinematographic limits of Platonism and mechanism. But for Bergson, the cinematographic illusion is not just a figure of philosophical critique, or of a critique of philosophy: it governs thought, perception and language. Moreover, as Deleuze demonstrates, this illusion is constitutive of human nature, by virtue of the latter's genesis in terms of a centred perspective on acentred universal variation. As such, in the terms Deleuze adopts from Bergson, the 'great Kantian reversal' can only take place with or as the elimination of the human as a centre of perception and action. Beckett's progressive purging of perception and action thus offers a figure for this 'reversal' given in terms of human experience and human thought, as the affection of self by self, the 'most terrifying'.

What Kant shows us is that this 'terror' is precisely the experience of time as change, as transformation. The doubling or duality of 'self' in the phrase 'the affection of self by self' presents this 'experience' in the form of a fracture or crack in thought and in the 'I' which thinks. This 'fracture' is analysed by Deleuze in *Kant's Critical Philosophy* in terms of Rimbaud's formula 'I is another'.[38] On the one hand, Deleuze says, there is the I of 'I think', for which thought appears as spontaneity, as 'an act which constantly carries out a synthesis of time, and of that which happens in time, by dividing up the present, the past and the future at every instant'.[39] On the other hand, however, the 'I' also exists *in* time, and thus as that which changes constantly, not as a function of my own action but because time is the form of change and movement itself. This 'I' experiences 'my' thoughts not as spontaneous action or power, but as an expression of time (time as the form of change, which the 'I' suffers or undergoes): 'I cannot therefore constitute myself as a unique and active subject, but as a passive ego which represents to itself only the activity of its own thought; that is to say, the *I*, as an other which affects it.'[40] Thus (as Deleuze explains in his account of this 'fractured I' in *Difference and Repetition*):

> the spontaneity of which I am conscious in the 'I think' cannot be understood as the attribute of a substantial and spontaneous being, but only as the affection of a passive self which experiences its own thought – its own intelligence, that by virtue of which it can say *I* – being exercised in it and upon it but not by it.[41]

The 'affection of self by self' is thus the experience of the 'I think' not as spontaneous action or power, but as something imposed from 'without' by or as time as the form of that which changes: thought as powerlessness or pure passivity, the exposure of the 'I' to time as transformation or self-differing difference. The affection of self by self as the 'most terrifying': thought as a suffering of time.

If Deleuze is able to place the Kantian reversal of the subordination of time to movement at the centre of his Bergsonian account of the cinema, it is because he finds or reaches that reversal in terms derived from Bergson, and not from Kant. He thus reconstructs or enters into the movement of Kantian thought in Bergsonian terms. This task must be understood in the context of Deleuze's wider project of rethinking or correcting Kant's transcendental idealism in line with Maimon's critique thereof (a project which finds its positive articulation in the form of Deleuze's own transcendental empiricism[42]). As Smith points out, 'Maimon's primary objection was that Kant had ignored the demands of a genetic method'[43] which, rather than assuming the 'facts of reason' *a priori* (as Kant does), would show how they are 'engendered immanently from reason alone as the necessary modes of its manifestation'.[44] Such a method 'requires the positing of a principle of difference in order to function . . . [since] it is difference that constitutes the genetic condition of real thought'.[45]

Bergson's role in Deleuze's response to Maimon's critique is by no means limited to the *Cinema* books, and lies in the very roots of the Deleuzian philosophical project. As Ansell-Pearson points out,

Bergson's importance to Deleuze was from the start tied to Deleuze's 'effort to radicalise the post-Kantian project commenced by Solomon Maimon ... [and] to pass from a transcendental philosophy to a genetic one'.[46] Indeed, we can trace this theme of genesis back to 'Bergson's Conception of Difference' itself, where it plays a role which is on the one hand indirect (in its relation to Kant) and utterly foundational (in its relation to the underlying principles of Deleuzian thought). The treatment offered in that essay of the relation between internal and external difference constitutes a genetic account of external difference, whereby it is 'deduced' from internal difference in so far as the former is a 'product' of the differing from itself of internal difference all the way to external difference. As we have seen, this pattern is pervasive in Deleuze's work, so much so that it might be called the ur-form of Deleuzian logic.

It should be no surprise then that Deleuze's return to Bergson in the *Cinema* books should also entail a return to this theme of genesis. Deleuze's deduction of perception, action and affection-images as products of a centred perspective on acentred universal variation must be understood in this context as the application of just such a genetic method. In particular, it offers itself as a genetic account of the human, and of the limits of the intellect in relation to the being of difference, that is nevertheless deduced on the basis of that being. Thus we can see that the emphasis Deleuze places in *Cinema 1* on the necessity of deducing the cinematographic illusion, rather than simply describing or asserting it, is a direct response to the demand for a genetic account of the human and of human thought.

But the 'facts of reason' that can be derived from this genesis are those of the dogmatic image of thought and the indirect image of time imposed by the cinematographic illusion. As such, the genesis of the human and of human thought in difference is obscured, suppressed, hidden behind that illusion. It is only with the stripping away of this mask that time as the form of change and as a principle of difference reveals itself *to* thought. In terms of this Bergsonian reformulation of Kant, the spontaneity of the 'I think', of thought as an active power, *is* cinematographic thought. It is an illusion that masks from thought the passivity of the 'I' that changes under the force of time. But where that power fails, this passivity begins to surface: the 'facts of reason' proper to the 'I think' are exposed to their genetic condition, to time as change, to the differing of being from itself. The 'affection of self by self' is precisely the *experience* of the exposure of the 'I think' to the passivity of the 'I' subject to time as change (to self-differing difference) as its very condition. The 'I think' here remains, but all that remains for it to think is its own absence from itself and the incapacity of its thought. In other words, the reversal enacted in Beckett's 'reverse proof' is nothing other than the 'great Kantian reversal', offered here not as a moment in the history of philosophy, but as the drama of thought itself in its struggle to think.

As I argued at the beginning of this chapter, the terms of relation between the classical and modern cinemas articulated by the totalisation of the whole are such that the thought of the modern cinema is given in terms of the impossibility *of* thought. In other words, the affection of self by self, and thus the crack in thought effected in the Kantian reversal of the relation of movement and time, must therefore be characteristic not only of the break *between* classical and modern cinemas, but of the modern cinema itself. This experience of thought no longer as a power one possesses, but as an incapacity or suffering one undergoes, is precisely what Deleuze finds in Antonin Artaud's conception of the cinema, which Deleuze argues prefigures that of the modern cinema, despite originating in the 1920s.[47] Artaud, he says, argues that the image 'has as its object the functioning of thought, and that the functioning of thought is also the real subject that brings us back to images'.[48]

In this Artaud shares a superficial similarity with Eisenstein, but where the latter attributes to montage the power of thinking the whole (as montage idea), and expressing that idea in images (internal monologue), Artaud 'overturns' the totality of cinema-thought relations such that 'on the one hand there is no longer a whole which is thinkable through montage, on the other hand there is no longer an internal monologue utterable through image'.[49] Far from thought thinking the whole under the shock of montage, for him this shock takes the form of a fundamental dissociation or dislocation of images and of thought, a delinking in which the 'spiritual automaton has become the Mummy, this dismantled, paralysed, petrified, frozen instance which testifies to "the impossibility of thinking that is thought"'.[50] This, according to Deleuze, is what Artaud 'recognises' as 'the real subject-object of the cinema. What cinema advances is not the power of thought, but its "impower", and thought has never had any other problem . . . [than] this difficulty of being, this powerlessness at the heart of thought.'[51]

Where Eisenstein sees in the cinema a means of constructing '*the sensory-motor relationship between world and man, nature and thought*'[52] that gives the whole *to* thought and expresses it *in* thought, for Artaud, the brain's 'innermost reality is not the Whole, but on the contrary a fissure, a crack'.[53] This constitutes a precise formulation of the 'fractured I' of the Kantian reversal and of the 'affection of self by self', or thought as the suffering of time (despite the fact that Kantian philosophy is most certainly not what is at stake here for Artaud). Thus

> it might be said that Artaud turns round Eisenstein's argument: if it is true that thought depends on a shock which gives birth to it (the nerve, brain matter), it can only think one thing, the fact that we are not thinking, the powerlessness to think the whole and to think oneself, thought which is always fossilized, dislocated, collapsed.[54]

Deleuze notes that 'A being of thought which is always to come is what Heidegger discovered in universal form, but it is what Artaud lived as the most singular problem, his own problem.'[55] That is to say, where Heidegger approaches this problem at a distance, abstractly and via (existential) analysis, for Artaud it concerns 'his own' lived experience, even if that experience is one of a fundamental dislocation of 'himself' and of thought, the anguish of which he describes as an 'absence like a gap, a kind of cold, imageless suffering, without feeling'.[56] To the extent that Heidegger places this experience at a distance as an object of his thought, he remains on the side of the illusory spontaneity of the 'I think' (he chooses to think about the impossibility of thought, but does not suffer it, does not suffer the thought which is not his own to think in him). It is the illusion of spontaneity that must be fractured for thought to think, even if all that is then left to thought is its own impossibility. It must be given as experience, not abstraction (that is, under the condition of *real*, rather than possible experience).

The limits of Heidegger's approach are simply those of the cinematographic limits of thought and language.[57] Artaud's poetry takes the form of language, to be sure – Deleuze's treatment of Artaud draws heavily on Blanchot's account of the famous correspondence between Artaud and Jacques Rivière concerning Artaud's poems[58] – but it is precisely the failure of those poems to think and to think the impossibility of thought, despite or as his anguish, that opens them onto the crack in thought and in the brain.[59] The value of the cinema in so far as it approaches this territory is that it does so without abstraction, in strictly concrete terms as image and in the relation between images (that is to say, montage).

Thus where Beckett achieves the 'affection of self by self' by means of the *elimination* of perception and action, the cinema of the time-image does so by means of their *delinking*. With the modern cinema, montage no longer constitutes itself as a gap that is crossed, no longer constructs a link and continuity between images that can be extended all the way to an Idea of the world as totality. The centre no longer holds and the aberration of movement returns to the cinema, not in the form of a world without man, but as man's experience of the absence of both the world and himself, the affection of self by self: 'it is here that the reversal is produced: movement is no longer simply aberrant, aberration is now valid in itself and designates time as its direct cause. "Time is out of joint": it is off the hinges assigned to it by behaviour in the world, but also by movements of world.'[60] The 'fractured I' or 'crack in the brain' thus appears in the modern cinema in the form of the interstice, or 'irrational cut', that opens up between images once they are no longer constrained by sensory-motor schemata, a crack which swallows both world and thought. Under these conditions

> the cinematographic image . . . carries out a *suspension of the world* or affects the visible with a *disturbance*, which far from making thought visible, as Eisenstein wanted, are on the contrary directed to what does not let itself be thought in thought, and equally to what does not let itself be seen in vision.[61]

With this 'suspension of the world', it is not just the 'I' that is fractured, it is the relationship between world and man, man and world itself. In or for the cinema of the time-image, the human is no longer an agent of action in a field of possibility, but a 'seer', 'prey to a vision, pursued by it or pursuing it, rather than engaged in an action'.[62]

If we can now justify the correlation of Beckett's elimination of perception and affection-images with the collapse of sensory-motor schemata, and the 'affection of self by self' with the 'great Kantian reversal' that gives rise to the classical cinema, there nevertheless remains the problem of history. As I've argued, if we locate the war and its attendant horrors as the concrete expression of the totalisation of the whole expressed in the classical cinema's articulation of cinematographic thought, we risk characterising those horrors as the direct result *of* that totalisation. We would then be left with the absurd and repugnant conclusion that the Holocaust could somehow be deduced on the basis of the powers of thought or cinema alone. We might justly reject this proposition and argue instead that the war, fascism, the death camps are the *cause* of thought's exposure to its own limits, and of the break between the classical and modern cinemas. However, to do so would be to act as if this exposure, this break, were a consequence, a reflection or representation of those events, and thus to subject the powers of both thought and cinema to a strictly external determination (that of the world historical events 'outside' both, which they are said to reflect or respond to).

To resolve this twofold problem, we must turn once more to Kant and to the 'great reversal' he effects within philosophy. This reversal is a historical event: it takes place as a moment in history, and particularly the history of philosophy: Kant is sitting at his desk one day, has an idea and writes it down. This is the spontaneity of the 'I think' acting in history and 'making history', and thus an articulation of thought as a power we (or in this case, Kant) possess. But what he thinks is this: the 'fractured I', thought not as spontaneity, but as a suffering of time. The reversal of the relation of time and movement that Kant thinks at this moment in history dislocates both history as linear progression and thought as power. This event of thought disrupts both philosophy (and especially the history of philosophy) and the spontaneity of thought proper to the philosopher who thinks it. It comes as no surprise then that 'Kant shrank away from the consequences of his discovery',[63] as Rodowick puts it. However, Deleuze's Bergsonian/cinematic reformulation of the Kantian project can, I think, be read as an attempt to follow through what Kant shies away from, by showing how both history and the spontaneity of thought *and* their dislocation can be deduced in genetic terms on the basis of the self-differing difference of being As such this 'Bergsonian/cinematic reformulation' bears directly on Deleuze's genetic and Maimonian reformulation of Kant's transcendental idealism.

Deleuze begins, of course, by deducing not the 'fractured I' or the reversal, but rather the human as centred perspective on acentred universal variation. The cinematographic condition of human being or human nature is such that it lives in and thinks the world as a field of action in which time is experienced as a passage from one moment to the next, a causal and linear chain of action and reaction. In other words, the mode of existence of the human as cinematographic is *historical*: we live 'in' history, as agents of history. Deleuze is thus able to account for 'history' and 'the historical' not in the form of the events of history as such, but rather as a *mode of existence* deduced from and on the basis of difference. Moreover, this mode of existence is inextricably intertwined with the (illusory) spontaneity of the 'I think': the spontaneity of thought (thought as a power we possess) is a product of the cinematographic condition of the human. That is to say, the spontaneity of the 'I think' only appears as a possibility, or as possibility, on the basis of the subordination of time to movement and thus as a moment in history itself. Here the sense of Deleuze's claim that the *Cinema* books do not constitute a history of the cinema becomes clear: in so far as 'history' plays a role therein, it does so in the form of a deduction *of* the historical as a product of the cinematographic genesis of the human.

Likewise, if the cinema recapitulates the history of philosophy, this is not because it reflects or represents that history: the spiritual automaton of the cinema enters into the movement of actualisation, of the genesis of the human and of human thought and philosophy by its own means and as a consequence of its own powers. History (including that of philosophy), and a grasp of the world in terms *of* history, is a product of the cinematographic human condition, of a world constructed in causal terms. Non-human cinema may dramatise or enter into that historical movement by its own means, but those means are non-cinematographic in essence. As such, they are non-historical, even if the products of cinema enter into history as a series of events in historical time – this or that film released in a particular year, watched at a certain day and time in a particular cinema, and written about by a given author, whose words are read by someone else at some later date.

As Brenez puts it, the cinema exists 'not as a simple reflection, the redoubling of something that already existed, but as *the emergence of a visionary critical activity*'.[64] Such a conception of the cinema not only responds directly to the exigencies of the '*Cahiers* axiom' discussed at the start of this book,[65] but also offers the cinema as an exemplar of the 'metaphysical auscultation' or 'diagnostic power' that Bergson and Deleuze respectively attribute to art in general. If the cinema is indeed a 'visionary critical activity', it is because its deduction of the human, and of the relation between man and world it explores in its diverse modes, constitutes the production not just of an experimental brain or brains, but also of experimental worlds (even when those worlds are ones of totality and closure). The products of the cinema and of the philosophical and ontological speculation they recapitulate neither cause nor represent the world, but *envision* it: if those visions bear on the historical world in which we live and act, it is only because they are deduced and constructed on the same basis *as* that world – on the basis of real difference as the genetic condition of experience.

The outcomes of these arguments are twofold. We can now see that the exposure to being that Beckett constructs by means of the reduction of the human to the experience of 'the affection of self by self' is reflected in terms valid for the whole of cinema, in terms of the collapse of sensory-motor schemata that precipitate the break between classical and modern cinemas. The gap between the two is constituted in terms of the fracturing of the spontaneity of thought under the force of time as change, given as the exposure to death as the human experience of the real difference of being. Furthermore, we can show that Deleuze's cinematic account of the trajectory of human thought towards its own fracture is able to deduce the historical mode of existence (and not the events of history as such) without being subject to strictly external historical determinations and thus reduced to a reflection or representation *of* the events of history.

But if the events of history cannot account for the trajectory of thought towards its own fracture – if it is not the experience of the war as such that exposes thought to the consequences of its totalising tendencies, nor the Holocaust that reveals the limits of cinematographic human thought in and as death – then what does? We must account for this trajectory and this exposure strictly in terms of the powers of thought itself, as derived from its cinematographic genesis. And since it is through the formal capacities of the cinema as such that Deleuze demonstrates this genesis and these powers, we must therefore do so *in terms of these formal capacities alone*. In other words, rather than the history of the cinema reflecting or expressing the war and its attendant horrors, that horror must be in some sense be found internal to the cinema, envisioned by it independently of the historical events of the world, and as a product of the cinema's own *formal* properties. The cinema must come face to face with 'death, immobility, blackness' on terms internal to it, and as a consequence *of* those terms.

'The Image, the Remains'

The key to this task lies in montage itself, and in the consequences of its organisation within the classical cinema according to sensory-motor schemata. That is to say, it is in terms of such schemata that cinematographic human being must be confronted with or exposed to its own limit or boundary in or as death. We can start by returning to Deleuze's claim that the cinema of the movement-image 'was from the beginning linked to the organisation of war, state propaganda, ordinary fascism' not only historically, but as a function of its own essence.[66] He extends this claim on the basis of the thesis of Paul Virilio's *War and Cinema*, which argues that technologies of perception are necessarily technologies of war, since for something to become a target it must first of all be *seen*.[67] In consequence, Deleuze says, 'the system of war mobilises perception as much as arms and actions: thus photo and cinema pass through war and are coupled together with arms'.[68]

This means not only that the space of conflict presents a veritable theatre of mise en scène and counter-mise en scène, which seeks to hide or reveal, display or dissemble the image as a (real or potential) target, but that the exercise of power and control in its broadest sense is tied essentially to visibility. You can't shoot, control or master what you can't see. Virilio cites Maurice Merleau-Ponty: 'The problem of knowing who is the subject of the state and war will be of exactly the same kind as the problem of knowing who is the subject of perception.'[69] This means not only that the subject of the state must be visible to the state if they are to be subjected, but that that control itself is exercised in and as the visible. For Deleuze, fascist Germany constitutes a key figure of this system of the visible, in which 'it is the whole of civil life which passes into the mode of the *mise-en-scène*, in the fascist system: "real power is henceforth shared between the logistics of arms and that of images and sounds"; and, to the very end, Goebbels dreamt of going beyond Hollywood'.[70] This 'fascism of images' means not only that every subject is a target, but that the organisation of images (Virilio's 'logistics of perception') renders 'civil life' as indiscernible from the organisation of war. But if the cinema is indeed linked *essentially*, and not just historically, to the organisation of war from its beginning, it is not enough account for this link in terms of a merely historical example (in this case, that of the 'cinematic' organisation of relations of state and subject in fascist Germany). Rather, it must be justified at the level of film form itself, in terms of the powers of frame, shot and montage and the composition of images they effect.

If, as Virilio suggests, 'to see' is merely a point along a trajectory towards 'to kill', then the proto-cinematic technology of Étienne-Jules Marey's chronophotographic rifle of 1882 serves as a figure for this violence at the heart of the cinema, as both 'precursor of the Lumière brothers' camera and direct descendent of the Colt revolvers and cylindrical guns'.[71] In it, the technological apparatus of seeing (the camera) and killing (the rifle) are fused in a prefiguration of the motion picture camera, in so far as its capacity to capture a sequence of images in rapid succession gives rise to a pre-cinematic analogue of the twenty-four frames a second captured by the motion picture camera. In fusing 'to see' with 'to kill', it poses the line of flight of the bullet as a figure for the classical cinema's organisation of images into a system of action and reaction, whose principle of organisation is that of death. The perception of the camera, its point of view or perspective, inscribes the line of flight of the bullet as it speeds towards its victim, such that the perspective so constructed is the organisation of a space of action as much as it is one of perception.

Massumi points out in his translation of *A Thousand Plateaus* that, in the context of the system of perspective associated with Renaissance painting, a 'line of flight' (or *ligne de fuite*) refers to the lines of perspective converging towards a painting's vanishing point, its *point de fuite* or 'point of flight'.[72] A line of flight, in this sense, is a principle of organisation that determines relations between elements as coherent; it keeps things quite literally 'in proportion'. If the bullet's line of flight is thus also a line of perspective, then its vanishing point, its point of flight, is the bullet-raddled body of its victim: gunman and prey are joined in a perspectival system, which, as much as it determines a scheme of vision also determines a scheme of action and reaction: I shoot, you die. Thus where the Renaissance system of spatial perspective maintains the proportionality of spatial perception within a single image, the cinema seeks to maintain the coherence and proportion between perception *and* action, across multiple shots and angles: 'Perception is organised in obstacles and distances to be crossed, while action invents the means to cross and surmount them.'[73]

It is in this sense that the line of flight of a bullet is a line of perspective; it determines the relation between a perception-image (the view through the gun sight) that gives the distance to be crossed, and an action-image (the firing of the gun) as the invention of the means to cross that distance. But where the perspectival system of painting produces an indirect image of spatial depth as a function of relative in-frame size, the coherence of the classical cinema lies in the fact that it organises the plane of movement-images into an indirect image of time as a function of movement. It produces, as Deleuze says, not a spatial but a *temporal* perspective.[74] The line of flight of the bullet is the articulation of a passage of time, an orderly causal procession from one moment to the next, one present to the next, so that the coherence of action and reaction from one shot to the next is temporal rather than spatial. You live, and then you die, in that order.[75]

The line of flight of the bullet thus serves as a figure for the sensory-motor organisation of images and for the cinematic dramatisation of the causal/historical mode of existence. The purpose of this sensory-motor mode of organisation is precisely to maintain the coherence of the relations between images – to ward off the aberration of movement – by constraining the disruptive force of time as change to a linear temporal perspective. The narrative space of the classical cinema, in its widest sense as the organisation of the space and time of action, is determined and organised in relation to the corpse that is the bullet's point of flight. As the point to which all (temporal) lines of perspective flow, the vanishing point, the corpse, is a principle of determination, orienting all possible relations between images in relation to that point and delimiting them as a function of it.

Of course, just as the vanishing point of a painting does not appear *in* that painting, but rather 'behind' it (and even then virtually) the 'corpse as vanishing point' does not refer to any specific image of violence or death that might appear on screen. Rather, it serves as both limit and principle of coherence. The line of flight of the bullet and the corpse towards which it flies thus offer a figure for the organising principle of a romantic comedy as much as a western or a war film (that is to say, for the classical cinema in its entirety) in so far as the action each presents is equally organised in sensory-motor terms as a causal series of action and reaction.

It's also worth noting that Deleuze and Guattari insist that the proportionality of images that the spatial perspective of a painting organises does not *represent* a pre-existing spatial order, but rather *constructs* it: 'Lines of flight as perspective lines, far from being made to represent depth, themselves invent the possibility of such a representation.'[76] This invention of depth is by the same measure the invention of a world ordered or constructed in spatial terms (the world of the painting), in the same way that the classical cinema 'invents' the temporal order that constructs its worlds as coherent spaces of action and reaction.

Moreover, what we find with the spatial perspective constructed in painting is that this construction is also and unavoidably the construction of the eye to and for which that world is given. Imagine a rectangular canvas with a line drawn from each corner towards the vanishing point which lies behind it; now extend those lines in the other direction, 'proceeding' in front of the canvas, rather than receding behind: the eye/I of the viewer constructed by the painting lies at the point where those lines intersect. The vanishing point towards which a painting's lines of perspective recede, which maintains the coherence of the spatial depth so constructed, is thus mirrored on the 'far' side of the image plane in the eye/I of an ideal viewer, in relation to whom the ordering of space effected in the image is constructed. The effect of this is, as John Berger points out, to centre 'everything on the eye of the beholder ... Perspective makes the single eye the centre of the visible world. Everything converges on to the eye as to the vanishing point of infinity. The visible world is arranged for the spectator as the universe was once thought to be arranged for God.'[77] The cinema repeats this same dynamic in terms not of space, but of time. In the system of temporal perspective organised by the classical cinema, the vanishing point of that perspective is mirrored in the genesis of the human as a centre of action. With this genesis, the world is organised around and in relation to the human as a centre of perception and action, just as the spatial perspective of painting centres 'everything on the eye of the beholder'. Thus this genesis constitutes the mirror image of the corpse as vanishing point, such that genesis and corpse exist in or as a condition of mutual presupposition (all that lives must die, and only those that die will have lived).

The bullet's line of flight and the corpse towards which it flies should thus be understood as serving to maintain or, more properly, restore or construct a properly human temporal order and continuity of perception and action within the cinema. Unlike the images of natural perception, those of the cinema are divorced from any centre of perception and thus lacking in any common scale or principle of organisation, and so inherently aberrant. Sensory-motor schemata (figured as a linear temporal perspective) serve to re-establish this lost proportion in a new mode or at a new level, restoring normality to aberrant movement and coherence to perception and action in relation to their *point de fuite*. Deleuze notes that 'Time as progression derives from the movement-image or successive shots. But time as unity or as totality depends on montage which still relates it back to movement or to the succession of shots.'[78] This mutual presupposition of succession and totality is simply the 'sensory-motor unity of man and world'.

This unity is articulated in the classical cinema in terms of an Idea of the world derived on the basis of sensory-motor schemata, which in turn justifies and assures the coherence and effectiveness of our action in and on the world. In doing so, it construes the whole as a closed totality in which action finds its principle of coherence in stillness and death: the unity of man and world, of the one and the many in the figure of the corpse (the mass graves and the ovens). What the figure of the line of flight of the bullet as a line of temporal perspective with the corpse as its vanishing point brings out is that this unity, this death, *is a function of the indirect image of time constructed by the classical cinema*. The montage Idea of the world as closed totality (the deathly stillness of Hegelian finality/fatality) is not a reproduction of the world, but neither is it the constitution of an autonomous world; it is the production or creation of the world *as an object of our thought and subject of our action*. This is what we find figured in the corpse, as the organising principle or vanishing point of the bullet's line of flight.

To suggest that the corpse serves to orient or determine the world as something which is both at our disposal and subject to our comprehension is simply to reiterate Blanchot's proposition that, 'as contemporary philosophies would have it, comprehension and knowing in man are linked to what we call finitude'[79] and that this finitude is given us by death as a border which delimits life and its world, and orients the passage of life's time in relation to that border. The corpse, as the organising and orienting principle of a sensory-motor schema is in this sense an image of action as mastery and of thought as a power at our disposal. But where, Blanchot asks 'is the finish? Granted, it is taken in or understood as the possibility which is death. But it is also "taken back" by this possibility, inasmuch as in death the possibility which is death dies too.'[80] We can recognise in this the same paradox located via Derrida in relation to the exposure to death constructed in Beckett's *Film*.[81] But where Beckett constructs this relation to death through the elimination of perception and action-images, and the reduction of the human to the 'terror' of the affection of self by self, here (with the figure of the corpse as vanishing point) 'death, immobility, blackness' are embedded in, derived from, the system of the classical cinema itself, in and as its formal principle of organisation.[82]

The corpse as vanishing point is that which organises the images of that cinema into a coherent temporal perspective, and towards which it moves in time (to live is to move, step by step, towards death). The Idea of the whole as totality derived from such schemata reveals the boundaries that determine the world of living action and give it its coherence *as those of death* ('"behind" the image [at the vanishing point] there was nothing to be seen but concentration camps'[83]). It implies that, at the literal unifying point of the sensory-motor schema (its vanishing point), there is an absence: the corpse not as a figure of death as the sovereign power of the negative, but as the 'impossibility of possibility' itself. The unity of the totalised or totalisable whole, which is constitutive of a world in which one knows how to act and react, rests finally on a gap, a 'hole in appearances'[84] opening onto the indeterminate, interminable presence of absence which corresponds to what Blanchot refers to as the 'outside'. Blanchot says of the 'cadaverous presence' that death

> suspends the relation to place, even though the deceased rests heavily in his spot as if upon the only basis that is left to him. To be precise, this basis lacks, the place is missing, the corpse is not in its place. Where is it? It is not here, and yet it is not anywhere else. Nowhere? But then nowhere is here. The cadaverous presence establishes a relation between here and nowhere.[85]

It is precisely this relation between here and nowhere that is to be found at the vanishing point: the presence of absence, the 'suspension of the world' nevertheless present as an image *in* the world.

Blanchot makes his comments on the corpse, and the ambivalence of its relation to the space it occupies, in a short essay titled 'The Two Versions of the Imaginary'.[86] The first version in question grasps the image as the 'life giving negation' of the thing, which places that thing at thought's disposal and thus subject to our mastery.[87] In so far as the corpse bears on such an image, it is as a figure of finitude, of closure and totalisation, and thus 'a formidable resource, reason's fecund power'.[88] The second version of the imaginary, and of the image, which haunts the first as its indivisible double, is precisely that which withdraws this 'fecund power' and leaves both action and thought bereft, disoriented, adrift.

The corpse that lies before us is, in this sense, infinitely far from the individual we once knew, despite being nothing other than that same person. In many respects it is the collapse of all the possibilities that once expanded before them, of the world organised around them as a space of actions and things at one's disposal. This corpse 'is neither the same person who was alive, nor is it any other person, nor is it anything else'.[89] It is in this sense that Blanchot tells us that 'the mourned deceased begins to *resemble himself*'.[90] Inasmuch as *himself* is no longer, all that remains is the cadaver, which is not that person and yet is nothing else. All that remains, all that the remains are, is the resemblance, the image of the person that once was. Thus

> the corpse is a reflection becoming master of the life it reflects – absorbing it, identifying substantively with it by moving it from its use value and from its truth value to something incredible – something neutral which there is no getting used to . . . It is the likeness, like to an absolute degree, overwhelming and marvelous. But what is it like? Nothing.[91]

The image, in this sense, is that which 'threatens constantly to relegate us, not to the absent thing, but to its absence as presence, to the neutral double of the object in which all belonging to the world is dissipated'.[92]

Blanchot likens it to the way a damaged tool ceases to be subsumed into its function and becomes its own image, in so far as it appears for itself rather than for its use or engagement with the world. Since it no longer refers or is referred to the world as a place of action, in its appearing as image there is no possibility of a response, an action or reaction by it or to it; the image is passive, indifferent, neutral. Moreover, inasmuch as the image is withdrawn or detached from what Blanchot calls 'practical life and the accomplishment of true tasks',[93] it is also withdrawn from any system of signification or meaning; it floats anonymous, indifferent, existing or more properly *appearing* solely for itself, with neither connection nor relation nor reference. The corpse establishes a relation between here and nowhere: appearing before us as its own image and yet infinitely or absolutely distant, it presses against us with 'the gaping intimacy of an undifferentiated nowhere which must nevertheless be located here'.[94]

What is essential in Blanchot's account is that these two versions of the image appear in the corpse *as the same and single image*. The name 'image' pertains to both versions in equal measure and neither can they be separated. Moreover, although it is the corpse that serves as his figure for the image, the 'two versions of the imaginary' in question describe the condition of the image *as such*, and not merely that of the corpse. This doubling or duplicity of the image is the condition of its appearing, and appears with and as the image: 'it is as if the choice between death as understanding's possibility and death as the horror of impossibility had also to be the choice between sterile truth and the prolixity of the non-true. It is as if comprehension were linked to penury and horror to fecundity.'[95]

Hence the ambivalence of the figure of the corpse which is the vanishing point of the bullet's line of flight: on the one hand, as a figure of finitude, it puts the image at our disposal as a tool; it is a figure of thought as a power the human possesses, and through which it possesses the world. On the other hand, despite all this, the corpse is precisely that which has ceased to be a thing, to be anything; no longer attached to or engaged with the world of action and reaction, the corpse is abandoned to the pure passivity of the image, dislocated from any system of signification, meaning or truth. It is the pure appearing of the image for itself, rather than for us, outside of all other reference, but nevertheless as an image, as an appearing within the phenomenal world of human action in terms that disrupt, destabilise, disfigure the possibility of that action. Indeed, what is essential in it is that it be an experience, a presence: the presence of absence, the experience of nothing taking place, taking our place, and any place or basis on which we might act or respond. To 'live an event as image is to be taken: to pass from the region of the real where we hold ourselves at a distance from things the better to order and use them into that other region where the distance holds us . . . It keeps us outside; it makes of this outside a presence where "I" does not recognize itself.'[96] Both time as passage and time as the form of change appear in and as the same 'vanishing point'. The living move step by step towards death, but their death, as their own, is impossible, '"taken back" by this possibility, inasmuch as in death the possibility which is death dies too'.[97]

But if the genesis of the human as a centred perspective on acentred universal variation is the 'mirror image' and presupposition of the corpse as vanishing point, this means that that centre, and that perspective, are given no less equally in relation to the corpse as a figure of the interminable, of prolixity and horror, the decentring of all centres: that which works to 'efface the living truth proper to every place and make it equivalent to the absolute neutrality of death'.[98] The foundation of our action, our condition of possibility, the constitution of ourselves as a centre, has as its immanent double unfounding, impossibility, dislocation; the spontaneity of the 'I think' is irremediably fractured, appearing to and for itself as pure passivity, the suffering of time. Thought as a power we possess is hollowed out by a thought outside itself, and an unthought within thought. In the *Cinema* books, Deleuze calls this doubling or duplicity of the image in or as the single and same image the *crystal-image*, 'the most fundamental operation of time'.[99]

No doubt this claim requires some unpacking. The acentred universal variation of being is what Bergson calls 'pure recollection' or 'pure past', which exists for itself as pure virtuality.[100] This is, as Rodowick puts it, the primary form of time, time in its pure state.[101] The actual, on the other hand, 'is always a present'.[102] The problem lies, of course, in how the present becomes the past, unless it is always and already in the past at the same time it is present in or as the present. Thus

> the image has to be present and past, still present and already past, at once and at the same time. If it was not already past at the same time as present, the present would never pass on. The past does not follow the present that it is no longer, it coexists with the present it was. The present is the actual image, and its contemporaneous past is the virtual image, the image in the mirror.[103]

'The present' is thus given as a split or fracture; on one side, the present as actual, which is constantly replaced or renewed as a present opening onto the future which is not yet; on the other the present which passes and is preserved in and as the (virtual) past. Deleuze describes it as a splitting of time into 'two dissymmetrical jets, one of which makes all the presents pass on [the actual], while the other preserves all the past [the virtual]. Time consists of this split, and it is this, it is time that we *see in the crystal-image*.'[104] What is essential here, however, is that these two 'states' of the present (that which passes and that which is preserved) cannot be distinguished from each other. Time as passage, and time as the form of change are indiscernible, indistinguishable, unassignable as actual and virtual. This is the crystal-image, the 'genetic element' of opsigns,[105] 'the point of indiscernibility of the two distinct images, the actual and the virtual . . . a bit of time in the pure state, the very distinction between the two which keeps on reconstituting itself'.[106]

Deleuze also makes it clear that the crystal-image corresponds directly to the 'fractured I' and the affection of self by self that 'appears' in and with the Kantian reversal of the relation of movement and time: 'The actual is always objective, but the virtual is subjective . . . time itself, pure virtuality which divides itself in two as affector and affected, "the affection of self by self as definition of time".'[107] The indiscernibility of time as passage and time as the form of change (the corpse as finitude and the corpse as dislocation or decentring) is such that the spontaneity of the 'I think' experiences its own thought as something 'exercised in it and upon it but not by it'.[108] As Bergson describes it,

> whoever becomes conscious of the continual duplicating of his present into perception and memory [the present which passes, and the present

which is preserved] ... will compare himself to an actor playing his part automatically, listening to himself and beholding himself play.[109]

Under these circumstances, the 'I think' is given to itself as the experience of the *failure* of thought to think, as the suffering of something outside itself which nevertheless can only be located inside the self, as the affection of self by self: 'what forces us to think is the "inpower of thought", the figure of nothingness, the inexistence of a whole which could be thought'.[110]

In so far as the cinema of the time-image finds its genesis in this cracked or fractured 'I', the spiritual automaton or experimental brain of the cinema is no longer (as in the classical cinema) constituted in the causal and rational linking of images or thoughts which follow each other in their place ('if this image, then this, then this', extended, even if only hypothetically, to the whole as totality). It offers instead the delinking of images and the irrational cuts which divides those images as much as it joins them ('this image *and* this image *and* this image...'). The modern cinema thus constitutes thought as that which 'seizes [thought] from the outside, as the unthinkable in thought ... It is the spiritual automatism of images which produces from the outside a thought which it imposes, as the unthinkable in our intellectual automatism.'[111] This constitutes an entirely new sense of the relation between man and world, nature and man. Where for the classical cinema the whole was the open (even if it was constrained or limited the whole as totality), for the modern cinema the whole is the *outside*:

> the whole undergoes a mutation, because it has ceased to be One-Being, in order to become the constitutive 'and' of things ... The whole thus merges with that Blanchot calls the force of 'dispersal of the Outside', or 'the vertigo of spacing': that void which is no longer a motor part of the image, and which the image would cross in order to continue, but is the radical calling into question of the image.[112]

The indiscernibility of the two versions of the imaginary, of the mutual presupposition of centre and vanishing point on the one hand, and that vanishing point as the dislocation of action, of self and of thought on the other, thus means that

> what Blanchot diagnoses everywhere in literature is particularly clear in cinema: on the one hand the presence of an unthinkable in thought, which would be both its source and barrier; on the other hand, the presence to infinity of another thinker in the thinker, who shatters every monologue of a thinking self.[113]

The Night, the Rain

It is in these terms that the impossibility of reading the two volumes of the *Cinema* books, either together or apart, as coherent or incoherent is to be accounted for simultaneously in terms of film form, of the powers of thought, *and* in terms of both world and film history. The 'great reversal' of the relation of movement and time (in philosophy as in cinema) exists as an event in history (Kant at his desk, the war and the horrors of the camps). But in this reversal, history, and the events of history, are unfounded, dislocated, disordered, such that in its happening the eventuality of the reversal cannot happen, does not happen. There is no history there where this reversal is: *the disaster*, 'advent of what does not happen, of what would come without arriving'[114] (the disaster, the outside: two of the 'names of thought, when it lets itself come undone'[115]).

The relation between the *Cinema* books themselves thus constitutes a crystal-image, in which the tension between the classical cinema's indirect image of time (time as causality, as history) and the modern cinema's direct image of time (time as the form of change) must be grasped in or as the *indiscernibility* of these respective images (the indiscernibility of founding and unfounding). Deleuze is able to deduce the human as a historical mode of existence on the basis of the formal properties of the cinema (which he has demonstrated correspond to the conceptual parameters of Bergsonian philosophy). But this deduction also demonstrates that this mode of existence is given its coherence and order only by treating the whole as a closed totality – that is to say, as finitude that is lived by the human in its relation to death as a boundary or border (the vanishing point figured in the image of the corpse). And this figure or image of death is also and indivisibly that of the disruptive form of time as change. History (causality, the classical cinema, the indirect image of time) opens itself to the outside, to the disaster, not as a result of history ('the Holocaust is *not a species* of the disaster'[116]) but on the basis of its own duplicitous condition.

It is not that 'history' is founded by finitude, and then unfounded by its dislocation. This would simply mark another historical passage of time between those two moments. Rather, the 'events' of history are doubled by their own absence from themselves and by their disordering in time. In *The Logic of Sense*, Deleuze offers us a different name for this eventuality of what does not happen, which is also perhaps another name for the crystal-image: the *event*. On the one hand, there is 'the event embodied in a state of affairs, an individual or person, the moment we designate by saying "here, the moment has come"'.[117] On the other hand, we find the event as counter-actualisation: 'the event considered in itself, sidestepping each present, being free of the limitations of a state of affairs, impersonal and pre-individual, neutral'.[118] Deleuze identifies this double structure or ambiguity of the event explicitly with death, and with Blanchot's analysis thereof:

> no one has shown better than Maurice Blanchot that this ambiguity is essentially that of the wound and of death, of the mortal wound ... Every event is like death, double and impersonal in its double. 'It is the abyss of the present, the time without present with which I have no relation, toward which I am unable to project myself. For in it *I* do not die. I forfeit the power of dying. In this abyss they die – they never cease to die, and they never succeed in dying.'[119]

'They die' here marks the impersonality, the dislocation of the 'I think' from itself in the exposure of the human to time as the form of change: the dispersal and fragmentation of the self in its confrontation with a death which can never be my own. In a striking figure, Deleuze compares this experience of the absence of and from self with the impersonality of 'it rains': 'How different is this "they" from that which we encounter in everyday banality. It is the "they" of impersonal and pre-individual singularities, the "they" of the pure event wherein *it* dies in the same way that *it* rains.'[120]

He returns to this figure in the *Cinema* books (attributing it this time to the cinema itself, by way of French film theorist Jean-Louis Schefer) to suggest that 'the condition of the cinema has only one equivalent, not imaginary participation, but the rain when you leave the auditorium: not dream, but the blackness and insomnia'.[121] In this summoning of insomnia, of the night and the rain as the condition of the cinema and of the event, we can hear the imperceptible voice of Levinas' *Il y a*, the 'there is' present in its absence.[122] '*There is*', Levinas tells us, 'is an impersonal form, like in it rains ... Its anonymity is essential.'[123] One of the key characteristics of Levinas' account is that it presents itself as an existential analysis of the 'there is' as a phenomenon within the field of experience. But that phenomenon, that experience, is one of anonymity, dispersal, dislocation, in which any 'I' that might be the subject of that experience is lost. The night as rest is given over to the day, as restoration and preparation for its labours; but in the night without sleep (the night which does not sleep) 'the vigilance of insomnia which keeps our eyes open has no subject. It is not the return of some presence into the void left by absence – not the return of some *thing*, but of a presence: it is the reawakening of the *there is*'.[124] It is the experience of an existence without existents: the presence of absence, and thus the absence of the world and of oneself.

It is impossible not to hear in Levinas' description of this experience the presence of the 'fractured I', the crystal-image, the absence of the world and of oneself. In the depths of insomniac night, in the 'there is', the

> mind does not find itself faced with an apprehended exterior. The exterior – if one insists on this term – remains uncorrelated with an interior. It is no longer given. It is no longer a world. What we call the I is itself submerged by the night, invaded, depersonalised, stifled by it. The disappearance of all things and of the I leaves what cannot disappear, the sheer fact of being in which one participates, whether one wants to or not, without having taken the initiative, anonymously.[125]

As I have pointed out, in his discussion of Beckett's *Film*, Deleuze notes in passing that the 'death, immobility, blackness' he projects beyond the end of the film is merely a 'means in relation to a more profound end. It is a question of attaining once more the world before man',[126] that is to say, being as real difference, being as it exists for itself and as itself. Beckett's elimination of the material moments of human subjectivity can never reach the 'world before man' since 'man' is already there as that which he seeks to eliminate. Indeed, he cannot even reach 'death, immobility, blackness' within his film, or as image: these must be 'projected' beyond its end.

What Beckett constructs in miniature is what Deleuze dramatises across the whole of the *Cinema* books, and particularly in the 'great reversal' that lies between their two volumes: the drama of thought in its attempts to think, and to think being in terms of being, and adequate to being (to attain the 'world before man'). This attempt is hobbled from the start by the cinematographic genesis of the human; overcoming this genesis requires the overcoming of the human, and thus the absence of the human and of human thought.

But the experience of the 'there is' (the fractured I, the crystal-image) offers another path (which is perhaps a non-path). Beginning with and from the human (or the cinematic construction thereof) Deleuze is able to show that the human (that is to say, the cinematographic) has as its duplicitous condition both finitude and prolixity, and that that condition is capable of presenting itself *as an image, as an experience*: this is the modern cinema, the cinema of the time-image – the experience of movement subordinated to time, of the great reversal, of the anonymity of the event (the event of one's own absence). And these are the only terms in which the human might be said to grasp the 'more profound end' of being in or as thought – not in its own terms, but in terms of the failure or incapacity of thought in its exposure to being, to time as the form of change.

The dramatisation of thought that Deleuze constructs by means of the cinema (the dramatisation of the struggle of thought to think, to become adequate to real movement) arrives at the cinema of the time-image as the experience of this exposure constructed in and as image: it is the drama of the unfounding of thought, the relation of man and world, world and man appearing in and as the 'suspension of the world' and the absence from oneself, presented in and as image.

> It is the suspension of the world, rather than movement, which gives the visible to thought, not as its object, but as an act which is constantly arising and being revealed in thought: 'not that it is here a matter of thought become visible, the visible is irremediably infected by the initial incoherence of thought, this inchoate quality'.[127]

The experience of the absence of oneself is as close as human being or the 'I think' can come to the overcoming of the human. This is not the experience of being *as* being, but of the *exposure* of human being to that being: the cinema, the night, the rain.

Notes

1. Deleuze, *Cinema 1*, 66.
2. Ibid.
3. Schneider, *Film*. To be precise, *Film*'s end credits identify it as 'by' Samuel Beckett (he wrote the screenplay) but 'directed by' Alan Schneider. To avoid unnecessary complication or confusion in the text, I follow Deleuze's attribution of the film to Beckett. However, as convention dictates, for citation purposes the film as such is attributed to Schneider.
4. Deleuze, *Cinema 1*, 66. This 'formula' appears at the beginning of Beckett's screenplay for the project, which he intended to be read along with the viewing of the film. Waugh and Daly, '*Film* by Samuel Beckett'.
5. Deleuze, *Cinema 1*, 67.
6. Ibid., 67–8. Emphasis in original.
7. Ibid., 68.

The Night, the Rain

8. Ibid.
9. Ibid.
10. The presentation I am offering here is a condensation of several typically dense pages of argument on Deleuze's part. Nevertheless, it must be said that Deleuze's account of experimental cinema remains schematic. This is perhaps unavoidable, given that the history of experimental cinema is more or less coextensive with that of cinema itself (an argument might be made for its origins in Georges Méliès fascination with cinema as 'special effect', but if not there, then at the very least we can find it certain aspects of French and Soviet cinema in the 1920s). Deleuze does respond to this complexity to some degree in his account, as for example in his discussion of Vertov as the 'father' of experimental cinema. Nevertheless, Deleuze's analysis is oriented by and towards a treatment of experimental cinema in the terms I deploy throughout this section. Ibid., 81–6.
11. Ibid., 82.
12. Ibid., 85.
13. Although there's no evidence of a direct Bergsonian influence on Brakhage, R. Bruce Elder nevertheless traces a chain of influences trickling down from Bergson to Alfred North Whitehead, to Charles Olson, and finally to Brakhage, placing the latter firmly in an 'American tradition' with substantive, albeit second-hand, links to Bergsonian philosophy. Elder, *The Films of Stan Brakhage in the American Tradition of Ezra Pound, Gertrud Stein and Charles Olson*, 511 n.444, and more generally 75–99 and 146–57.
14. Deleuze, *Cinema 1*, 81.
15. Ibid., 83.
16. If the tendency of experimental cinema that Deleuze focuses on is capable of fulfilling the conditions for Bergsonian intuition, it is to the extent that it seeks to install itself directly within the aberrant movement that is the product of the cinema's non-human eye.
17. Levinas uses this particular phrase in relation to Blanchot's *Thomas l'Obscure*, and the latter's account of the *il y a* there in terms of 'The presence of absence, the night, the dissolution of the subject in the night, the horror of being, the return of being to the heart of every negative moment, the reality of irreality.' *Existence and Existents*, n.1, 58.
18. Ibid., 51–2.
19. This underlying logic is what I think Hallward is pointing towards when he argues that 'one of the most characteristic features of Deleuze's work is his tendency to present what initially appears as a binary relation in such a way as to show that this relation is in fact determined by only one of its two "terms"'. Hallward, *Out of This World*, 82 and 156–7.

20. The case of experimental cinema differs from these cases inasmuch as it does not need to overcome the human, since the cinema is non-human to begin with. Rather, the cinema begins with being and then deduces beings on that basis (experimental cinema/the *gramme* as the point of genesis of the taxonomy of cinematic signs = material moments of human subjectivity).
21. Were the task of the *Cinema* books to provide a full accounting of the possibilities of the cinema, this would constitute a serious omission. Its absence reflects the nature of the properly philosophical task Deleuze essays therein, which as we will see in a moment concerns the human in its relation to being (where experimental cinema treats of the cinema's capacity to construct a 'world without man').
22. Deleuze, *Cinema 2*, 272.
23. Deleuze, *Cinema 1*, 68.
24. Ibid., 98.
25. Haase and Large, *Maurice Blanchot*, 38.
26. Ibid., 43.
27. Ibid., 47–8.
28. Deleuze, *Cinema 2*, 209.
29. Variants of this figure appear in Aeschylus, *Agamemnon*, Lines 1078–80; Sophocles' *Oedipus Rex*, *The Three Theban Plays: Antigone, Oedipus the King, Oedipus at Colonus*, Line 1529; Herodotus, *The Histories*, Book 1, Chapters 30–4. For all that this formulation is ancient, it retains an absolutely contemporary currency. By way of strictly autobiographical evidence, my first encounter with it was in a song by Tom Waits: 'The higher that the monkey can climb / the more he shows his tail / call no man happy till he dies / there's no milk at the bottom of the pail.' 'Misery is the River of the World'.
30. The account I have offered here is necessarily a traduction of Derrida's characteristically subtle, elusive and complex analysis of this theme, and particularly of his treatment of Heidegger. Nevertheless, the following passage captures what is essential for my purposes: 'I cannot consider myself happy, or even believe myself to have been happy, before having crossed, passed, and surpassed the last instant of my own life, even if up to that point I have been happy in a life that will have been, in any case, so short. What, then, is it to cross the ultimate border? What is it to pass the term of one's life (*terma tou biou*)? Is it possible? Who has ever done it and who can testify to it? The "I enter", crossing the threshold, this "I pass" (*perao*) puts us on the path, if I may say, of the *aporos* or of the *aporia*: the difficult or the impracticable, here the impossible, passage, the refused, denied, or prohibited passage, indeed the nonpassage, which can in fact be something else, the event of a coming or of a future advent, which no longer has the form of the movement that consists in passing, traversing, or

transiting. It would be the "coming to pass" of an event that would no longer have the form or the appearance of a *pas*: in sum, a coming without *pas*' (*Aporias*, 7–8).

31. Ibid., 77.
32. Haase and Large, *Maurice Blanchot*, 53.
33. The correlation between totalisation as a *general* condition for action, and my death as that which is most *particular*, most especially 'mine' (even if and as it removes the possibility of any possession) may seem an unfortunate slippage. But this is part of death's particularity: it is my uttermost possibility, and thus absolutely and particularly mine, and yet it is the most banal of generalities, since everything that lives must die.
34. Deleuze, *Kant's Critical Philosophy*, vii.
35. It is all the more so for the fact that it only 'appears' explicitly and directly in the respective introductions to *Cinema 1*, and *Cinema 2*. Deleuze, *Cinema 1*, ix; Deleuze, *Cinema 2*, xi.
36. Deleuze, *Kant's Critical Philosophy*, viii.
37. Ibid.
38. Ibid., viii–ix.
39. Ibid., viii.
40. Ibid., viii–ix.
41. Deleuze, *Difference and Repetition*, 86.
42. As Smith puts it, the 'two demands laid down by Maimon – the search for *the genetic elements of real experience* and the positing of a *principle of difference* as the fulfilment of this condition – could be said to be the two primary components of what Deleuze came to call his *transcendental empiricism*'. Smith, *Essays on Deleuze*, 238. Emphasis in original.
43. Ibid., 111.
44. Ibid.
45. Ibid.
46. Ansell-Pearson, 'Beyond the Human Condition', 58.
47. Deleuze notes that Artaud rejects as a dead end both abstract experimental *and* classical narrative cinema (both of which were developing in the 1920s as the latter was working through his ideas on cinema). In this Artaud shares a certain commonality with Deleuze. As we've seen, the latter finds the experimental cinema of only minor relevance to his project in the *Cinema* books (notwithstanding the *gramme*'s position as the point of genesis of the taxonomy of signs of the classical cinema). And although the classical cinema certainly is of interest to Deleuze, I would argue that this interest lies primarily in the manner in which it sets up the conditions for the appearance of the time-image, in so far as the latter appears with and in the disordering and decentring of the image of thought the classical cinema constructs. Deleuze, *Cinema 2*, 165.

48. Ibid.
49. Ibid., 167.
50. Ibid., 166. Deleuze is citing here from Blanchot's discussion of the famous Artaud-Rivière correspondence. Blanchot, *The Book to Come*, 36–7.
51. Deleuze, *Cinema 2*, 166.
52. Ibid., 163. Emphasis in original.
53. Ibid., 167.
54. Ibid.
55. Ibid.
56. Quoted in Blanchot, *The Book to Come*, 36.
57. Though we must certainly acknowledge Heidegger's etymological excavations as an effort to 'force' language to reveal that which lies beyond (or perhaps within) it.
58. Ibid., 34–40.
59. And as his notorious translation of Lewis Carroll's *Jabberwocky* demonstrates, Artaud's struggle to think leads him to attempt force language beyond its own limits just as Bergson demands, and far more radically than Bergson himself. Deleuze discusses Artaud's treatment of Carroll at length in the 'Thirteenth Series of the Schizophrenic and the Little Girl', in Deleuze, *The Logic of Sense*, 82–93.
60. Deleuze, *Cinema 2*, 41.
61. Deleuze attributes this formulation to Jean-Louis Schefer. Ibid., 168. Emphasis in original.
62. Ibid., 3.
63. Rodowick, *Gilles Deleuze's Time Machine*, 130.
64. Brenez, 'The Ultimate Journey'. Emphasis altered.
65. 'The Cahiers axiom is this: that the cinema has a fundamental rapport with reality and that the real is not what is represented – and that's final.' Andrew, *What Cinema Is!*, 4–5.
66. Deleuze, *Cinema 2*, 165.
67. Virilio, *War and Cinema*.
68. Deleuze, *Cinema 2*, 309 n.16.
69. Virilio, *War and Cinema*, 2–3.
70. Deleuze, *Cinema 2*, 309 n.16.
71. Virilio, *War and Cinema*, 86.
72. The reader should note that although Massumi raises this point in the context of Deleuze and Guattari's concept of 'deterritorialisation', I do not seek to invoke that concept directly in the discussion that follows. Deleuze and Guattari, *A Thousand Plateaus*, 298.
73. Deleuze, *Cinema 2*, 40.
74. Deleuze, *Cinema 1*, 68.
75. The fact that the classical cinema often presents narrative events out of chronological order (i.e., through flashbacks) does not alter this,

since they are only 'out of order' with reference to the linear temporal perspective it constructs.
76. They further point out that 'lines of flight as perspective lines' are the reterritorialisation of lines of flight understood in their broader Deleuzoguattarian sense as lines of deterritorialisation and escape. Deleuze and Guattari, *A Thousand Plateaus*, 298.
77. Berger, *Ways of Seeing*, 16.
78. Deleuze, *Cinema 2*, 271.
79. Blanchot, *The Space of Literature*, 261.
80. Ibid.
81. Perhaps unsurprisingly, given Blanchot's place in that analysis.
82. And more generally, from the terms of the genesis of the human as a centered and thus cinematographic perspective on the acentered universal variation of being.
83. Deleuze, *Negotiations*, 69.
84. Deleuze, *Cinema 2*, 167.
85. Blanchot, *The Space of Literature*, 256.
86. Ibid., 254–63.
87. Ibid., 260.
88. Ibid. The Deleuzian equivalent here would be the perception, affection and action-images the brain/screen 'subtracts' from the universal variation of the whole in order to act in and on it. 'Subtraction' is not negation per se, but certainly in so far as what appears in this subtraction is the actual, it becomes subject to the possibility of negation.
89. Ibid., 256.
90. Ibid., 257. Emphasis in original. Deleuze might say 'begins to differ from himself' in so far as 'resemblance ... is the identity of what differs from itself'. Deleuze, 'Bergson's Conception of Difference', 51.
91. Blanchot, *The Space of Literature*, 258.
92. Ibid., 262.
93. Ibid., 260.
94. Ibid., 257.
95. Ibid., 261.
96. Ibid., 261–2.
97. Ibid., 261.
98. Ibid., 259.
99. Deleuze, *Cinema 2*, 81.
100. Ibid., 79.
101. Rodowick, *Gilles Deleuze's Time Machine*, 123. And since time is the form of change or difference, we can also identify acentred universal variation with the differing from itself of being.
102. Deleuze, *Cinema 2*, 78.
103. Ibid., 79.
104. Ibid., 81. Emphasis in original.

105. Bogue, *Deleuze on Cinema*, 120.
106. Deleuze, *Cinema 2*, 82–3.
107. Ibid., 83.
108. Deleuze, *Difference and Repetition*, 86.
109. Quoted in Rodowick, *Gilles Deleuze's Time Machine*, 126; original source Bergson, *Mind-Energy*, 168–9.
110. Deleuze, *Cinema 2*, 168.
111. Ibid., 178–9.
112. Ibid., 180.
113. Ibid., 168.
114. Blanchot, *The Writing of the Disaster*, 1.
115. Ibid., 57–8.
116. Bruns, *Maurice Blanchot: The Refusal of Philosophy*, 123.
117. Deleuze, *The Logic of Sense*, 151.
118. Ibid.
119. Ibid., 151–2.
120. Deleuze, *Cinema 2*, 152.
121. Ibid., 168.
122. Neither Deleuze nor Schefer summons Levinas by name, although perhaps he is present at one remove (for Deleuze at least) in the figure of Blanchot.
123. Levinas, *Existence and Existents*, 53.
124. Ibid., 62.
125. Ibid., 53.
126. Deleuze, *Cinema 1*, 67.
127. Deleuze, *Cinema 2*, 169.

8

Conclusion: The Crystal-Image of Philosophy

Why does Deleuze write about the cinema, as a philosopher? What are the properly philosophical problems to which the cinema offers him the means to respond in a way that philosophy itself cannot? Put simply, these problems concern the relation of man and world, world and man. The problem here turns on the adequacy or otherwise of thought to the task of thinking the world in its own terms. For Deleuze these terms are those of difference itself, of movement in so far as it is an expression of duration, or time as the form of change. This problem is figured in the cinematographic illusion in so far as that illusion is a consequence of the genesis of the human as a centred perspective on the acentred universal variation of being. Since the cinematographic condition of the human is such that we grasp the world in relation to our own needs, and not as it is for itself, the natural metaphysics of human thought is thereby oriented towards totalisation and a grasp of being as a closed totality, even if the genesis *of* that thought is deduced on the basis of difference and the openness of the whole. To think the world in its own terms thus requires the overcoming of the human, and of the cinematographic limits of human thought.

Deleuzian philosophy offers a direct response to this demand in terms of a montage thought that seeks to enter into the real movement of being. By fragmenting and recomposing the elements given cinematographically in experience, it seeks to enter into their movement of actualisation in 'reverse', and so counter-actualise them in order to reascend towards the differing from itself of the virtual. But although this 'cinematic' method offers philosophy the means by which it might overcome the human and so approach being in its own terms, in doing so it leaves the human 'behind' and positions it simply as a barrier to thought that thought must seek to surpass. As such, it leaves Deleuzian philosophy open to the criticisms that Hallward directs at it: that the human has no place there, such that it offers nothing to the human, or to properly human concerns. The nuance, or specificity, of the *Cinema* books within the heterogenesis of Deleuze's philosophy of difference is precisely the focus it offers on the human *as* human, and on the 'thought of the world' understood in terms of the human *relation* to difference, to being as acentred universal variation.

Thus the problem that the *Cinema* books address is, in a sense, the inverse of that which requires Deleuzian philosophy to overcome the cinematographic limits of human thought: how can the relation of the human to being, to difference, be accounted for and thought in terms *of* the human and of human thought rather than those of its overcoming? The cinema offers Deleuze the means to respond to this problem because it is able to deduce the human and the operations of human thought on the basis of its own non-human mode of thought, the essence of which is to think in terms of real movement and thus of real difference. In other words, it can think the problem of human thought and its relation to being in terms not subject to the limits of that thought. Through the composition of its formal elements – frame, shot and montage – the cinema possesses the tools to dramatise not only human thought, but the relation of that thought to being as difference, the relation of man and world, world and man.

In so far as it thinks human thought in non-human terms, the cinema enables Deleuze to account for the products of the dogmatic image of thought in the terms of his own philosophy of difference. This is what we find in the classical cinema's recapitulation of classical philosophy in cinematic terms. In this, the argument of the *Cinema* books repeats the logic by which he accounts for external difference in terms of the differing from itself of internal difference, and thereby accounts for finalism, mechanism and ultimately the Hegelian dialectic in terms of real difference. But where 'Bergson's Conception of Difference' presents this relation abstractly or 'in principle', *Cinema 1* does so concretely and directly, as and in the history of the classical cinema itself.

Thus in the history of the classical cinema, Deleuze finds the dramatisation of the history of thought as spontaneity and power, a history oriented by and towards the thought of the whole as totality. But what it reveals is that this totality constitutes the unfounding of that power and spontaneity: to the extent that it completes its goal or end in the totality of the one, it exposes thought to its own horror, the failure and incapacity of thought to respond to, master or think its own end. Action, the historical as the mode of being of the human, moves on a trajectory towards death as that which both determines and delimits life and meaning, and at the same time exposes the

Conclusion: The Crystal-Image of Philosophy

human and human thought to its own absence in terms that disrupt and decentre both thought and history itself. This is the Deleuzian formulation of the relation of philosophy to death: the exposure of the human and of human thought to being as it is for itself and not for us.

If the cinema thus offers Deleuze the non-human means to think the human relation to being, what the cinema's recapitulation of the history of philosophy reveals is that this exposure is also (*contra* Hallward) profoundly and utterly political. Totality, totalisation, are realised in the realm of the human in the *presence* of the people: the 'dream' of the people as One, as unity and totality whose extremes are realised in totalitarianism and as fascism. The Holocaust lies at the centre and break between the cinemas of the movement-image and time-image and between the two volumes of the *Cinema* books as a figure of totality itself, of the people as one in the deathly stillness and unity of the mass grave. If philosophy is constituted in the relation to death as thought's vanishing point (its *point de fuite*), and thus as both the ground of its possibility and its exposure to the impossibility of possibility itself, what the cinema reveals is that the political, as the organisation of the world of human action, is in its turn constituted in relation to totalitarianism as its completion and its horror. It is here, Blanchot tells us, at or with this completion,

> outside the sovereignty of the One and the Whole, outside of the Universe and also of its beyond, and when all is accomplished (when death finally comes, in the form of a life fulfilled), the demand without any rights, the demand of the other (the multiple, the impoverished, the lost) presses as never before, as that which has always escaped realization.[1]

The philosophy of difference bears on the political not in terms of prescriptions for action or the search for justice, but in the form of this 'demand without rights', the demand of the other which not only *has* escaped realisation, but *must* – for in its realisation, it would fall once again into the realm of always totalised or totalisable action and power. When Deleuze tells us that 'the people are missing',[2] this absence is not a void to be filled, a project yet to be completed. It is the condition for the confrontation of the political itself, of identity and dominion with the demand of the other, a demand that cannot be met or affirmed in any unity or presence of the people joined together 'as one'. Thus, to summon up Blanchot once more,

> for thought which has reached its culmination – for thought whose completion has put it to sleep – the wakeful and incessant obsession with

others is confirmed. The affirmation is void, and the obsession is with others in their un-presence. Moreover thought does not know how to acknowledge this obsession. But it knows that this nocturnal disaster is thought's due and is conferred upon thought in order that thought might be assigned a disjointed perpetuity.[3]

We wait for the people to arrive, for possibility or for the possibility of thought, but our waiting is and must be interminable, never to be met by any arrival – the 'obsession with others in their un-presence' as thought's 'disjointed perpetuity.'

If Kant's 'great reversal' of the relation of movement and time lies at the heart of the philosophical problem that Deleuze turns to the cinema to resolve, and of the *Cinema* books themselves as the break or gap that joins and divides them, it is because this reversal is in itself disastrous, experienced in and for thought as the suffering of time, as the impossibility and 'impower' of thought figured in the fractured 'I'. But this fracture is also that of the unity of man and world, of the reciprocal determination of thought as a power we possess and the Idea of the world as totality on the basis of which that thought is derived and justified. As Deleuze puts it, in the 'modern world'

> the link between man and world is broken. Henceforth this link must become an object of belief: it is the impossible which can only be restored within a faith. Belief is no longer addressed to a different or transformed world. Man is in the world as if in a pure optical and sound situation. The reaction of which man has been dispossessed can only be replaced by belief. Only belief in the world can reconnect man to what he sees and hears. *The cinema must film, not the world, but belief in this world, our only link.*[4]

If this belief concerns the modern cinema, as our only relation to the pure optical and sound situations that have replaced the Idea of the world as totality, it concerns philosophy no less. Deleuze points out that this 'transformation in belief' within the cinema 'was already a great turning-point in philosophy, from Pascal to Nietzsche: to replace the model of knowledge with belief. But belief replaces knowledge only when it becomes belief in this world, as it is.'[5] The Nietzschean character Deleuze attributes to the modern cinema is articulated at the level of film form in its transformation of narrative – that is to say, in its mode of composition of images. Classical narration sought to construct an Idea of the world as closed totality, and thus as an object of thought, subject to human knowledge and power in the form of truth or judgement. However, in so far as thought

Conclusion: The Crystal-Image of Philosophy

presents itself in the modern cinema as the passive experience of time as the form of change, we 'no longer have a chronological time which can be overturned by movements which are contingently abnormal; we have a chronic non-chronological time which produces movements necessarily "abnormal", essentially "false"'.[6] Narration thus takes on a 'new status' and 'ceases to be truthful, that is, to claim to be true, and becomes fundamentally falsifying'.[7] The 'crack' in thought produced by the reversal of the relation of movement and time is such that our relation to the world presents itself in the form of the powers of the false, which 'cannot be separated from an irreducible multiplicity. "I is another" . . . has replaced Ego = Ego.'[8]

In so far as the 'great Kantian reversal' that gives rise to the modern cinema substitutes knowledge as a power we possess with a Nietzschean affirmation of belief, it turns this reversal against Kantian philosophy itself, as a continuation of Deleuze's post-Kantian and Maimonian response to it.[9] For Kant, it is the noumenon, the world as it is, that cannot be known directly, while time (and space) constitute the *a priori* form of being known of things as they appear. It is on this basis that the entire architectonic of human knowledge and of philosophy unfolds. For Deleuze, however, time itself (or more precisely, duration as temporalised difference) takes the place of the Kantian noumenal. The (Bergsonian) terms in which the cinematographic genesis of the human and of human thought are deduced on the basis of this temporalised difference are such that, just as with Kant, the world (the being of difference) cannot be *known* in human terms. But where for Kant this eliminates any possible relation of thought to the world as it is, for Deleuze it opens up the possibility of a relation based not on knowledge, truth or adequation but rather on the affirmation of the powers of the false, and of *belief* in this world as the link, the relation between man and world, world and man. The thought of the world cannot, for Deleuze, take the form of judgement or truth, but can only become adequate to the world in the form of the affirmation of the world *as it is*. This is not the affirmation of things as they appear (the actual, the present) but, rather, of the becoming other *of* the now: time as the form of change, the unceasing creation of the being of difference.

To *believe in this world as it is*, then, means neither submission to the existing reality or the cynicism of *realpolitik*, nor a messianic faith in a world or a people to come. It is, rather, to affirm being as vital difference, as creation. Against the powers of horror, of the totalisation of thought and world and the totalitarianism of politics, we must place a belief in creation and difference not as the possibility of the new, but as the condition of its reality. To believe in the world is to affirm the people, not in their presence now or to come, but in or as their absence, understood as their unceasing becoming other. To believe in the people to come is not to put one's faith in the future, but in *the becoming other of the present*, in time as the form of change.

The cinematographic genesis of human nature and human being is such that we will always grasp the new in terms of the possibilities of action it presents, grasp it as an object of knowledge, a tool to be deployed within the realms of closure and finitude (in other words, treat it as merely actual, and thereby divorce it from its real movement of actualisation). But 'to believe in the world as it is' is not to believe in this or that new thing, event or idea, but rather to affirm the differing from itself of being. It is to affirm the openness of the whole, to hold that openness against the human and cinematographic orientation towards totalisation and closure, towards violence and death. We must believe in the world, in the people, not as a unity or totality given or possible to us, but as the differing from itself in which we find the condition for the creation of the new: the new as a becoming other which of necessity escapes us, our mastery, our totalising grasp.

The relation of human being and human thought to being as difference, our relation to the world *as it is*, thus constitutes a problem for Deleuze not in the form of something to be solved or overcome, but rather as the impossibility of thought that forces thought to think what it cannot know but can only affirm. This is the disaster at the heart of thought, the fracturing of the 'I' as an event belonging not to me or to my thought, but to the '"they" of impersonal and pre-individual singularities, the "they" of the pure event wherein *it* dies in the same way *it* rains'.[10] Here the 'impersonality of dying' indicates 'the event in which death loses itself in itself, and also the figure which the most singular life takes on in order to substitute itself for me'.[11] This problem, this event, this exposure of the human to being is what Deleuze finds in the modern cinema that arises in or with the collapse of the sensory-motor whole of the classical cinema:

> the sensory-motor break makes man a seer who finds himself struck by something intolerable in the world, and confronted by something unthinkable in thought ... For it is not in the name of a better or truer world that thought captures the intolerable in this world, but on the contrary, it is because this world is intolerable that it can no longer think a world or itself ... Which then is the subtle way out? To believe, not in a

different world, but in a link between man and the world, in love or life, to believe in this as in the impossible, the unthinkable, which nonetheless cannot but be thought . . . it is this belief that makes the unthought the specific power of thought.[12]

The cinema's thought of the world, then, constitutes the dramatisation of thought's struggle to think, to become adequate to being and the thought of being, not as mastery or power unto death, but as belief in the world as the creation of the new. If the modern cinema offers this to us, to our thought and to philosophy, it is as the exposure to being, to difference, to time as the form of change: the event as a 'most singular life' which substitutes itself for me, for my thought.

In his final essay, 'Immanence: A Life', Deleuze takes up the theme of this 'singular life' that reveals itself in or as the exposure to death. Here, at the end, we find what might be read as an obscure or indirect commentary on an approach to a death that will never have been his own. There is no biography here, no attempt at a final summation of *his* life, his achievements, his failures, to determine whether he, like the ancient Greeks, might at last call himself happy. We shouldn't, he says, seek to 'enclose life in the single moment when individual life confronts universal death'.[13] Rather, in approaching death, 'individuality fades away in favour of the singular life immanent to a man who no longer has a name, though he can be mistaken for no other'.[14] This 'singular life' is not my life, but *a* life. The impersonality of the indefinite article here, like that of 'it dies' or 'it rains', marks the exposure of 'my' life to a pure becoming other in or as my relation to death.

The relationship posed in 'Immanence: A Life' between 'my' life and *a* life mirrors the relation I have posited between the life of action, the life of actual events, and death as 'the figure which the most singular life takes on in order to substitute itself for me'. In other words, what Deleuze offers us in this essay is another figure for the cracked 'I', for the affection of self by self and for the crystal-image. Just as time, as the form of change, imposes on the spontaneity of the 'I' a thought exercised in it and on it but not by it, in the approach towards death, my life, my name, find themselves substituted for by the impersonality of *a* life which nevertheless 'can be mistaken for no other'. Death figures here not in the bleakness of an end that will always have come too soon, but in or as the crystalline relation in which 'my' life becomes indiscernible from *a* life, from the creative power of the unceasing becoming other of being itself. The substitution of belief for knowledge here takes the form of the indiscernibility of the 'I' that thinks its own power and the I that experiences its own thought as the suffering of time in the affection of self by self.

But as such, this relation also serves as a final, properly Deleuzian formulation of the figure of philosophy itself as thought's relation to death. Philosophy as a thought driven by the impossibility of its own thinking cannot *know* its own thought, but can only affirm the becoming other of a thought it can never grasp or master as its own. And this is precisely the drama of thought enacted by the *Cinema* books themselves. In the crystal-image constructed by the impossible relation between its two volumes, between the movement-image and the time-image, between the classical and modern cinemas, we are given the drama of thought in its struggle to think. Here, then, is what Deleuze offers us in and with the *Cinema* books: the montage thought of the cinema and its thought of the world as the crystal-image of philosophy itself.

Notes

1. Blanchot, *The Writing of the Disaster*, 130.
2. Deleuze, *Cinema 2*, 215.
3. Blanchot, *The Writing of the Disaster*, 130.
4. Deleuze, *Cinema 2*, 171–2. Emphasis added.
5. Ibid., 172.
6. Ibid., 129.
7. Ibid., 131.
8. Ibid., 133.
9. It's worth noting that the Bergsonian basis of Deleuze's treatment of both Kant and Nietzsche in the movement of the *Cinema* books is prefigured to some degree in 'Bergson's Conception of Difference'. Not only does Deleuze's early treatment of Bergson lay the foundations for his 'genetic' critique of Kant, as Ansell-Pearson points out, but, as Boradorri argues, the 'temporalization of movement' effected in that essay underpins Deleuze's treatment of Nietzsche in its entirety. As such, the 'Bergson–Kant–Nietzsche' axis mapped out in the *Cinema* books must be regarded as a 'nuance' of Deleuze's relation to and treatment of all three across his entire career. Ansell-Pearson, 'Beyond the Human Condition', 58; Borradori, 'The Temporalization of Difference', 10–14.
10. Deleuze, *The Logic of Sense*, 152.
11. Ibid., 153.

12. Deleuze, *Cinema 2*, 169–70.
13. Deleuze, *Pure Immanence*, 29.
14. Ibid.

References

Aeschylus. *Agamemnon*. Trans. E. D. A. Morshead. Harvard Classics. New York: PF Collier & Son, 1909 <www.bartleby.com/8/1> (last accessed 24 July 2017).
Alliez, Éric. 'On Deleuze's Bergsonism'. *Discourse* 20, no. 3 (Fall 1998): 226–46.
Alliez, Éric. *The Signature of the World: What Is Deleuze and Guattari's Philosophy?* Trans. Eliot Ross Albert. New York and London: Continuum, 2004.
Andrew, Dudley. *André Bazin*. New York and Oxford: Columbia University Press, 1978.
Andrew, Dudley. *What Cinema Is!* Malden, MA: Wiley-Blackwell, 2010.
Andrew, Dudley and Hervé Joubert-Laurencin. 'A Binocular Preface'. In *Opening Bazin: Postwar Theory and Its Afterlife*, ed. Dudley Andrew and Hervé Joubert-Laurencin. New York: Oxford University Press, 2011, ix–xix.
Andrew, Dudley and Hervé Joubert-Laurencin, eds. *Opening Bazin: Postwar Film Theory and Its Afterlife*. New York: Oxford University Press, 2011.
Ansell-Pearson, Keith. 'Beyond the Human Condition: An Introduction to Deleuze's Lecture Course'. *SubStance* #114, 36, no. 3 (2007): 57–71.
Ansell-Pearson, Keith and John Mullarkey. 'Chronology of Life and Works'. In *Henri Bergson: Key Writings*, ed. Keith Ansell Pearson and John Mullarkey. New York and London: Continuum, 2002, viii–xi.
Ansell-Pearson, Keith and John Mullarkey, eds. *Henri Bergson: Key Writings*. New York and London: Continuum, 2002.
Badiou, Alain. *Deleuze: The Clamour of Being*. Trans. Louise Burchill. Minneapolis and London: University of Minnesota Press, 2000.
Bazin, André. *What Is Cinema?* Trans. Hugh Grey. Vol. 1. 2 vols. Berkeley, Los Angeles and London: University of California Press, 2005.
Beasley-Murray, John. 'Whatever Happened to Neo-Realism? – Bazin, Deleuze, and Tarkovsky's Long Take'. *Iris: A Journal of Theory on Image and Sound* 23 (1997): 37–52.
Bellour, Raymond. 'Thinking, Recounting: The Cinema of Gilles Deleuze'. *Discourse* 20, no. 3 (Fall 1998): 56–75.
Benda, Julien. *The Treason of the Intellectuals*. New York: Norton, 1969.
Berger, John. *Ways of Seeing*. London: BBC and Penguin Books, 1972.

References

Bergson, Henri. 'Bergson–James Correspondence'. In *Henri Bergson: Key Writings*, ed. Keith Ansell Pearson and John Mullarkey, trans. Melissa McMahon. New York and London: Continuum, 2002, 357–65.

Bergson, Henri. *Creative Evolution*. Trans. Arthur Mitchell. New York: Henry Holt, 1911. New York: Dover, 1998.

Bergson, Henri. *Laughter: An Essay on the Meaning of the Comic*. Trans. Cloudsley Brereton. Milton Keynes: Lightning Source, 2010.

Bergson, Henri. 'Letter to Floris Delattre, 24th December 1935'. In *Henri Bergson: Selected Writings*, ed. Keith Ansell Pearson and John Mullarkey, trans. Melissa McMahon. New York and London: Continuum, 2002, 369–71.

Bergson, Henri. *Matter and Memory*. Trans. Nancy Margaret Paul. London: George Allen and Unwin, 1911. New York: Zone, 1991.

Bergson, Henri. *Mélanges*. Paris: Presses Universitaires de France, 1972.

Bergson, Henri. *Mind-Energy: Lectures and Essays*. Trans. H. Wildon Carr. New York: Henry Holt & Company, 1920.

Bergson, Henri. *The Creative Mind: An Introduction to Metaphysics*. New York: Citadel, 1992.

Bergson, Henri. 'The Life and Works of Ravaisson'. In *The Creative Mind*. New York: Citadel, 1992, 220–52.

Bergson, Henri. *The Meaning of War: Life and Matter in Conflict*. London: T Fisher Unwin, 1915 <http://www.gutenberg.org/etext/17111> (last accessed 24 July 2017).

Bergson, Henri. *Time and Free Will: An Essay on the Immediate Data of Consciousness*. Trans. F. L. Pogson. Mineola, NY: Dover Publications, 2001.

Blanchot, Maurice. *The Book to Come*. Trans. Charlotte Mandell. Stanford: Stanford University Press, 2003.

Blanchot, Maurice. *The Space of Literature*. Trans. Ann Smock. Lincoln and London: University of Nebraska Press, 1982.

Blanchot, Maurice. *The Writing of the Disaster*. Trans. Ann Smock. Lincoln and London: University of Nebraska Press, 1995.

Bogue, Ronald. *Deleuze and Guattari*. London and New York: Routledge, 1989.

Bogue, Ronald. *Deleuze on Cinema*. London and New York: Routledge, 2003.

Boljkovac, Nadine. *Untimely Affects: Gilles Deleuze and an Ethics of Cinema*. Edinburgh: Edinburgh University Press, 2013.

Bordwell, David. 'Lowering the Stakes: Prospects for a Historical Poetics of Cinema'. *Iris* 1, no. 1 (1983): 5–18.

Bordwell, David. *On the History of Film Style*. Cambridge, MA and London: Harvard University Press, 1997.

Borradori, Giovanna. 'The Temporalization of Difference: Reflections on

Deleuze's Interpretation of Bergson'. *Continental Philosophy Review* 34 (2001): 1–20.

Boundas, Constantin V. 'Deleuze-Bergson: An Ontology of the Virtual'. In *Deleuze: A Critical Reader*, ed. Paul Patton. Oxford and Massachusetts: Blackwell, 1996, 81–106.

Boyer, Carl B. *A History of Mathematics*. New York, London and Sydney: John Wiley & Sons, 1968.

Braidotti, Rosi. 'Becoming Woman: Or Sexual Difference Revisited'. *Theory, Culture & Society* 20, no. 3 (2003): 43–64.

Brenez, Nicole. 'The Ultimate Journey: Remarks on Contemporary Theory'. Trans. William D. Routt. *Screening the Past* 2 (1997): n.p. <www.screeningthepast.com/2014/12/the-ultimate-journey-remarks-on-contemporary-theory/> (last accessed 24 July 2017).

Bruns, Gerald L. *Maurice Blanchot: The Refusal of Philosophy*. Baltimore and London: Johns Hopkins University Press, 1997.

Buchanan, Ian and Claire Colebrook, eds. *Deleuze and Feminist Theory*. Edinburgh: Edinburgh University Press, 2000.

Buchanan, Ian and Patricia MacCormack, eds. *Deleuze and the Schizoanalysis of Cinema*. London and New York: Continuum, 2008.

Burchill, Louise. 'Becoming-Woman: A Metamorphosis in the Present Relegating Repetition of Gendered Time to the Past'. *Time & Society* 19, no. 1 (2010): 81–97.

Butler, Judith P. *Subjects of Desire: Hegelian Reflections in Twentieth-Century France*. New York: Columbia University Press, 1987.

Calasso, Roberto. *K*. Trans. Geoffrey Brock. New York: Vintage, 2005.

Colebrook, Claire. *Deleuze: A Guide for the Perplexed*. London and New York: Continuum, 2006.

Conley, Tom. 'Film Theory "After" Deleuze'. *Film–Philosophy* 5, no. 31 (2015): n.p. <www.film-philosophy.com/vol5-2001/n31conley> (last accessed 24 July 2017).

Daney, Serge. *L'Exercise a Été Profitable, Monsieur*. Paris: Pol, 1993.

Davis, Nick. *The Desiring-Image: Gilles Deleuze and Contemporary Queer Cinema*. Oxford and New York: Oxford University Press, 2013.

Deamer, David. *Deleuze, Japanese Cinema, and the Atom Bomb: The Spectre of Impossibility*. New York: Bloomsbury, 2014.

Deamer, David. *Deleuze's Cinema Books: Three Introductions to the Taxonomy of Images*. Edinburgh: Edinburgh University Press, 2016.

del Río, Elena. *Deleuze and the Cinemas of Performance: Powers of Affection*. Edinburgh: Edinburgh University Press, 2012.

Deleuze, Gilles. *Bergsonism*. Trans. Hugh Tomlinson and Barbara Habberjam. New York: Zone Books, 1991.

Deleuze, Gilles. 'Bergson's Conception of Difference'. In *The New Bergson*, ed. John Mullarkey, trans. Melissa McMahon. Manchester and New York: Manchester University Press, 1999, 42–65.

References

Deleuze, Gilles. *Cinema 1: The Movement-Image*. Trans. Hugh Tomlinson. Minneapolis: University of Minnesota Press, 1986.

Deleuze, Gilles. *Cinema 2: The Time-Image*. Trans. Hugh Tomlinson. Minneapolis: University of Minnesota Press, 1989.

Deleuze, Gilles. 'Cours Vincennes, 21/3/1978'. Trans. Melissa McMahon, <https://www.webdeleuze.com/textes/67> (last accessed 24 July 2017).

Deleuze, Gilles. 'Cours Vincennes: Synthesis and Time', 14/3/1978'. Trans. Melissa McMahon, <https://www.webdeleuze.com/textes/66> (last accessed 24 July 2017).

Deleuze, Gilles. *Difference and Repetition*. Trans. Paul Patton. New York: Columbia University Press, 1994.

Deleuze, Gilles. *Essays Critical and Clinical*. Trans. Daniel W. Smith. London and New York: Verso, 1998.

Deleuze, Gilles. *Kant's Critical Philosophy*. Trans. Hugh Tomlinson. Minneapolis: University of Minnesota Press, 1984.

Deleuze, Gilles. '"Le Cerveau, C'est L'écran", Entretien Avec Gilles Deleuze'. *Cahiers Du Cinéma*, no. 380 (February 1986): 24–32.

Deleuze, Gilles. 'Mysticism and Masochism'. In *Desert Islands and Other Texts: 1953–1974*, ed. David Lapoujade, trans. Michael Taormina. Los Angeles and New York: Semiotext(e), 2004, 131–4.

Deleuze, Gilles. *Negotiations 1972–1990*. Trans. Martin Joughin. New York: Columbia University Press, 1995.

Deleuze, Gilles. *Nietzsche and Philosophy*. Trans. Hugh Tomlinson. New York: Columbia University Press, 1983.

Deleuze, Gilles. *Pure Immanence: Essays on a Life*. Trans. Anne Boyman. New York: Zone, 2001.

Deleuze, Gilles. 'The Brain Is the Screen: An Interview with Gilles Deleuze'. In *The Brain Is the Screen: Deleuze and the Philosophy of Cinema*, ed. Gregory Flaxman, trans. Marie Therese Guirgis. Minneapolis and London: University of Minnesota Press, 2000, 365–73.

Deleuze, Gilles. *The Logic of Sense*. Trans. Mark Lester with Charles Stivale. New York: Columbia University Press, 1990.

Deleuze, Gilles. 'The Method of Dramatization'. In *Desert Islands and Other Texts, 1953–1974*, ed. David Lapoujade, trans. Michael Taormina. Los Angeles and New York: Semiotext(e), 2004, 94–116.

Deleuze, Gilles. 'What Is the Creative Act?' In *Two Regimes of Madness: Texts and Interviews 1975–1995*, ed. David Lapoujade and Michael Taormina, trans. Ames Hodges. Los Angeles and New York: Semiotext(e), 2006, 312–24.

Deleuze, Gilles and Félix Guattari. *A Thousand Plateaus: Capitalism and Schizophrenia*. Trans. Brian Massumi. Minneapolis and London: University of Minnesota Press, 1987.

Deleuze, Gilles and Félix Guattari. *What Is Philosophy?* Trans. Hugh Tomlinson. New York: Columbia University Press, 1994.

Derrida, Jacques. *Aporias: Dying – Awaiting (One Another at) the 'Limits of Truth'*. Trans. Thomas Dutoit. Stanford: Stanford University Press, 1993.

Descombes, Vincent. *Modern French Philosophy*. Trans. L. Scott-Fox and J. Harding. Cambridge: Cambridge University Press, 1980.

Dillet, Benoît. 'What Is Called Thinking? When Deleuze Walks along Heideggerian Paths'. *Deleuze Studies* 7 (2013): 250–74.

Douglass, Paul. 'Bergson and Cinema: Friends or Foes?' In *The New Bergson*, ed. John Mullarkey. Manchester and New York: Manchester University Press, 1999, 209–27.

Dowd, Garin. 'Pedagogies of the Image Between Daney and Deleuze'. *New Review of Film and Television Studies* 8, no. 1 (2010): 41–56.

Elder, R. Bruce. *The Films of Stan Brakhage in the American Tradition of Ezra Pound, Gertrud Stein and Charles Olson*. Waterloo, ON: Wilfrid Laurier University Press, 1998.

Ellrich, Lutz. 'Negativity and Difference: On Gilles Deleuze's Criticism of Dialectics'. *MLN* 111, no. 3 (1996): 463–87.

Elsaesser, Thomas. 'A Bazinian Half-Century'. In *Opening Bazin*, ed. Dudley Andrew and Hervé Joubert-Laurencin. Oxford and New York: Oxford University Press, 2011, 3–12.

Elsaesser, Thomas, ed. *Early Cinema: Space, Time, Narration*. London: BFI, 1990.

Elsaesser, Thomas and Malte Hagener. *Film Theory: An Introduction through the Senses*. New York: Routledge, 2010.

Fell, John L. *Film Before Griffith*. Berkeley, Los Angeles and London: University of California Press, 1983.

Film. Film. Directed by Alan Schneider. Screenplay by Samuel Beckett. USA: Milestone Film & Video, 1966.

Fisher, Jaimey. 'Deleuze in a Ruinous Context: German Rubble-Film and Italian Neo-Realism'. *Iris: A Journal of Theory on Image and Sound* 23 (1997): 53–74.

Flaxman, Gregory. 'Cinema Year Zero'. In *The Brain Is the Screen: Deleuze and the Philosophy of Cinema*, ed. Gregory Flaxman. Minneapolis and London: University of Minnesota Press, 2000, 87–108.

Flaxman, Gregory. 'Introduction'. In *The Brain Is the Screen: Deleuze and the Philosophy of Cinema*, ed. Gregory Flaxman. Minneapolis and London: University of Minnesota Press, 2000, 1–57.

Foucault, Michel. *The Order of Things: An Archaeology of the Human Sciences*. Routledge Classics. London and New York: Routledge, 2002.

Foucault, Michel and Gilles Deleuze. 'Intellectuals and Power'. In *Language, Counter-Memory, Practice: Selected Essays and Interviews*, ed. D. F. Bouchard. Ithaca: Cornell University Press, 1977, 205–17.

Frampton, Daniel. *Filmosophy*. London and New York: Wallflower Press, 2006.

References

Frenzy. Film. Directed by Alfred Hitchcock. USA: Universal Pictures, 1972.

Grosz, Elizabeth. *Volatile Bodies: Towards a Corporeal Feminism*. St Leonards: Allen & Unwin, 1994.

Gunning, Tom. 'The Cinema of Attractions: Early Film, Its Spectator and the Avant-Garde'. In *Early Cinema: Space, Frame, Narrative*, ed. Thomas Elsaesser with Adam Barker. London: BFI, 1990, 56–62.

Haase, Ullrich M. and William Large. *Maurice Blanchot*. London and New York: Routledge, 2001.

Hallward, Peter. *Out of This World: Deleuze and the Philosophy of Creation*. London and New York: Verso, 2006.

Hardt, Michael. *Gilles Deleuze: An Apprenticeship in Philosophy*. Minneapolis: University of Minnesota Press, 1993.

Herodotus. *The Histories*. Trans. Aubrey De Sélincourt, and John Marincola. London and New York: Penguin Books, 1996.

Huggett, Nick. 'Zeno: Commentary'. In *Space from Zeno to Einstein: Classic Readings with a Contemporary Commentary*, ed. Nick Huggett. Cambridge, MA and London: MIT Press, 1999, 37–51.

Kern, Stephen. *The Culture of Time and Space: 1880–1918*. Cambridge, MA: Harvard University Press, 1983.

Kerslake, Christian. 'Transcendental Cinema: Deleuze, Time and Modernity'. *Radical Philosophy* 130 (March 2005): 7–19.

Kovács, András Bálint. 'The Film History of Thought'. In *The Brain Is the Screen: Deleuze and the Philosophy of Cinema*, ed. Gregory Flaxman, trans. Sándor Hervey. Minneapolis and London: University of Minnesota Press, 2000, 153–70.

Kracauer, Siegfried. *Nature of Film: The Redemption of Physical Reality*. London: Dennis Dobson, 1961.

L'Arrivée D'un Train À La Ciotat. Film. Auguste Lumière and Louis Lumière. France. 1896.

Lambert, Gregg. 'Cinema and the Outside'. In *The Brain Is the Screen: Deleuze and the Philosophy of Cinema*, ed. Gregory Flaxman. Minneapolis and London: University of Minnesota Press, 2000, 253–92.

Lattre, Alain de. *Bergson: Une Ontologie de La Perplexité*. Paris: Presses Universitaires de France, 1990.

Lawlor, Leonard. *The Challenge of Bergsonism: Phenomenology, Ontology, Ethics*. London and New York: Continuum, 2003.

Levinas, Emmanuel. *Existence and Existents*. Trans. Alphonso Lingis. The Hague: Martinus Nijhoff, 1978.

L'Herbier, Marcel. 'Hermes and Silence'. In *French Film Theory and Criticism: A History/Anthology 1907–39*, ed. Richard Abel, 1: 1907–1929. Princeton: Princeton University Press, 1988, 147–55.

Lindsay, Vachel. *The Art of the Moving Picture*. New York: Liveright, 1970.

Loiperdinger, Martin. 'Lumière's Arrival of the Train: Cinema's Founding Myth'. *The Moving Image* 4, no. 1 (2004): 89–118.

Lyotard, Jean-François. *The Postmodern Condition: A Report on Knowledge*. Trans. Geoff Bennington. Manchester: Manchester University Press, 1984.

Marks, Laura U. *The Skin of the Film: Intercultural Cinema, Embodiment, and the Senses*. Durham and London: Duke University Press, 2000.

Marrati, Paola. *Gilles Deleuze: Cinema and Philosophy*. Trans. Alisa Hartz. Baltimore: Johns Hopkins University Press, 2008.

Martin-Jones, David. *Deleuze and World Cinemas*. London and New York: Continuum, 2011.

Martin-Jones, David. *Deleuze, Cinema and National Identity*. Edinburgh: Edinburgh University Press, 2006.

Marx, Karl. 'Critique of the Gotha Program'. In *Marx Today: Selected Works and Recent Debates*, ed. John F. Stilton. New York: Palgrave Macmillan, 2010, 145–7.

Marx, Karl. 'On Hegel's "Concrete Universal"'. In *From Hegel to Marx: Studies in the Intellectual Development of Karl Marx*, ed. and trans. Sidney Hook. University of Michigan Press, 1962, 312–14.

Massumi, Brian. *A User's Guide to Capitalism and Schizophrenia: Deviations from Deleuze and Guattari*. Cambridge, MA: MIT Press, 1992.

Massumi, Brian. 'Translator's Foreword: The Pleasures of Philosophy'. In *A Thousand Plateaus: Capitalism and Schizophrenia*. Minneapolis and London: University of Minnesota Press, 1987, ix–xv.

Méliès, Georges. 'Cinematographic Views'. *October* 29 (Summer 1984): 23–31.

Ménil, Alain. 'Deleuze et Le Bergsonisme Du Cinéma'. *Philosophie* 47, no. 1 (September 1995).

Ménil, Alain. 'The Time(s) of the Cinema'. In *An Introduction to the Philosophy of Gilles Deleuze*, ed. Jean Khalfa and Kevin Nolan, trans. Jean Khalfa. London and New York: Continuum, 2003, 85–104.

'Misery is the River of the World', *Blood Money*, Compact Disc, Tom Waits. USA: Anti, 2002.

Mothlight. Film. Directed by Stan Brakhage. USA, 1963.

Moullet, Luc. 'The Green Garbage Bins of Gilles Deleuze'. Trans. William D. Routt. *Rouge* 6 (2005): n.p. <http://www.rouge.com.au/6/deleuze.html> (last accessed 24 July 2017).

Mullarkey, John. *Bergson and Philosophy*. Edinburgh: Edinburgh University Press, 1999.

Mullarkey, John. 'Introduction: La Philosophie Nouvelle, or Change in Philosophy'. In *The New Bergson*, ed. John Mullarkey. Manchester and New York: Manchester University Press, 1999, 1–16.

Nancy, Jean-Luc. 'The Deleuzian Fold of Thought'. In *Deleuze: A Critical Reader*, ed. Paul Patton and Anthony Uhlmann, trans.

Tom Gibson. Blackwell Critical Readers. Oxford: Blackwell, 1996, 107–13.
Nancy, Jean-Luc and Abbas Kiarostami. *L'Évidence Du Film/The Evidence of Film*. Trans. Christine Irizarry. Bruxelles: Yves Gevaert Éditeur, 2001.
Nietzsche, Friedrich. 'The Philosopher as Cultural Physician'. In *Philosophy and Truth*, ed. Daniel Brezeale. Atlantic Highlands, NJ: Humanities Press, 1979, 67–76.
Patton, Paul. *Deleuze and the Political*. London and New York: Routledge, 2000.
Perkins, Claire. 'Cinephilia and Monstrosity: The Problem of Cinema in Deleuze's *Cinema* Books'. *Senses of Cinema*, no. 8, July–August (2000): n.p. <http://sensesofcinema.com/2000/book-reviews/deleuze/> (last accessed 24 July 2017).
Pisters, Patricia. *The Neuro-Image: A Deleuzian Film-Philosophy of Digital Screen Culture*. Stanford: Stanford University Press, 2012.
Popper, Karl. *The Open Society and Its Enemies*. Vol. 2, *The High Tide of Prophecy: Hegel and Marx*. 2 vols. London: Routledge Classics, 2003.
Rancière, Jacques. *Film Fables*. Trans. Emiliano Battista. Oxford and New York: Berg, 2006.
Restivo, Angelo. 'Into the Breach: Between The Movement-Image and The Time-Image'. In *The Brain Is the Screen: Deleuze and the Philosophy of Cinema*, ed. Gregory Flaxman. Minneapolis and London: University of Minnesota Press, 2000, 171–92.
Rodowick, D. N. *Gilles Deleuze's Time Machine*. Durham and London: Duke University Press, 1997.
Roffe, Jon. *Badiou's Deleuze*. Durham: Acumen, 2012.
Ropars-Wuilleumier, Marie-Claire. 'The Cinema, Reader of Gilles Deleuze'. In *Gilles Deleuze and the Theatre of Philosophy*, ed. Constantin Boundas and Dorothea Olkowski. New York and London: Routledge, 1994, 255–61.
Roud, Richard. *A Passion for Films: Henri Langlois and the Cinémathèque Française*. Baltimore and London: Johns Hopkins University Press, 1983.
Routt, William D. 'Poubelle, Ma Belle'. *Rouge* 6 (2005): n.p. <www.rouge.com.au/6/poubelle.html> (last accessed 24 July 2017).
Routt, William D. 'The Madness of Images and Thinking Cinema'. *Postmodern Culture* 8, no. 2 (1998) <http://muse.jhu.edu/journals/pmc/v008/8.2routt.html> (last accessed 24 July 2017).
Salmon, Wesley C. 'Introduction'. In *Zeno's Paradoxes*, ed. Wesley C. Salmon. Indianapolis and New York: Bobbs-Merrill, 1970, 5–44.
Sinnerbrink, Robert. *New Philosophies of Film: Thinking Images*. London and New York: Continuum, 2011.
Smith, Daniel W. *Essays on Deleuze*. Edinburgh: Edinburgh University Press, 2012.
Somers-Hall, Henry. 'Transcendental Illusion and Antinomy in Kant and

Deleuze'. In *Thinking Between Deleuze and Kant: A Strange Encounter*, ed. Edward Willatt and Matt Lee. London and New York: Continuum, 2009, 128–49.

Sophocles. *The Three Theban Plays: Antigone, Oedipus the King, Oedipus at Colonus*. Trans. Robert Fagles. London: Penguin Books, 1984.

Stam, Robert. *Film Theory: An Introduction*. Oxford: Blackwell, 2000.

Strike. Film. Directed by Sergei Eisenstein. USSR, 1925.

Thomas, Allan James. 'Fascism, Irrationalism and Creative Evolution, or Deleuze, Running Away'. *Bulletin de La Société Américaine de Philosophie de Langue Français* 15, no. 2 (Fall 2005): 1–27.

'V as in Voyage', *Gilles Deleuze from A to Z*. DVD. Directed by Pierre-André Boutang. Subtitles trans. Charles J. Stivale. Semiotext(e) Foreign Agents, 2011.

Vaughan, Dai. 'Let There Be Lumière'. In *Early Cinema: Space, Frame, Narration*, ed. Thomas Elsaesser with Adam Barker. London: BFI, 1990, 63–7.

Virilio, Paul. *War and Cinema: The Logistics of Perception*. Trans. Patrick Camille. London and New York: Verso, 1989.

Waugh, Katherine, and Fergus Daly. 'Film by Samuel Beckett'. *Film West: Ireland's Film Quarterly*, no. 20 (15 December 2015): n.p. <www.iol.ie/~galfilm/filmwest/20beckett.htm> (last accessed 24 July 2017).

Worms, Frédéric. '*Matter and Memory* on Mind and Body: Final Statements and New Perspectives'. In *The New Bergson*, ed. John Mullarkey, trans. Pelagia Goulimari. Manchester and New York: Manchester University Press, 1999, 88–98.

Yacavone, Daniel. *Film Worlds: A Philosophical Aesthetics of Cinema*. New York: Columbia University Press, 2015.

Index

Note: 'n' indicates chapter notes.

aberrant movement, 29–31, 39, 42, 140, 143, 154, 157n73, 163–5, 183–4, 189–90, 192, 202, 207–8, 211, 221, 228, 239n16
absolute movement, 128, 144, 147–9, 159n97, 165, 184
action, 86–8, 92, 94, 110, 123–4, 163–5, 169, 173–4, 187, 190, 193, 202, 210, 212–14, 217, 221, 229, 246–7
action and reaction, 23–4, 27–32, 34, 41, 123–4, 169, 222, 227, 232
action-image, 34, 36, 125–9, 132–3, 164, 167, 182, 205, 207, 212, 215, 226, 229, 243n88
action-thought, 187–9, 191, 193
actual, 72–5, 84n96, 84n99, 84n104, 99–102, 108–10, 150, 157n71, 170, 173, 211, 233, 243n88, 249
actualisation, 72–5, 84n99, 100–2, 173, 223, 236, 245, 250
affection, 127–8, 212, 216–17, 219–21, 224, 229, 233–4, 251–2
affection-image, 36, 125–9, 132–3, 167, 195n4, 204–5, 207, 212, 218, 221
Alliez, Éric, 105
American cinema, 158n80, 180, 188–9, 195n6, 207, 239n13; see also experimental cinema
Andrew, Dudley, 2, 17n5, 18n10, 20n27
Ansell-Pearson, Keith, 155n5, 176, 178, 217–18, 252n9

any-instants-whatever, 56–8
Arrivée d'un Train à la Ciotat, L' (Lumière and Lumière), 23–33, 48n2, 49n5, 136, 225–6
arrow paradox see Zeno's paradoxes
art, 5, 91, 96–103, 109, 116n54, 223, 226
Artaud, Antonin, 219–20, 241n47, 242n59
ascent, 208–13, 245
auteur, 104, 106, 196n30

Badiou, Alain, 8–9, 12–13, 16, 20n35, 108
Bazin, André, 2, 7, 17n5, 20n27
Beasley-Murray, Jon, 35
Beckett, Samuel, *Film*, 205–12, 214–15, 219–21, 224, 229, 237, 238n3, 238n4
becoming, 14–16, 75, 84n99, 85–8, 94–7, 100–1, 109–11, 159n89, 249–52
becoming-woman, 110–11
being, 16–17, 22n63, 48, 62–3, 66, 68, 71–4, 80n43, 86–95, 100–1, 109–10, 119–32, 140, 165–6, 168, 209, 213, 224, 232–3, 246–7, 249; see also human being
being-for-itself, 128, 209
belief, 47, 248–52
Bellour, Raymond, 2, 8, 11, 13, 15, 19n17, 83n81, 106, 115n50, 118n82
Berger, John, 228

Bergson, Henri-Louis, 10–11,
    20n36, 44–8, 53–68, 79n9,
    80n42, 82n76, 85–97, 99, 102,
    108, 113, 113n1, 115n49,
    116n54, 117n65, 119–23, 145,
    155n5, 155n7, 176, 192, 194,
    201–2, 209, 216–18, 222–3,
    232–4
  Creative Evolution, 72, 78n3,
    83n84, 85–6, 90, 128–33, 139,
    141–2, 156n47, 158n77, 160,
    201
  Matter and Memory, 46, 85–8,
    114n7, 119–20, 130–5,
    139–42, 158n84, 201
  see also Deleuze, Gilles:
    Bergsonism; 'Bergson's
    Conception of Difference'
Biran, Maine de, 212
blackness, 206, 209, 212, 224, 229,
    236–7
Blanchot, Maurice, 42–3, 46–7,
    51n78, 65, 166, 179, 201–3,
    210, 214, 220, 229–31, 236,
    239n17, 242n50, 244n122,
    247–8
Bogue, Ronald, 3, 73, 80n42,
    158n86, 159n97
Boljkovac, Nadine, 7
Bordwell, David, 5–6, 38, 104, 106
Borradori, Giovanna, 61–3, 80n48,
    197n72, 252n9
Braidotti, Rosi, 111
brain/screen, 122–30, 140, 147,
    178, 205, 243n88
Brakhage, Stan, 158n80, 207,
    239n13
break, 10–11, 15–16, 36, 39–40,
    42–4, 82n77, 144–5, 154, 160,
    166, 179, 182–3, 194, 202–5,
    215–16, 222, 224, 247–8; *see
    also* gap
Brenez, Nicole, 45, 223
Bruns, Gerald L., 43
Buchanan, Ian, 18n16
bullets, 226–9, 231–2
Butler, Judith, 65
Butler, Samuel, 114n22

Cahiers axiom, 1–10, 223, 242n65
Cahiers du cinéma (journal), 2,
    17n5, 18n8, 18n10, 18n13
camera mobility, 26–9, 37, 143–4,
    152–3, 157n69, 162, 164–6,
    192, 202, 207–8, 226
capitalism, 186
causality, 41, 56–8, 62, 66, 163,
    169–71, 178, 180, 195n10,
    203, 235
cause and effect, 40–1, 101, 163–5,
    169, 216
Cavell, Stanley, 19n26
cinema, history of, 5, 15, 19n23,
    25–6, 28, 35–40, 106–7, 134,
    138, 195n9, 246; *see also*
    classical cinema; modern
    cinema; primitive cinema
cinema studies, 1, 3–7, 11, 17n5,
    18n8
cinematograph, 53, 85, 132, 135,
    142, 157n53
cinematographic illusion, 53–7,
    64, 66, 69–70, 75–8, 85–92,
    94, 103, 109–10, 113, 113n1,
    128–36, 138–42, 145, 154,
    158n77, 160, 162, 164–5, 179,
    181, 189–92, 201–2, 211, 216,
    218, 245
classical cinema, 24, 32–3, 35–6,
    40–2, 44–6, 160–84, 188,
    190–2, 202–3, 205, 207–8,
    215–16, 219, 221–2, 224–5,
    228, 241n47, 242n75, 246,
    250, 252
closed set, 28, 45, 59–61, 76, 145,
    148–51, 158n86, 159n97, 160,
    162, 166–70, 176, 181–2, 192,
    213
closed whole, 27, 58, 63–4, 147,
    166–71, 173–4, 180–1, 201–2,
    208, 214, 229, 235, 245, 248
Colebrook, Claire, 112, 115n38
concepts, 5, 7–9, 15, 38, 67–8, 70,
    72, 89–91, 94–101, 103–8,
    116n58, 116n64, 170, 174–5,
    201
Conley, Tom, 19n19

Index

consciousness, 93, 122–5, 129, 131–2, 155n19, 213
contestation, 75, 118n93
corpse, 227–33, 235
creation, 8, 12–14, 21n47, 58, 60, 62, 66, 73–6, 96–100, 103–5, 108, 116n58, 150, 209, 211, 249–50
crystal-image, 232–3, 235, 237, 251–2
crystalline regime, 38–9
cuts, 15, 33, 40–3, 51n56, 76, 82n76, 86–7, 108–9, 141, 149, 151, 163, 186–7, 221, 234

Daney, Serge, 2–3, 18n8, 44, 190, 193
darkness, 206–7, 209–10, 212, 215
Davis, Nick, 7
Deamer, David, 7
death, 191, 193, 202, 209–10, 212–14, 224, 227, 229–32, 237, 240n29, 240n30, 241n33, 246–7, 250–2
decentring, 16, 39, 41, 43, 137, 140, 154, 158n75, 165–6, 169, 181, 190, 192, 232–3, 241n47, 247
Dedekind, Richard, 40, 51n56
degrees of difference, 70–3, 82n79, 147, 156n21, 173
Del Rio, Elena, 7
Deleuze, Gilles
  Bergsonism, 57, 67, 70, 72, 78, 78n5, 93–4, 100, 102, 115n37, 173
  'Bergson's Conception of Difference', 61–6, 70–2, 78, 80n38, 80n39, 80n48, 80n49, 82n75, 173, 177, 196n46, 210, 218, 246, 252n9
  Difference and Repetition, 15, 20n36, 67–8, 75, 84n96, 173, 217
  Essays Critical and Clinical, 97–8
  'Immanence: A Life', 251
  Kant's Critical Philosophy, 216
  'Letter to a Harsh Critic', 71
  'Letter to Serge Daney', 44
  The Logic of Sense, 235–6
  'The Brain Is the Screen', 18n13
  What is Philosophy? (and Felix Guattari), 17n2, 91, 98–9, 102–4, 117n68, 174–6, 227
Derrida, Jacques, 214, 229, 240n30
Descombes, Vincent, 65
deterritorialisation, 211, 242n72, 243n76
dialectic, 14, 16, 27, 50n51, 64–8, 71, 75–7, 81n55, 81n57, 108, 112, 117n68, 133, 169, 180, 184–5, 187–8, 190, 195n6, 198n95, 246
difference, 4, 7–17, 27, 33, 61–75, 80n49, 82n75, 84n96, 147–8, 172–3, 177, 196n45, 197n72, 204–6, 209–11, 217–18, 222, 224, 237, 241n42, 245–7, 249–51; *see also* external difference; internal difference
difference of degree, 70–3, 83n79, 147, 156n21, 173
Dillet, Benoît, 183
disease, 98–9, 101, 116n56
Douglass, Paul, 90, 134–5, 140, 157n59
Dowd, Garin, 18n8
dramatisation, 14–17, 112, 237–8, 246, 251–2
dream, 45, 182–3, 188–91, 236, 247
duration, 4, 9, 23, 27, 45–6, 54, 57–61, 63–4, 66, 68–72, 86, 88–90, 92, 94–6, 103, 108, 113, 114n21, 130, 140, 145, 147–51, 153–4, 161–2, 165–9, 209, 216, 245, 249

Eisenstein, Sergei Mikhailovich, 27, 162, 184–90, 192, 198n95, 219–20
Elder, R. Bruce, 239n13
Ellrich, Lutz, 81n55
Elsaesser, Thomas, 18n12, 20n27
empiricism *see* transcendental empiricism

Epstein, Jean, 139–40, 157n73
evolution, 72–3, 83n84, 113n1
experience, 108, 170–4, 194, 206, 210–13, 237–8; see also human experience
experimental cinema, 158n80, 207–8, 211, 239n10, 239n16, 240n20, 241n47
Expressionism, 36, 180, 188, 195n6
external difference, 63–4, 66–7, 70, 77, 83n84, 158n83, 173, 196n46, 198n95, 210, 218, 246

fascism, 191–3, 199n124, 202, 204, 222, 225, 247
Fell, John L., 48n2
film theory, 1, 10, 106, 110, 138–9
film-philosophy, 7, 19n26
finalism, 55–8, 62, 64, 66, 70, 74–5, 81n59, 187, 191, 246
Fisher, Jaimey, 37, 39
Flaxman, Gregory, 18n13, 18n16, 39, 53, 76, 195n5
form, 145, 180, 194, 225, 235, 246
Foucault, Michel, 18n8, 106, 117n77
frame, 29, 44, 124, 141, 145, 149, 168, 192
freedom, 193–4
French Impressionist cinema, 180, 188, 195n6, 239n10

gap, 10, 15, 26, 33–5, 41–2, 47, 128, 141, 164, 194, 203–4, 206, 221, 224, 248; see also break
genesis, 75–7, 109, 111–13, 119–20, 129, 132, 154, 155n5, 157n71, 173, 178–9, 207–8, 210, 213, 217–18, 222–4, 232, 234, 237, 243n82, 245, 249–50
German Expressionism, 36, 180, 188, 195n6
Griffith, D. W., 26–7, 36, 180
Guattari, Felix, 17n2, 91, 98–9, 102–4, 117n68, 174–6, 227
Gunning, Tom, 25

Haase, Ullrich, 213
Hagener, Malte, 18n12
Hallward, Peter, 12–14, 21n51, 61–2, 77, 84n105, 193, 239n19, 245
Hardt, Michael, 9, 12, 61–2, 64–7, 71, 76, 81n55, 81n57
Hegel, Georg Wilhelm Friedrich, 14, 61, 64–8, 71–2, 75–7, 81n55, 81n57, 81n59, 104, 108, 162, 198n95, 199n110, 199n124, 213, 229, 246
Hegelianism, 6, 14, 16, 37–9, 50n51, 65–8, 70–1, 75, 81n57, 81n68, 109, 133, 191, 199n124; see also dialectic
Heidegger, Martin, 183–4, 213–14, 220, 242n57
heterogenesis, 8, 72, 83n81, 211, 245–6
history/the historical, 134, 222–4, 235, 246–7
Hitchcock, Aldred, 36, 37, 153
Holocaust, 43–5, 191, 193, 202, 204, 221–2, 224, 230, 235, 247
Horace, 53
horror, 44–5, 190, 193, 202, 215, 221, 224, 231–2, 235, 239n17, 246–7, 249
human, 21n51, 93, 113, 145, 154, 156n32, 158n75, 165–6, 176, 178, 181, 190, 192–4, 201–4, 207–11, 213–16, 218, 221–4, 228–9, 232, 235–8, 240n20, 240n21, 243n82, 245–7, 249–50
human being, 16–17, 88–9, 92, 109–13, 119, 128, 134, 166, 193–4, 208–9, 214–15, 222, 224, 238, 246–7, 250
human condition, 88, 201, 207, 210, 223
human experience, 93, 101, 108, 144, 193–4, 209, 211, 213, 215–16, 224
human nature, 119, 140, 145, 192–3, 206, 216, 222, 250

Index

human perception, 95, 152–3, 157n53, 161, 170, 207, 216
human perspective, 152, 161, 170, 184, 209
human subjectivity, 161, 201, 204–6, 209–10, 237, 240n20
human thought, 110, 112–13, 125, 132, 134, 141, 152, 154, 156n32, 161, 165–6, 169–70, 178–9, 183, 186, 192–3, 201–4, 207, 209, 215–16, 218, 223–4, 237, 245–7, 249–50

'I', 216–18, 220–3, 233–4, 236–8, 248, 250–2
Idea, 15, 169–74, 176, 178, 180, 185, 188–90, 192, 197n67, 202, 208, 213, 221, 228–9, 248
Idea of the whole, 169–70, 180, 185, 208, 213, 229
Idea of the world, 170–4, 176, 178, 180, 185, 189–90, 192, 197n67, 202, 221, 228–9, 248
idealism, 86, 120–1, 155n5, 172, 187, 217, 222
identity, 8, 14, 48, 61–2, 68, 75, 77, 111, 120–1, 133, 142, 148–9, 154, 165, 187, 210–11, 214, 247
impower/inpower (*impouvoir*), 16, 21n61, 110, 165–6, 175, 219, 234, 248
Impressionism, 180, 188, 195n6
internal difference, 63–4, 67, 70–2, 82, 83n84, 137, 158n83, 167, 172–3, 210, 218, 246
interval, 15–16, 33–5, 41–4, 47, 54, 123–4, 127–8, 147, 164; *see also* gap; break
intuition, 89–90, 92–5, 97, 102, 115n28, 115n45, 207, 209, 211, 239n16
Italian neo-realism, 2, 31

Joubert-Laurencin, Hervé, 20n27

Kant, Immanuel, 77, 80n48, 134, 155n5, 162–4, 170–3, 176–9, 196n46, 215–22, 233, 235, 237, 248–9, 252n9
Kern, Stephen, 48n3
Kerslake, Christian, 15, 195n5
Kiarostami, Abbas, 150
killing, 186, 225–6
Kojève, Alexandre, 65
Kovács, András Bálint, 35, 37
Kracauer, Siegfried, 30, 49n26

Lambert, Greg, 38
Langlois, Henri, 2, 18n6
language, 85–90, 92, 95–6, 102, 108–13, 116n51, 128, 161, 220, 242n57, 242n59
Large, William, 213
Lawlor, Leonard, 115n45, 117n68
Levinas, Emmanuel, 210, 212, 214, 236–7, 239n17, 244n122
Lindsay, Vachel, 45, 158n84
line of flight (*ligne de fuite*), 226–9, 231–2, 243n76
literature, 97–9, 101
Loiperdinger, Martin, 48n2
Lumière, Auguste and Louis, 23–33, 48n2, 49n5, 136, 225–6
Lyotard, Jean-François, 50n35

MacCormack, Patricia, 18n16
Maimon, Solomon, 155n5, 177–8, 196n47, 217, 222, 241n42, 249
man, 110–11, 191, 245
Marey, Étienne-Jules, 226
Marks, Laura, 7
Marrati, Paola, 3, 122
Martin-Jones, David, 7
Marx, Karl, 82n68, 199n109
Massumi, Brian, 20n32, 110–11, 118n90, 226, 242n72
mastery, 16, 37, 94, 103, 110, 173, 190–1, 193, 214, 229–30, 250–1
mathematics, 5, 40, 51n56, 54–6, 78n9, 180, 197n79
mechanism, 56–8, 62–7, 70, 74, 85, 109, 191, 216, 246
Méliès, Georges, 157n69
Ménil, Alain, 38, 85

Merleau-Ponty, Maurice, 225
metacinema, 119–25, 133, 135, 178
metaphysics, 85, 89, 91–104, 108, 189, 192, 223, 245
Metz, Christian, 25, 194n2
mimesis, 96
mise en scène, 2–3, 225
mobile camera *see* camera mobility
modern cinema, 10–11, 15, 24, 31–7, 40–2, 44–5, 160, 164–6, 175, 179, 182, 194, 203, 207, 216, 219, 222, 224, 234–5, 237, 248–52
monism, 77
montage, 2–3, 10, 15, 26–31, 33–44, 108, 136–7, 141, 143–5, 149, 151–3, 161–6, 169, 171, 174, 180–1, 184–9, 192, 198n95, 202, 207–8, 219, 221, 224, 229, 245
montage 'schools', 36, 174, 185, 188, 195n6, 196n30
Moulett, Luc, 19n20, 106–7, 118n80
movement, 13–17, 45, 53–64, 69–72, 75–8, 80n49, 88–9, 92, 94, 96, 101, 108, 133–4, 136, 141–54, 161–3, 165–8, 179, 183–4, 217, 233, 245, 248; *see also* aberrant movement; absolute movement; relative movement
movement-image, 23–42, 46, 86, 95, 121, 125–34, 140, 143, 151, 160–1, 166–70, 179, 183–4, 189, 191–2, 195n4, 201–4, 209, 225–6, 228, 247, 252
Mullarkey, John, 89, 94–6, 115n28
Mummy, the, 16, 219

Nancy, Jean-Luc, 108, 118n85, 150
narrative, 25–8, 50n35, 160–3, 169, 171, 174–5, 181, 186, 194n2, 227, 241n47, 242n75, 248–9
natural perception, 131, 134, 136–44, 152, 154, 165, 170, 195n13, 228

naturalism, 107, 118n82
negation, 61–2, 65–8, 71, 75–8, 80n43, 81n59, 109, 133, 142, 148, 157n71, 230, 243n88
neo-realism, 2, 31, 116n51
neuro-image, 7, 20n29
Nietzsche, Friedrich, 10–11, 80n48, 98–9, 114n17, 248–9, 252n9
non-human, 120, 141, 154, 161, 170, 192, 202, 207–9, 211, 223, 230n16, 246–7
nuance, 9, 13, 17, 67–72, 94, 110, 167, 178, 196n46, 210–11, 245, 252n9

ontology, 17, 20n35, 22n63, 44, 48, 62–4, 66, 68, 72, 76–7, 87, 91–2, 108–10, 112, 119, 121–4, 133, 135, 146, 153, 161, 167–9, 176, 181, 183, 189, 192–3, 223
open whole, 27–8, 30, 45–7, 58–61, 76, 83n84, 111, 114n21, 128, 143, 146–50, 159n89, 159n97, 162, 165–6, 172–4, 181, 192, 198n87, 201–3, 207
opsign, 31–2, 233
organic, 26–7, 32, 36, 38–40, 167, 174, 180, 188–90, 195n6, 197n79
out-of-field, 146, 168

painting, 226–8
Patton, Paul, 116n58
perception, 26, 28–9, 34, 85–8, 108, 120–3, 136–40, 157n53, 161–5, 169, 192, 195n4, 205, 212, 228–9, 243n88
perception-for-itself, 122, 129, 143
perception-image, 34, 36, 125–30, 132–3, 164, 167, 205, 207, 212, 226
Perkins, Claire, 105
perspective, 132–4, 140, 142, 151–2, 161–3, 165, 170, 184, 209, 222, 226–9, 232, 243n82, 245; *see also* point of view
philosophers, 98, 101, 104

Index

philosophy, 4–6, 63, 85, 91–5, 103, 109, 112–13, 116n54, 116n58, 139, 174–5, 178–9, 213, 216, 222–3, 245–9, 251–2
philosophy, history of, 1, 8, 15–16, 19n23, 105, 107, 119, 133–4, 161–2, 174, 176, 179, 195n17, 213, 223, 247
photogrammes, 135–6
photography, 69–70, 82n76
Pierce, Charles Sanders, 36
Pisters, Patricia, 7, 20n29
plane of immanence, 121, 174–6, 205–6
Plato, 55, 62–4, 66–7, 71, 81n59, 85, 103, 109, 116n56, 213, 216
point of view, 137–8, 140, 142–3, 149, 151–2, 158n75, 165, 184, 226
politics, 3, 111, 118n90, 183, 186, 190, 192–3, 199n124, 247, 249–50
Popper, Karl, 199n124
Porter, Edwin S., 26
postmodern, 50n35
post-war cinema *see* modern cinema
power, 11, 16, 117n67, 165–6, 169, 190–3, 202, 210, 217, 219, 225, 229–30, 232, 246–9, 251–2
powerlessness, 16, 21n61, 35, 94, 166, 179, 202–3, 217, 219
powers of the false, 11, 175, 249
pre-war cinema *see* classical cinema
primitive cinema, 25–6, 28–9, 33, 37–8, 50n30, 113n1, 136, 138–9, 141–54, 160, 181, 195n13
projector, 57, 135, 137–8, 140–3, 152, 154, 157n65, 158n75, 162, 164–5, 184, 191, 202
propaganda, 189–91, 225
Proust, Marcel, 24, 73, 98

Rancière, Jacques, 18n8, 154
Ravaisson, Jean Gaspard Felix, 115n49

realism, 86, 95, 120–1, 155n5
reason, 163, 172, 177–8, 218
recentring, 164–5, 182, 192
relative movement, 142–5, 147–50, 159n97, 165
Renoir, Jean, 20n27
representation, 2–3, 8, 14, 90, 96, 99, 172, 189, 211, 227
Restivo, Angelo, 33, 44
reterritorialisation, 211, 243n76
reverse proof, 204–5, 207, 209, 219
Rivière, Jacques, 220
Rodowick, David, 3–5, 7, 19n20, 21n43, 39, 50n30, 106, 134–6, 138, 167–9, 176, 188–9, 222, 233
Roffe, Jon, 20n35
Ropars-Wuilleumier, Marie-Claire, 39–40, 104–5, 181
Routt, William D., 18n6, 107, 158n84
Russell's paradox, 79n34, 146, 159n89

Sadoul, Georges, 30
Salmon, Wesley C., 54, 79n10
Schneider, Alan, 238n3
science, 5, 56–8, 60, 91, 113n1, 129
semiology, 99
sensory-motor schema, 23–30, 32, 34, 41, 43, 50n35, 163–5, 169–71, 173–4, 176–7, 179–82, 185–6, 191–2, 202, 205, 207, 215, 221, 224–5, 227–30, 250
set, 28, 51n56, 59–61, 79n31, 79n34, 146, 148, 159n89, 167–8–170, 173, 192, 196n33, 213–14
set theory, 51n56, 79n31, 159n89
Shakespeare, William, 15–16
shock to thought, 184–7, 189, 191
shot, 28–30, 34, 37, 44, 141, 144–9, 151, 153, 160–1, 164–5, 167, 169–71, 186, 192, 195n10
sign *see* taxonomy
silence, 202, 210, 215
single shot film, 29–32, 136
Sinnerbrink, Robert, 7, 19n26

Smith, Daniel W., 8, 98, 170, 172, 176–8, 196n47, 217, 241n42
Snow, Michael, 207
Somers-Hall, Henry, 171–2, 177
sonsign, 31
Soviet cinema, 26, 36, 180, 184, 195n6, 239n10
specificity, 4–5, 9–11, 17, 33, 35, 68, 75, 83n82, 91, 94–5, 99, 110, 245
Spinoza, Baruch, 10–11
spontaneity, 216–18, 220, 222–4, 232–3, 246
Stam, Robert, 49n26
stillness, 202, 209–10, 212, 229, 247
subjectivity, 111, 125, 128, 133, 140, 161, 201, 204–5, 209–10, 212, 214, 237, 240n20; *see also* human subjectivity
subtraction, 122–3, 125–6, 243n88
symptomatology, 98–9, 101, 105–6, 108, 116n64, 211
system, 8, 23, 26–32, 34, 37–8, 58, 113, 114n21, 125–6, 129–30, 142–3, 148, 168, 225–6, 228–9

taxonomy, 106–7, 125–6, 129, 158n80, 162, 182, 201, 204–5, 208
teleology, 6, 37–9, 47, 55–6, 58, 63, 81n59, 187–8, 191
thought, 7, 14–17, 21n47, 43, 76–7, 85–96, 108–13, 115n38, 130, 133–4, 141–2, 156n32, 158n32, 158n75, 161, 165–6, 169, 179, 184–5, 190–1, 201, 210, 213, 217–24, 234, 245–6, 248–9, 252; *see also* human thought
thought of the world, 17, 112–13, 124, 173, 187–90, 246, 249–52
time, 4, 15–16, 23, 27, 37, 45, 48n3, 163–5, 177, 179, 215–18, 224, 228, 243n101, 248, 250–1
time-image, 16, 23–4, 29–43, 46–7, 50n30, 50n35, 93, 160, 164–6,
175, 179, 203, 207, 221, 234, 238, 241n47, 247, 252
totalisation, 167–8, 182, 190–2, 202–3, 215, 219, 221, 224, 241n33, 247, 249–50
totalitarianism, 190, 192, 199n124, 247, 249
totality, 56–8, 167–83, 188–90, 192, 201, 213–14, 229, 246–8
transcendence, 17, 170–4, 176, 178–9, 189, 191–2, 196n46, 211, 217, 222
transcendental empiricism, 1–10, 99–100, 104–13, 217, 241n42
transformation, 27–8, 35, 44–6, 58–60, 143, 147, 149–53, 165, 209, 216–17, 248
Truth, 43, 188–9

universal variation, 121, 125, 130, 137, 143–4, 149, 167, 169, 173, 176, 178, 184, 191, 204, 206, 208–9, 216, 218, 222, 232, 243n88, 243n101, 245–6

vanishing point (point of flight/ *point de fuite*), 226–32, 234–5, 247
Vaughan, Dai, 24–5, 30
violence, 43–8, 71, 92–3, 186, 191–3, 202, 225–7, 250
Virilio, Paul, 225–6
virtual, 33, 72–5, 84n96, 84n104, 98–104, 106–7, 109–10, 116n56, 121–3, 126, 147, 149–50, 167, 170, 173, 209, 233, 245
visibility, 225–8

waiting, 23–4, 32–3, 59, 93–4, 248
war, 191, 202, 204, 221–2, 224–5
whiteness, 68–70, 82n74
whole, 27–8, 31–5, 39, 45–7, 56–61, 80n34, 146–51, 166, 168–9, 180, 184–5, 188–9, 201, 219–21, 229

Index

world, 2–3, 17, 28–35, 46–7, 86–8, 94–103, 108–11, 172–4, 193, 210, 212, 215, 223–4, 229–32, 234–5, 237–8, 245–52
    thought of the world, 17, 112–13, 124, 173, 187–90, 246, 249–52

World War Two, 24, 34, 36, 40, 190–1, 193; *see also* Holocaust

Worms, Frédéric, 123

Zeno's paradoxes, 54–5, 60, 69, 79n10

EU representative:
Easy Access System Europe
Mustamäe tee 50, 10621 Tallinn, Estonia
Gpsr.requests@easproject.com